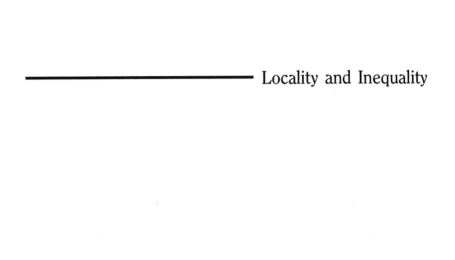

Locality and Inequality

SUNY Series on the New Inequalities

A. Gary Dworkin, Editor

Locality and Inequality

Farm and Industry Structure and Socioeconomic Conditions

Linda M. Lobao

The State University of New York Press

Cover Photo: Lloyd Lemmermann

Published by
State University of New York Press, Albany

For information, address State University of New York
Press, State University Plaza, Albany, N.Y., 12246

Library of Congress Cataloging-in-Publication Data

Lobao, Linda M., 1952-
    Locality and inequality : farm and industry structure and
socioeconomic conditions / by Linda M. Lobao.
        p.   cm.—(SUNY series on the new inequalities)
    Includes bibliographical references.
    ISBN 0-7914-0475-7 (alk. paper) — ISBN 0-7914-0476-5 (pbk. :
alk. paper)
    1. Agriculture—Economic aspects—United States. 2. Farms, Small—
United States. 3. Farmers—United States—Economic conditions.
4. United States—Rural conditions. 5. United States—Economic
conditions—1981-   —Regional disparities. I. Title. II. Series:
SUNY series in the new inequalities.
HD1765.L63 1990
338.1'0973—dc20   90-30

10   9   8   7   6   5   4   3   2   1

To my son Erick,
who has brought much joy into my life.

Contents

List of Tables

List of Figures

Acknowledgments

I wish to express my gratitude to the many people and organizations that contributed to this research. From the Department of Sociology, Anthropology, and Social Work at North Carolina State University, Michael D. Schulman, Donald Tomaskovic-Devey, and Ronald C. Wimberley greatly influenced my conceptual focus and pursuit of the entire project. Robert L. Moxley from the Department of Sociology, Anthropology, and Social Work, Charles Proctor from the Department of Statistics, and Richard Slatta from the Department of History, also at North Carolina State, provided valuable comments during the initial undertaking of this research.

At The Ohio State University, Eugene Jones and Donald W. Thomas from the Department of Agricultural Economics and Rural Sociology, and Jian He, Department of Sociology, shared their time and ideas regarding technical aspects of the study. This manuscript further benefitted from the thoughtful advice and encouragement of Lawrence A. Brown, Department of Geography.

In the Department of Agricultural Economics and Rural Sociology, Ohio State, I am indebted to Maurice Klein for his help with references and research material, Eilise J. Semons for her excellent secretarial support and proofreading, Jan Geary for secretarial assistance, and Janice DiCarolis for her graphics work. I also appreciate the general support I received from my colleagues in the Department and for the research time that was afforded me.

I owe a debt of gratitude to colleagues at other institutions as well. Michael J. Belyea, now at the University of North Carolina, Chapel Hill, provided excellent commentary on the research design and a steady stream of support. Discussions with Martin Kenney, now in the Department of Applied Social Sciences, University of California, Davis, advanced the theoretical aims of the manuscript. Bill Falk, in the Department of Sociology, University of Maryland, provided helpful reviews and encouragement. And discussions with Gerhard Lenski, Department of Sociology, University of North Carolina, Chapel Hill, illuminated the topic of inequality to me as a graduate student.

Many colleagues generously shared their data and I would especially like to thank Glenn Fuguitt, Department of Rural Sociology, University of Wisconsin; Thomas A. Carlin and Bernal L. Green, United States Department of Agriculture, Economic Research Service; and William B. Clifford, Department of Sociology, Anthropology, and Social Work at North Carolina State University. This research was supported by my participation in a series of regional research projects which provided resources, time, and most significantly, diverse and stimulating colleagues: Project S-198, "Socioeconomic Dimensions of Technological Change, Natural Resource Use, and Agriculture Structure;" S-229, "The Changing Structure of Local Labor Markets in Nonmetropolitan Areas;" and NCR-127, "North Central Regional Research Committee on Rural Health."

The efforts of those involved in seeing the manuscript through the publication process, particularly editors A. Gary Dworkin, Lois Patton, Megeen Mulholland, and Carol Newhouse are much appreciated. In addition, the reviewers of my prospectus and draft manuscript provided thoughtful suggestions that improved the final copy.

Most importantly, I owe thanks to my family: my father George, a family farmer and later a machinist; my mother Helen; and sisters Susan and Lisa. In addition, I want to acknowledge my grandmother, Mary Baschuk, whose courage in independently supporting her family through factory work and domestic service I've long admired and whose warmth and support I'll always cherish. My family instilled a sense of pride in my working class origins and a consciousness that I hope always to retain even as I move away from them. Finally, my son Erick, to whom this book is dedicated, deserves the greatest thanks for being patient with the paths I have chosen to follow.

Introduction and Overview

This book explores how the organization of economic production in farming and industry generates socioeconomic inequality across different localities in the United States. Socioeconomic inequality, or the way in which resources are differently allocated and life chances presented, is an issue that crosses social science disciplines, theoretical perspectives, and research traditions. As individuals witness and try to make sense of the uneven distribution of prosperity and impoverishment around them, inequality is a significant popular concern as well as catalyst for political action. In this study, I attempt to integrate perspectives on the organization of farming and industry into a broad conceptual framework that seeks to understand the structural forces creating inequality at the local level. However, I give primary attention to farming, the raising of food and fiber. Why focus on this sector?

First, the farm sector has experienced fundamental restructuring and has been recently in the midst of a profound crisis. Moderate-size family farms, the mainstay of American agriculture, have declined during the postwar era and confronted widespread financial stress in the 1980s. Large-scale farms—the "factories in the field" often run by corporations and dependent upon hired labor—are expanding their share of agricultural sales.[1] The effects of these changes have been debated vigorously. Many social scientists and economic development specialists charge that the growth of large farms and decline of smaller, family operations jeopardize local well-being. Although restructuring of the farm sector has been evident for several decades and throughout all regions of the United States, the consequences of this process are virtually unstudied at the national level.

Second, farming is a vital economic activity that particularly affects the fortunes of rural areas and contributes to nearly all metropolitan economies as well. Farming is the foundation of the agricultural system, the nation's largest industry and its major employer, incorporating nearly one-quarter of the labor force (The National Commission on Agricultural Trade and Export Policy, 1986). Although the farm population has declined to about two percent, farming remains a dominant economic sector in more than a fifth of all U.S. counties (Bender et al., 1985). Changes in farming reverberate throughout the community,

affecting the livelihood of the people and businesses directly and indirectly connected to this sector. In rural areas, the restructuring of the farm sector has been
accompanied by declines in other traditional industries, such as mining, forestry,
and labor intensive manufacturing. The combination of these changes has led
to a general rural economic crisis and rising inequality in jobs, income, and living
standards between urban and rural areas in recent years. As the *Wall Street Journal*
(August 4, 1988:1) reports: "...the U.S. has been suffering more than a farm
crisis... It is in the midst of a coast-to-coast, border-to-border collapse of much
of its rural economy."

A third reason for focusing on farming is that this sector has been poorly
understood and relatively neglected in studies on the organization of economic
production. Theory and research on economic structure in first world societies
center mainly on service and manufacturing industries and on urban locations.
The primacy of urbanized, industrial sectors as an object of investigation and
as a setting from which to examine the dynamics of economic development dates
back to the time of the classical social theorists. In contrast, farming is more
often relegated to studies of preindustrial eras. By extending inquiry into the
agricultural sector and into rural areas, this book broadens and redirects general
social science concern with economic structure.

Finally, by examining farming as well as industry, I hope to bridge social
science perspectives and research traditions in both substantive areas. The
organization of contemporary economic production and its effects on individuals'
life chances have been studied mainly by sociologists, economists, and geographers.
In each discipline, agriculture and industry are distinct subfields. The literature
in industrial sociology and in the sociology of agriculture is particularly relevant
to the issues addressed in this book. Despite mutual concern with the effects
of economic structure on socioeconomic conditions, agricultural and industrial
sociologists tend to disregard one another's work. As a consequence, industrial
sociologists generally treat farming as a homogenous sector while agricultural
sociologists overemphasize the uniqueness of agricultural production and its
importance in determining local socioeconomic conditions. Examining farm and
industry structure allows comparisons to be drawn regarding patterns of development, production differences, and socioeconomic impacts that illuminate the
dynamics of both sectors.

FARM STRUCTURE AND SOCIOECONOMIC CONDITIONS: AN OVERVIEW AND EXTENSION

The control of farm production by large-scale corporate farms has long
concerned social scientists. In a study originally completed during the 1940s,
Walter Goldschmidt (1968, 1979a) addressed this issue through a comparison
of two rural California communities. One community was characterized by large-

scale farms employing extensive hired labor, the other by family owned and operated farms of small to moderate size. Goldschmidt found poorer socio-economic conditions in the large-farm community: residents had less education, lower income, and lower levels of living. There were few civic and social organizations. Because the owners of the large farms did not live in the community but controlled the fiscal and political structure, schools and other municipal services were less numerous and of low quality. In contrast, the community with family operated farms had better socioeconomic conditions, a thriving nonfarm business sector, numerous local organizations, and an active community polity. Goldschmidt attributed the differences in the two communities to the type of farm operations. Smaller, family operated farms result in a community of middle class individuals with higher, more evenly distributed incomes and a strong interest in their community. The differences observed by Goldschmidt have endured: in 1977 a team of researchers from the Small Farm Viability Project revisited the communities and reported surprisingly similar findings.

From the time of Goldschmidt's study to the present, analysts have continued to debate whether or not larger farms lead to greater inequality and lower quality of life as compared to family operations. The 1980s farm crisis heightened interest in the issue. Rural people, policy makers, and academics question seriously the consequences of a decline in moderate-size family operations and their potential replacement by other types of farms, such as large, industrial farms or even small, part-time farms.

Despite decades of research, a number of questions about the Goldschmidt hypothesis, as it is called, remain unanswered. First, in light of dramatic postwar changes, such as the massive reduction in the number of farms, movement to a service economy, and growing state welfare expenditures, to what extent is the Goldschmidt hypothesis still relevant? Do localities with many large-scale farms have poorer conditions today? Another question is whether the effects of farm structure are confined only to particular areas. Because virtually all studies center on specific states or regions, little is known about the effects of farm structure which is generalizable to the national level.

Beyond these questions, more significant conceptual issues remain. Although Goldschmidt argued that nonfarm characteristics such as population size, locational advantages, and other resources also influenced community quality and needed to be held constant, subsequent studies have often failed to examine important factors external to farming. Over time, the importance of farming as an economic base has decreased while that of manufacturing and service industry has grown. Today, about a half of all farm operators report their principal occupation to be a nonfarm one. Yet nearly all studies on the effects of farm structure neglect local industrial structure. This has consequences beyond the methodological level, that is, beyond the failure to control for a potentially confounding factor. By omitting industrial structure, analysts lose a piece of reality essential for understanding local inequality.

The research question addressed by studies in the Goldschmidt tradition is also framed narrowly in terms of theory and scope. It is rarely linked to literatures outside rural sociology or agricultural economics and it is defined as a problem unique to the farm sector. Rather, the fundamental question addressed by the Goldschmidt studies is about the relationship between the economy and socioeconomic inequities, a broad issue with a long tradition of theory and research behind it in the social sciences. Moreover, industrial sociologists and labor economists have taken a parallel approach by focusing on how industrial structure affects socioeconomic differentials. In both cases, structural interpretations are presented. That is, the source of inequality is seen as situated largely in the organization of economic production. The issues raised by Goldschmidt are thus deeply connected to wider theoretical concerns about the relationship between the economy and inequality and about the origins of inequality itself.

But despite these interdisciplinary substantive and theoretical linkages, the Goldschmidt question has rarely been cast into a broader conceptual framework. By focusing on economic structure, whether farming or industry, we gain an understanding of how the conditions of production in a particular locality affect life chances. However, local inequality also results from other social forces, such as what individuals themselves do or have done in the past to modify the conditions of their existence, and from less mutable factors such as geographical region and other spatial characteristics. Thus, to understand how economic structure generates patterns of inequality it, too, must be seen as only one piece of a larger puzzle.

PURPOSE OF THE BOOK

This book is a response to the preceding questions and issues. While it explores how the structure of both farming and industry shape the patterns and levels of local inequality, the focus is primarily on farming. Much has been written about contemporary industrial restructuring and issues such as plant closings, geographical shifting of operations, and changes in job stratification and the labor process. The farm sector, however, has also undergone a dramatic and parallel restructuring with repercussions for local communities that have been debated extensively but less studied. I broaden previous work on this issue in several ways.

First, the effects of farm structure are examined across the United States and across major agricultural regions. This allows a view of relationships at the national level and permits comparison among regions and between regions and the nation as a whole.

Second, I extend the analysis of farm structure to local industrial structure, comparing the two sectors regarding patterns of development and influences on local socioeconomic conditions. Interrelationships between farming and industry are also explored.

Third, I situate the Goldschmidt hypothesis in the context of broader social science theoretical perspectives. I start from the premise that the Goldschmidt hypothesis is really about how the local economy generates inequality and, in an even more fundamental sense, about how inequality itself comes to be generated across localities. Reformulating the issue in this way grounds the Goldschmidt debate into traditional social science concerns, allowing it to be linked to other literatures and disciplines.

Finally and most importantly, I develop a conceptual framework that ties farming and industry structure and other structural factors to inequalities in socioeconomic conditions across localities. This involves the interplay of three sets of forces: economic structure, spatial or locational structure, and human agency in the form of characteristics that empower workers and their households. My perspective is developed through a synthesis of political economy and other structural approaches. Political economy deals with the distribution and accumulation of economic surplus and how these activities are influenced by social and political arrangements. It is therefore useful in explaining the development and impact of economic sectors. The insights generated by Marxian political economists are particularly relevant because they situate economic change and development into a broad, historically based theory.

Although the issues addressed in this book involve social science theory and ongoing disciplinary debates, they are not confined to the academic setting. The research problem is grounded in everyday life for millions of Americans. What does it mean to live in a community where large-scale, industrialized farms control employment opportunities and land, water, and other local resources or where most jobs are in fast-food restaurants, retail chains, and other low wage industries? What alternatives and bases of resistance do individuals and communities have in the face of low paying jobs or no jobs or when confronted with the loss of autonomy in traditional work activities? Economic development specialists, planners, policy makers, and working people and their organizations grapple with such questions every day. The motivation for this book comes out of real concern for the people these issues touch.

The study is situated in the 1970–1980 period. Major economic changes were occurring during this decade which constituted a significant break with previous periods. These changes are ongoing and still unresolved today. During the 1970s, farming continued to follow postwar trends toward increasing scale, decreasing farm numbers, and declining middle sector of traditional family farms. These changes occurred within a domestic and global economic climate that brought relative prosperity to the farm sector. Midway through the decade, however, a series of strains erupted in the wider economy which eventually undermined this prosperity. The postwar, fordist epoch of high mass consumption, mass production, high wages and family incomes, and liberal welfare state entered into crisis. The consequences were felt first in the nonfarm economy through rising unemployment, declining real earnings, and growing poverty. By the next decade, rural areas and the farm sector were engulfed by a parallel crisis. In order to understand contemporary changes in agriculture, industry, and levels of inequality, the 1970–1980 period is a critical starting point.

The remainder of this chapter centers on the theoretical perspectives that attempt to account for socioeconomic inequality. I review critically the conventional social science explanations that rest on neoclassical economic and functionalist assumptions. The structural perspective, within which political economy falls, challenges conventional explanations by addressing the macrosociological origins of inequality. I examine structural perspectives on industry, farming, and local labor markets, which consider the relationship between economic structure and socioeconomic outcomes across space. My perspective on local inequality is developed from a critique and synthesis of this literature.

THEORETICAL PERSPECTIVES ON SOCIOECONOMIC INEQUALITY

Functionalism and Human Capital Theory

The sources of socioeconomic inequality have long concerned social scientists. While there have been a variety of approaches to the study of inequality, two general perspectives have emerged, one based on conventional sociological and economic assumptions, the other developed as a counter to these (Tomaskovic-Devey, 1987; Horan and Tolbert, 1984). The conventional approach has emerged from neoclassical economic theory, specifically human capital theory, and its sociological counterpart, functionalism, which share similar assumptions and ideology. These theories tend to view socioeconomic differences as a consequence of personal attributes and qualifications. Functionalism assumes that differential rewards (such as earnings, prestige, and power) must be associated with occupational positions in order to ensure that the most capable people fill these positions (Davis and Moore, 1945). Similarly, human capital theory views differential rewards (earnings) as resulting from an exchange process in which those workers with appropriate supply attributes (education, skills) are rewarded to the extent they meet the demand requirements of employers. Both perspectives assume that workers and employers are rational economic actors and that workers exercise free and informed choice about career objectives. Socioeconomic differentials are regarded not only as necessary for the operation of the economic system but also as fundamentally just because individuals' positions in the socioeconomic order are seen to signify their productivity or social value.

In explaining socioeconomic differences, functionalism and human capital theory point to individuals' characteristics and the choices they make. Some explanations focus on cultural attributes, such as Lewis's (1968) "culture of poverty" in which social and psychological adaptations to poverty are seen as enmeshing the poor in a web of cultural attributes that limit their advance. Sociologists (Blau and Duncan, 1967; Hauser and Featherman, 1977) have developed status attainment models that focus on education and other personal background characteristics. Human capital theorists (Becker, 1964; Mincer, 1970) examine factors that enhance or inhibit workers' competitiveness, such as education, skills, motivation, and experience. Both functionalism and human capital theory see personal investment in education and training as a key determinant of job position and earnings, thus stressing the "supply" characteristics of the labor force. Some revision of this general argument has occurred as a response to obvious differences in earnings between men and women or between whites and minorities. Economists have relaxed competitive market assumptions by recognizing employers' tastes for discrimination. Perceived as less desirable workers by employers, blacks and women are said to be last in the labor market line, thus confronting fewer and poorer paid positions (Thurow, 1975).

Human capital theory and functionalist perspectives on inequality and poverty have been criticized from an empirical (Beeghley, 1983; Blaug, 1976; Schiller, 1980) as well as ideological basis. The ideological underpinnings of these perspectives serve to justify and explain the privileged positions of the middle and upper class (Gans, 1972; Schiller, 1980; Tomaskovic-Devey, 1988b). Policy prescriptions to reduce poverty and other inequities take the form of upgrading individual characteristics or human capital through education and training, since the individual rather than society is perceived as flawed. Such policies are ideologically and economically appealing because they imply that society is doing all it can do to help the poor and that further government expenditures and larger social structural changes are unnecessary (Schiller, 1980).

Recent Structural Perspectives

Functionalism and human capital theory have been challenged by the new structuralism. This approach can be considered an umbrella for a variety of recent perspectives some of which are rooted in Marxian political economy. The structural approach focuses on the context in which inequality is created, that is, on the social order that constrains individuals' choices and generates the positions individuals occupy. The opportunities provided by the organization of economic production, specifically in the quality and quantity of employment, are considered key factors in explaining socioeconomic differentials. The structural perspective is thus more concerned with the demand aspect of the labor market (Tomaskovic-Devey, 1988c). Most income is employment related. Employers rather than employees determine the number of jobs and the rewards associated with them. Socioeconomic differences are therefore a structural issue which cannot be understood by reference to individual characteristics alone (Hodge and Laslett, 1980:129).

For example, Tomaskovic-Devey (1987) persuasively argues that individual characteristics, such as race, gender, and education are not the cause of the amount of poverty in a locality. Rather, these characteristics are the basis for allocating poverty, in part, because employers use them as a screening device when hiring employees. Suppose all Americans became white, college-educated men. As Tomaskovic-Devey notes, the amount of poverty would not change because the quality and quantity of employment had remained unchanged. This argument also challenges policy prescriptions central to functionalist and human capital perspectives which have stressed job training and schooling as a solution to low wages and poverty. Rather than reduce poverty, such programs merely "reshuffle the queue of people waiting for available jobs" (Tomaskovic-Devey, 1987:59). Bowles and Gintis (1976) also have shown that the link between educational achievement and workplace rewards is tenuous. Socioeconomic background is a major determinant of both educational level and labor market position.

Three strains of literature grounded in the structural approach are relevant for developing a conceptual framework on locality and inequality. The first centers on the industrial sector and examines the effects of stratification among industries, firms, and jobs on workers' earnings and related employment conditions. Most of this literature is aspatial in the sense that it does not deal with relationships occurring across place. The second strain of literature focuses on the single industry of farming and examines the consequences of variations among different farm units for community and household levels of inequality. This literature is characterized by the numerous studies addressing the Goldschmidt hypothesis. The final strain, labor market research, situates the analysis of inequality into a spatial context. It particularly focuses on how the industrial structure and labor force characteristics of different locales determine variations in workers' earnings and other employment outcomes.

Structural Perspectives: Industry. Much of the new structuralist literature is based upon the assumption that the economy is composed of distinct sectors that vary in the rewards and opportunities they provide workers (Doeringer and Piore, 1971; Edwards, 1979; Gordon, 1972; Gordon et al., 1982; O'Connor, 1973). This approach is often referred to as segmented or dual economy theory. According to segmented economy theory, the uneven development of production has resulted in two distinct privatized sectors and their specific firms. One is the peripheral or competitive sector; the other is the core or oligopoly and monopoly sector. In the core sector, firms tend to be large and have a major share of production in their home industries, elaborate divisions of labor, internal job ladders, and stable employment. Core firms generate higher skilled and remunerated occupational positions. The converse conditions are found in the periphery. Firms in this sector have smaller labor forces and informally organized divisions of labor. They generate lower paid, less skilled positions. In addition to the organization of production in the two privatized sectors, or those organized by capital, many segmented economy theorists (O'Connor, 1973; Hodson, 1978; Schervish, 1983) recognize a third sector, that organized by the state. The state functions as part of the business sector by producing goods and services and by acting as an employer. It also provides the distinct function of mediating relationships in the privatized economy. Earnings in the state sector are said to be relatively high, falling between the core and periphery (Hodson, 1978).

Segmented economy theory is an established part of labor economics and the sociology of industry with a literature spanning at least two decades. Fine (1987) traces early elements of the theory back to Adam Smith and John Stuart Mill. However, it is by no means a coherent theory and can best be considered an ordering framework for the analysis of inequality. Most research on the segmented economy centers on job outcomes such as earnings and benefits (Beck et al., 1978; Hodson, 1978, 1983; Tigges, 1988). Relatively few studies have examined the effects of economic segmentation on local socioeconomic conditions (for exceptions see Reif, 1987; Tomaskovic-Devey, 1987; Bloomquist and Summers, 1982).

Structural Perspectives: Farming. The agricultural sector involves the entire system of food and fiber production. It encompasses three types of activities: the provision of agricultural inputs; farming; and the processing, transporting, and marketing of farm products. Farming was originally a self-sufficient enterprise in which producers performed all three types of activities. As the market economy developed, agricultural functions not directly associated with food and fiber production shifted to nonfarm enterprises or agribusiness.

Economic segmentation theorists generally consider farming part of the peripheral sector. Paid farm employment does tend to be casual, relatively unskilled, and low wage (Glover, 1984; Mamer, 1984). However, classifying farming as peripheral employment obscures fundamental differences between farming and other industries in patterns of development (Goss et al., 1980), production dynamics (Mann and Dickinson, 1978), degree of state intervention (Schervish, 1983), and use of unpaid, family labor. This view also ignores differences among production units in farming that affect socioeconomic disparities. As a result, a study of farming must focus on variations within this single industry as well as the position of farming itself in the segmented economy.

That local socioeconomic conditions are a consequence, in part, of the opportunities generated by the economic system was recognized as early as the 1930s by agricultural sociologists (Tetreau, 1938; Goldschmidt, 1978a). The structural perspective in agriculture focuses on the uneven development of the farm sector and on the socioeconomic impacts of various farm structures. Researchers have been concerned with postwar, long-term structural trends toward larger and fewer farms, and particularly with the growth of large-scale, hired labor dependent farms. As noted previoulsy, Walter Goldschmidt's (1978a) work has been a starting point for the numerous studies on this issue. The Goldschmidt hypothesis that large-scale industrial-like farming has detrimental community impacts, while smaller scale family operated units improve community life, has been tested over various time periods and locations. Although recent studies have reported divergences, much of the literature supports the hypothesis.

A second conceptual tack in analyzing the effects of farm structure has been taken in research on the farm financial crisis of the 1980s. Like studies in the Goldschmidt tradition, these are concerned with the same structural trend toward larger and fewer farms. However, they emphasize the accelerated pace with which midsize, family operated farms have declined in the face of the farm crisis, rather than the growth of large-scale industrial farming. The decline of midsize family farms implies a loss of middle class independent producers sustaining community institutions, with a consequent decline in community well-being unless factors such as opportunities for nonfarm employment intervene. Most studies on the farm crisis center on the farm household rather than the rural community so that the extent to which community well-being has been jeopardized is still largely unknown.

The Local Labor Market. With the exception of studies on farming, much of the research from structural perspectives does not focus on localities or other aggregate spatial units. The local labor market is an important concept for understanding inequality because it links social relations to place. However, there is no uniform meaning for this concept (Horan and Tolbert, 1984:9), and labor market research is a rubric for diverse studies and conceptual (albeit mainly structural) frameworks. Labor markets involve particular types of social relations in a locality, relationships of exchange between workers and employers.

Horan and Tolbert (1984:10) define the local labor market as a geographic area "within which transactions between buyers and sellers of labor are situated and occur on a regular basis." The local labor market is a center of employment opportunities. It is structured by industries with their respective firms and job positions and by a labor force with varying skills and qualifications. Labor markets thus embody structural constraints which circumscribe and shape individuals' economic opportunities. Labor markets vary in the extent to which interaction between employers and employees is self-contained and to which employment parameters constrain the mobility of some categories of workers, such as the less skilled, more than others (Horan and Tolbert, 1984:11). A continuing methodological issue has been the operational definition of the labor market. Those typically employed include: standard metropolitan statistical areas (SMSAs), counties, states, and Bureau of Economic Analysis economic areas based on commuting-to-work patterns (Horan and Tolbert, 1984).

Labor market research is generally directed to the consequences of local labor market organization for workers. Labor markets offering better employment opportunities tend to result in better economic rewards for all workers and in greater returns to human capital investments. Most commonly, models of individuals' earnings are estimated as a function of individual characteristics, such as age, education, and race, and contextual characteristics of the local labor market, such as racial composition, unemployment rates, and industrial and occupational structure (Hanushek, 1973; Parcel 1979; Parcel and Mueller, 1983).

In addition to labor market approaches that use the individual as the unit of analysis, a few studies have examined the effects of labor market structure on socioeconomic outcomes at the aggregate level. Studies of nonmetropolitan industrialization have found that the effects of incoming industry on local well-being depend upon the type of industry and the employment opportunities generated (Summers et al., 1976; Shaffer, 1979). A few researchers have also examined the effects of segmented industrial structures across labor markets (Tomaskovic-Devey, 1987, 1988a; Horan and Tolbert, 1984; Bloomquist and Summers, 1982; Reif, 1987). These studies have found that high wage core industries result in better local socioeconomic conditions, such as higher income and lower poverty. Labor market research adds a spatial dimension to the analysis of inequality and can therefore advance structural perspectives.

In sum, research from the structural perspectives in agriculture and in industry shows that the organization of economic production has developed unevenly, resulting in economic structures that offer different rewards and opportunities for individuals. Structural perspectives are a counter to conventional social science theories such as functionalism and human capital theory because they address the macrosociological origins of inequality rather than idividuals' labor market defects and choices. They thus shift emphasis to the context in which individual choices are made, demonstrating that good jobs and high incomes are unattainable for many Americans as a consequence of economic structure.

A CRITIQUE OF LABOR MARKET RESEARCH AND STRUCTURAL APPROACHES

Studies from the structural approach (including labor market research) do an important job of documenting how economic structure produces inequality. However, they have tended to give less attention to what people do to shape the conditions of their existence. Recently, researchers have argued that the forces that allow individuals to set the terms and conditions of their employment—their market capacity—must be incorporated into structural perspectives (Bradley and Lowe, 1984; Tigges, 1988; Tomaskovic-Devey, 1987). In part, this means reinterpreting human capital characteristics, such as age, education, and skill levels, from factors that enhance an individual's chance of job rewards to factors which provide greater bargaining power for groups of workers vis-à-vis employers

(Tigges, 1988). It also means recognizing that the allocation of rewards on the basis of race and gender goes beyond individual employer tastes for discrimination and is rooted in social structural factors, particularly the need for pools of low-wage, available labor. Finally, it means consideration of organizations, such as unions, that empower workers and of social welfare programs and policies that allow workers greater options in the face of low-wage employment (Tomaskovic-Devey, 1987). The incorporation of the market capacity of labor into structural perspectives counters some of the critiques of this literature, specifically the focus on the demand side of the labor market and the rigidity of a top-down approach that ignores the frame of human action.

Although labor market and other research from structural perspectives contribute enormously to an understanding of how social inequities become attached to forms of the organization of production, there are a number of shortcomings with the literature. First, it tends to focus on exchange processes between employers and employees without regard to their sociopolitical context. While structural perspectives do challenge human capital and functionalist assumptions by recognizing that individuals' labor market options are constrained by social structural factors, the sale of labor power tends to be viewed within a context of formal legal equality. Market relations and mutual dependencies between workers and employers are emphasized over relations of coercion or exploitation. These assumptions are evident in the solutions prescribed to industrial restructuring, generally framed in efforts to recapitalize localities, rather than in social changes which fundamentally alter the relationship between capital and labor (Fine, 1987).

Beyond the set of assumptions governing much of the structuralist research, a second issue concerns theoretical development. There have been few attempts to situate the analysis of economic structure (whether in farming or industry) into wider social theory: the uneven development of economic structures over space and differentiated effects on individuals and their localities have not been explored in any coherent framework. Rather, much of the literature tends to be empirically driven and loosely connected to the broader sociopolitical context.

A third set of issues revolves around the scope of research. Beyond the Goldschmidt literature, there has been little attempt to examine employment outside formal wage labor, such as farming and other forms of self-employment (for an exception, see Deseran and Dellenbarger, 1988). Most studies also center on the privatized sector with its underlying market assumptions rather than the state sector, which is governed by a different set of political economic forces (O'Connor, 1973). If the state is analyzed at all, it is generally in its role as an employer. The political economic role of the state, to mediate in the privatized sector and facilitate accumulation, is generally neglected (Fine, 1987).

Finally, the labor market tends to be viewed as a locus of production rather than as a concomitant locus of consumption and site of reproduction of labor power. Labor market outcomes in the industrial sector are most always analyzed in production-related terms, such as earnings. There have been few attempts to study the effects of labor market structures on health, education, and other extra-economic indicators, although this would be a logical research extension that could contribute to a broader understanding of local quality of life.

TOWARD A POLITICAL ECONOMY OF LOCALITY AND INEQUALITY

Political economy addresses the limitations of other structural perspectives and provides the conceptual tools for developing a general approach to the study of locality and inequality. Marxist political economy situates the origins and development of the organization of economic production into the sociopolitical context. It directs attention to the salient aspects of economic structure and related factors which have a bearing on local inequality. It also organizes empirical inquiry through delineating relevant concepts for empirical observation and structuring the interpretation of research findings. Under the capitalist mode of production, Marx recognized the evolution of two contending classes: the capitalist class or bourgeoisie who owns and controls the means of production; and workers or the proletariat who have only labor power or the ability to sell their work. From Marx's perspective, the fundamental basis for inequality in a society comes from this differential social relationship between capital and labor.

Marx saw the control of capitalists over the means of production as giving them unequal power over workers in the marketplace, creating the basis for inequalities in other areas of life (Smith, 1977). According to Marx, the value of commodities is equal to the value of three factors required to produce them: constant capital, or raw materials and machinery; variable capital, or the value of labor power which depends on the costs of subsistence, or food, clothing, and other necessities needed for reproducing the labor force; and surplus value, which reflects the unpaid contribution of labor to the commodity. Upon selling the commodity, the capitalist realizes surplus value that, in its money form, can be reinvested into production, providing the basis for successive expansions of production and accumulation of capital. The more capitalists are able to reduce the market price of labor power or wages to subsistence levels, the higher will be the rate of extraction of surplus value. The actual rate at which capitalists extract surplus value depends upon the nature of the production process and on historical and political factors.[2]

Wood (1986:7) summarizes the Marxian perspective on wage differentials and general economic inequality.

Wage levels therefore reflect the broader political, social and historical dimensions of the relationship between capital and labor as social classes, over and above the technical makeup of the production process and necessary subsistence levels. Generally, it is the relationship between the

speed and extent of capitalist development and the number of available
jobs on the one hand, and the supply of available labor power on the other
that will determine the relative strengths of capital and labor, rates of
exploitation, and wage levels. The ability of a strong working class to
organize in order to control the influx of labor into a particular industry
may increase wage levels significantly above the value of labor power. On
the other hand, a large excess of labor power will allow capital to reduce
wages toward or even below their value, transforming the workers' fund
for necessary consumption into a fund for the accumulation of capital. . .The
struggle between capital and labor. . .over the rate of surplus value. . .is
not only the basis of class conflict in capitalist society but also the major
determinant of the amount of profit, the rate of capital accumulation, and
general living standards.

A major contribution of Marx's perspective is that socioeconomic inequality
is shown to be an alterable and unnecessary societal feature that stems from the
social relations of production (Townsend, 1979:80). But although Marx directs
our attention to the origins of inequality, the classical Marxist perspective must
be broadened to account for current socioeconomic inequalities. First, income
differentials and general living standards within or between classes were not a
focus of Marx's work. Marx emphasized the polarizing nature of production and
the development of distinct classes rather than the "more graduated character
of consumption" (Townsend, 1979:80), which was an assumed but largely unex-
plored consequence of class location. Second, Marx did not anticipate the increase
of intermediate class groupings, neither fully capitalist nor working class, such
as part-time farmers, managers, and others in contradictory class locations (Wright,
1978; Mooney, 1983). Not all individuals in a society have a definitive position
in the structure of production, and individuals may occupy more than one position at one time. Third, in addition to class relations, race, gender, age, and other
asymmetrical relationships affect the allocation of wages and resources. Fourth,
as is often noted, Marx focused on a competitive capitalist environment rather
than the current stage of monopoly capitalism. The development of a segmented
economy and the persistence of simple commodity production such as family
labor farming were largely unanticipated. State intervention to counter the
destabilizing effects of the economy was also assumed minimal. Finally, the
geographic mobility of capital, the ability of capital to seek out new markets and
labor pools and to take advantage of changing conditions of accumulation has
occurred on a more rapid and global scale than envisioned by Marx.

In developing a political economic account of the effects of current economic
structure on local inequality, I therefore reach into areas not fully treated by Marx.
As a consequence, this involves consideration of recent studies dealing with issues
of comparatively less concern to Marx, such as agriculture and inequalities in

the sphere of consumption. It also involves analyses of advanced captialism, which focus on economic segmentation, the role of the state, and uneven spatial development. An overview of the key elements and issues involved in understanding current local inequality is presented in the following section.

Locality and Inequality: A Conceptual Framework

Most theory in economics and sociology is constructed as if people lived in a spatial vacuum. Classical economic and early Marxist perspectives centered on the uniformity of the development process and assumed that spatial differences among localities, regions, and nations would diminish as development proceeded. Because labor was considered relatively mobile, its attachment to place was generally not an important issue. Contemporary social science theory, including segmented economy theory and general theories of stratification (Collins, 1974, Wright, 1978; Poulantzos, 1974), as well as empirical research in these areas also centers on individuals independent of their locality. Yet social relations are inextricably tied to a spatial context and cannot be fully understood without reference to this context. As others have succinctly put it, "space makes a difference" (Savage et al., 1987:30).

By 'locality,' I refer to the local social system or to the system of social relations existing in a geographically defined locality (Bradley and Lowe, 1984).[3] Localities are settings of social interaction, specific to time and place, where structures and institutions shape and are shaped by the activity of their inhabitants (Jonas, 1988:3). Localities reflect social relations and organizational structures found in the larger society but these emerge differentially, due to the unique pattern of development of a specific area. Nonlocal or national processes, such as industrial restructuring and welfare policies, are mediated and reconstituted by these prior local variations. In a sense, localities can be viewed as purveyors of the various contingent conditions under which general social processes operate (Jonas, 1988:1).[4]

The locality as a unit of analysis contributes in several ways to an understanding of how the organization of economic production engenders inequality. First, the effects of industry and farming cannot be properly understood without situating them into a spatial context (Urry and Ward, 1985). The distribution of these sectors as well as their restructuring occurs unevenly across localities so that the costs and benefits of economic change likewise take on an uneven form. This means that individuals' life chances come to be differentially constrained by the place in which they live. Second, the locality is an appropriate level at which to observe inequality because it is not only the site of production but also the site of consumption activities. The effects of economic restructuring are not limited to workers and earnings but extend to households and consumption levels. State efforts to counteract the destabilizing effects of economic change also occur at this level. State programs redistribute benefits on the basis of local demographic characteristics, and social welfare policies are informally implemented through local offices. Finally, Urry (1984) argues that current economic restructuring has intensified the political importance of local systems of stratification. Classes have become more politically fragmented, and distributional struggles have moved from workplace to consumption issues. The locality is increasingly the site for political action for the redistribution of rewards.

Historical changes in the accumulation process have given rise to distinct economic structures in advanced capitalism, which affect local inequality. The development of economic segmentation has served to differentiate the core, periphery, and state sectors and their respective labor market segments (O'Connor, 1973; Edwards, 1979; Hodson, 1978, 1983; Gordon et al., 1982). However, in contrast to non-Marxian structural perspectives (e.g. Averitt, 1968; Doeringer and Piore, 1971), economic segmentation is grounded in the conflicting interests of capital and labor over the terms and conditions of work and the nature of the production process (Fine, 1987:11).[5]

The development of the farm sector proceeded somewhat differently from the nonfarm economy. While the concentration and centralization of capital also resulted in the tendency toward large-scale production units using hired labor, capital encountered barriers in farming related to land and biological production to which the nonfarm sector had generally not been subject. A holistic theory of the development of the farm sector under advanced capitalism has yet to emerge, but most current explanations center on the ways in which capital subsumes farmers in the accumulation process and on the obstacles to capitalist investment in farming (Mann and Dickinson, 1978; FitzSimmons, 1986; Friedmann, 1981). Kautsky (1988) explained how the development of farming takes on the daulistic pattern noted by contemporary observers (Stockdale, 1982; Goss et al., 1980). As the market economy expands, nonfarm capital comes to penetrate the farm sector, enmeshing producers into networks of exchange, for example, through the purchase of farm inputs and marketing of farm products. The previously homogenous farm stratum undergoes a process of differentiation or internal stratification in which some farmers come to resemble wage-laborers and others, large-scale capitalist producers. This internal stratification is reflected in recent farm changes. Small, part-time farms have increased in number; large-scale industrial type farms have come to account for a greater proportion of agricultural sales; and moderate-size farms based upon family labor have declined in number while those remaining have become highly capital-intensive and market oriented (Stockdale, 1982).

The uneven development of farming and industry structure has important implications for socioeconomic inequality. Income and general living standards reflect levels of consumption needed to reproduce labor power. Capital has differential stakes and abilities to support the consumption levels of particular workers and their families. High wages in the core sector are a viable strategy for securing a stable, skilled, and reliable work force. The strength of labor organizations in the core sector also ensures that a larger share of the total product in the form of wages will be paid to workers. Capital will thus tend to be more progressive in support of workers' consumption interests in the core. In contrast, where workers are more easily replaced and profits lower, as in the peripheral sector, employers have less need and ability to support high income and standards of living. When segments of the labor force are unable to reproduce themselves on the basis of the wage exclusively, state-sponsored social welfare bridges the gap between wages and costs on consumption (Wayne, 1986).[6]

Large farms dependent upon hired labor are similar to peripheral sector firms in that they generally require relatively unskilled, low-wage labor and provide unstable employment and limited benefits. Owners of such farms have little need to provide high income and consumption levels, particularly where much farm labor is seasonal and not tied to any particular enterprise. In contrast, because family farmers are not entirely proletarianized, they occupy different class positions than farm laborers, positions associated with generally better socioeconomic conditions.

The absence of the wage relationship (or hired labor dependency) within family farming means that capital subsumes such farmers in different ways than industrial workers or workers on large farms. Family farmers are integrated into circuits of exchange through the use of finance capital, farm inputs, processing and marketing facilities, and the land market. They struggle with fractions of large capital over the amount of surplus product (through pricing, interest rates) that remains to the household. Smaller farms may also be linked to capital through employment off the farm. These linkages, in turn, affect farmers' class locations. Family farmers who own their means of production and whose means of subsistence is derived mainly from farming are considered simple commodity producers or part of the petty bourgeoisie. Those who vary on the previous criteria, such as part-time farmers, tenants, and contract farmers, occupy contradictory class locations (Mooney, 1983). Because most family farmers are situated in these latter positions, living standards or consumption levels cannot facilely be read off from class position. Rather, inequalities *within* the family farm sector must be seen as an empirical question which depends upon the specific sociohistorical context (Mann and Dickinson, 1978).[7]

The economic power of capital—whether over farm and industrial workers through the wage relationship or over family farmers in the sphere of exchange— produces inequalities in other areas of social life. For example, levels of health, education, social disruption such as crime and suicide, and other social characteristics are directly affected by the level of economic well-being in an area (Smith, 1982; Morrill and Wohlenberg, 1971). Local politics may also be subject to control by particular fractions of capital, jeopardizing community interests in areas such as service provisions, environmental regulations, and tax policies (Falk and Lyson, 1988; Bluestone and Harrison, 1982). The implications of economic control thus extend to the extraeconomic arena.

Local inequality is not only a consequence of economic structure but also of the power of a population to set the terms and conditions under which its workers sell their labor power. According to Tomaskovic-Devey (1988a), three key factors empower workers vis-à-vis capital, enabling them to resist low wage employment. The first reflects the social wage, the "amalgam of benefits, worker protections, and legal rights" as well as worker organizational initiatives that "generally increase the social security of the working class" (Bluestone and Harrison, 1982:133). For example, labor organizations and nonlabor market guarantees such as welfare provided by the state are resources that facilitate workers' control over employment conditions and protect them from capital. While unionization has been viewed as the co-optation of workers by capital and welfare programs as the co-optation of workers by the state, it is increasingly argued that these represent real gains made by the working class (Block, 1987; Piven and Cloward, 1987). An organized workforce permits labor to confront capital on a more equal basis in the marketplace, and welfare and similar state programs allow workers to withhold their labor power when faced with low wage employment. A second factor empowering workers is the availability of employment. When the number of jobs exceeds job seekers, labor has greater ability to demand higher wages (Tomaskovic-Devey, 1988a). The final factor involves characteristics of the labor force. Historically, employers have used ascribed characteristics such as race and gender to discriminate in the allocation of jobs and to balkanize the labor force. Discrimination not only makes those who are discriminated against vulnerable to low wages but also undercuts the solidarity and bargaining power of other labor (Tomaskovic-Devey, 1988a). Education functions similarly as a device to screen out workers deemed less desirable. The power of a labor force to resist low paying jobs thus depends in part on its internal composition.

A final element to be included in a theory of locality and inequality is space, considered in terms of geographic context. Space affects social relations for at least a couple of reasons. First, it circumscribes the movement of capital and labor, presenting opportunities for and constraints on human action. Economic structures and levels of inequality vary spatially because capital continually searches out new opportunities for profits which generates "spontaneous, unregulated patterns of growth and contraction, which are by their very nature unbalanced" (Rees, 1984:31). At specific historical points, certain locations offer capital more accumulation advantages than others. For example, core industries have historically located in the urban Frost Belt to take advantage of labor and product markets. Routinization of production technology at the later stages of the product life cycle is frequently accompanied by a shift from urban to rural areas where expenses are lower and labor less organized (Falk and Lyson, 1988). As the global economy has changed, working class gains in areas such as the urban Frost Belt have become increasingly less tolerable, engendering the typical response of capital flight. In the face of capitalist gains, labor confronts a similar dilemma, either to migrate or to remain in the same location and organize.

In general, the importance of land as a factor of production and other ecological requirements have constrained the movement of agriculture more than industry. However, these constraints appear to be diminishing over time as capital circumvents ecological barriers through the creation of new technologies. Indeed, Rees (1984:33) argues that the spatial configuration of farm structure results from the same social forces governing the nonfarm economy:

> "Rural localities" may be viewed as the outcome of the use of space by particular fractions of capital. The predominance of agricultural production in given areas is the result of investment patterns reflecting specific dimensions of the accumulation process and the searching out of profits... In other words, agricultural production and its associated spatial manifestations are nothing more than a particular instance of much more general trends with capitalist production and the uneven spatial development thereby engendered. Indeed, it is perhaps doubtful that agriculture has even the degrees of specificity which Newby claims for it (i.e., in terms of the significance of land) when compared with other branches of capitalist production such as coal-mining, iron and steel production and so forth.

The spatial intersection of farming and industry has implications for local economic development. Historically, there has been a steady encroachment of industry and urbanization into farming areas with resultant costs and benefits for farmers, notably, rising land values, which constrain entry into farming and farm expansion, greater potential for environmental pollution, and increasing opportunities for off-farm employment. Farming, in turn, shapes the development of local industry because it helps underwrite the costs of reproducing the labor force by providing alternative means of subsistence.

Second, space affects social relations because historical conditions are embodied in location. Uneven development within and between regions means that wealth and poverty are differently dispersed. Moreover, capital tends to build upon pre-existing inequalities, which leads to their further entrenchment. Rural areas have continued to lag behind urban areas on virtually all socioeconomic indicators (Smith, 1982; Howes and Markusen, 1981), and recently the gap has widened. Poorer socioeconomic conditions in the South have been argued to result from the response of capital to historical regional inequalities in the attempt to extract surplus value (Wood, 1986). In sum, different areas present certain opportunities for workers and capital as a result of previous historical conditions. Rural regions and areas with a long tradition of resistance to labor organizations and a history of institutionalized discrimination, offer more limited life conditions for their inhabitants.

Inequality thus arises from the ways in which surplus is appropriated and resources necessary for consumption distributed and from the competition between capital and labor that structures these processes. Local inequality is viewed as a consequence of three factors: the economic structure of farming and industry, the power of labor vis-à-vis capital, and spatial characteristics. These factors order the conceptual perspective presented here as well as structure the interpretation of the empirical analysis.

A perspective on local inequality finally needs to be situated in the context of wider sociopolitical conditions during the period of study. The nature of the accumulation process at a particular historical point affects the shape and structure of industry (Gordon et al., 1982; Edwards, 1979), farming (Kenney et al., 1989), and general well-being. During the 1970–1980 period, farm incomes and land values were high. The agricultural system was appropriately integrated with the industrial system in that production and markets expanded, food costs as a percentage of workers' incomes remained low, and government subsidies were manageable (Kenney et al., 1989). In the nonfarm industrial sector, however, prior strains in the economy coupled with the 1973 oil crisis began to erode postwar fordism. From the mid-1970s, real personal income decreased, unemployment began to rise and rates of productivity declined (Kenney et al., 1989; Gordon et al., 1982; Blumberg, 1980). The U.S. economy became increasingly uncompetitive and in 1981 entered into the worst recession since the 1930s. The power of unions declined (Goldfield, 1987) and formerly protected, well-compensated workers in the core sector lost positions and wage guarantees in the face of deindustrialization (Bluestone and Harrison, 1982). Crisis in the farm sector was manifested somewhat later as the monetarist defeat of inflation launched by the Reagan presidency lowered land values and as worldwide recession and a sharp rise in the value of the dollar reduced the demand for farm exports during the early 1980s (Kenney et al., 1989; Leistritz and Murdock, 1988). By 1986, about one-fifth of all farmers were considered to be under severe financial stress, and farm bankruptcies and foreclosures were occurring at a rate several times that of the historical average (Murdock and Leistritz, 1988:1). The next chapter presents a closer look at the issues and events that have led to crisis and restructuring of the farm and nonfarm economy.

THE PLAN OF THE BOOK

The remainder of the book draws out conceptually and empirically the perspective on inequality articulated above. Chapter 2 discusses the political economic processes that underlie the development of farming and industry. Temporal and spatial aspects of the uneven development of both sectors, particularly recent patterns of restructuring are described. In Chapter 3, I evaluate critically the previous research on the effects of farm structure on local inequality. I probe the reasons for discrepant findings and continued debate about the effects of large farms and outline new directions for research. Chapter 4 examines the non-farm factors that affect inequality, with major focus on the structure of industry, factors affecting the balance of power of labor and capital, and spatial characteristics. Data and methods are presented in Chapter 5. The conceptual model of local inequality is presented and tested for the nation as a whole in Chapter 6 and by region in Chapter 7. The relationship between farming and other local characteristics, particularly the nonfarm industrial economy, is explored in Chapter 8. In the final chapter, I discuss the implications of the findings for research and policy. I also outline new directions for local development efforts in the context of contemporary economic restructuring.

The Uneven Development of
Farm and Industrial Structure

Our understanding of economic development in first world societies has been almost exclusively shaped by reference to the industrial economy. An enormous body of literature centers on the structure of manufacturing and service industries, organizational characteristics of enterprises, occupational hierarchies, and the incumbents who fill labor force positions. This focus has resulted in the neglect of productive activities outside enterprises employing paid labor, such as farming, production of services and goods in the home, and other forms of self-employment. The internal dynamics of these types of production and their relationship to changes in the wider economy broaden our knowledge about the process of economic development. Moreover, productive activities outside paid employment are increasingly important as household survival strategies and as bases for political mobilization under deindustrialization (Urry, 1985). This chapter discusses the political economic processes that shape the development of contemporary agriculture and industry. The evolution of farming is contrasted with that of industry and recent temporal and spatial patterns in the restructuring of both sectors are outlined.

The organization of production in agriculture and industry can be described as taking two ideal forms (Friedmann, 1981). First, capitalist enterprises are defined by the presence of two classes, one that owns and controls the means of production and one that has only labor power. Capitalist enterprises, ranging from small, competitive industries employing wage labor to oligopolistic and monopolistic structures are readily apparent in the industrial sector. Capitalist agricultural enterprises include vertically integrated agribusiness firms, which extend across input, farming, and marketing stages; and horizontal structures, which specialize in a few commodities, with separate ownership, management, and wage labor functions (Goss et al., 1980:100). The second form is simple commodity production in which "producers own their own means of production, hire little or no labor, and [where] commodities are exchanged for money which is used to provide the bulk of the family's subsistence or livelihood" (Buttel, 1980b:10). This form of production typifies family labor farming and, in the industrial sector, particularly in early capitalism, independent artisanry. The distinguishing feature between simple commodity and capitalist production is the absence of wage-labor dependency or the capital-labor relationship in the former. The development of contemporary economic structure involves the rise of segmentation among capitalist enterprises in the industrial sector and the differentiation of simple commodity producers in the farm sector.

THE DEVELOPMENT OF A SEGMENTED INDUSTRIAL STRUCTURE

Until the late nineteenth century, the U.S. economy was characterized by a competitive capitalist environment (Edwards, 1979; Hodson, 1983). Most firms were owned and managed by families or organized as partnerships, with few workers and a simple division of labor, a system that in many respects resembled that of contemporary farming. By the turn of the twentieth century, competition within major industries tended to eliminate small and inefficient firms, and finance capital made possible the growth of large corporations. The economy was dramatically transformed by the growth of big business. Firm expansion and market concentration produced an economic system whereby large firms came to dominate the most profitable industrial sectors,while smaller, generally more recently established firms were left in competitive markets.

Economic segmentation theorists see two distinct types of privatized economic sectors as arising under advanced capitalism: the competitive sector, composed of peripheral firms; and the monopoly or oligopoly sector, composed of core firms (Edwards, 1979; Gordon et al., 1982; Hodson, 1978; O'Connor, 1973). A third sector, representing production organized by the state, is interrelated with these privatized sectors.

According to economic segmentation theory, core firms are large-scale and operate in industries with limited competition. They tend to be vertically integrated and to have national markets and diversified product lines. Profits tend to be higher and risks of failure lower in the core as compared to peripheral sector. Compared to peripheral firms, core firms have a number of advantages that facilitate their growth: they can better capture economies of scale; they have greater access to credit since their probability of long-term survival is greater; and they can benefit from competition among the peripheral firms that compete for the services and contracts they offer (Jacobs, 1985; Edwards, 1979). These firms dominate in industries such as chemicals, petroleum, motor vehicles, aircraft, fabricated metal, and household appliances and in some services such as life insurance and commerical banking (Edwards, 1979:74–75). Industrial unionism tended to take hold in the core sector because union demands are less likely to weaken employers' positions in concentrated markets. Higher profits, lower risks, and the strength of labor organizations affect the quality of jobs, so that core sector employment tends to be relatively high paying, stable, and with internal career ladders (Gordon et al., 1982: Chapter 5).

In contrast to the few hundred core firms with enormous market power, Edwards (1979:72) estimates that about twelve million small and medium-size firms exist in the peripheral sector, in industries or branches of industries not yet controlled by corporations such as in retail and wholesale trade, light manufacturing, and personal and business services. These firms confront many competing sellers in their home product markets while facing monopolized markets everywhere else (Edwards, 1979:72). Thus peripheral firms may only be able to sell to a few large firms, as in the case of auto parts suppliers; they may use products available only from a few manufacturers, as in the case of food franchises; or they may depend on larger enterprises for financing, for granting subcontracts, or for retailing their products (Edwards, 1979:72-73). Peripheral firms have survived in advanced capitalism because some of their productive activities are not profitable for direct investment by the core. Core firms can also enhance their own profitability through exerting monopoly power over the periphery (Gordon et al., 1982:191). In comparison to core firms, peripheral firms have smaller, less unionized labor forces and more informally organized divisions of labor. Peripheral firms are said to draw from those segments of the labor force that have received the lowest wages historically, such as women and minorities.

Production organized by the state is a third sector recognized by segmentation theorists (O'Connor, 1973; Hodson, 1978; Schervish, 1983; Tolbert, 1983; Devine, 1985). The state facilitates the accumulation process by responding to the demands and distributive needs of capital. It also attempts to legitimize the social system through ameliorating some of the inequities and potential political instability produced by the market (Devine, 1985; O'Connor, 1973). The state intervenes in the privatized economy by providing money and in kind transfers, by formulating monetary policy, and by providing subsidies, regulations, and labor legislation (Hodson, 1983:17). As a result of "the demands by capital that the state underwrite monopoly accumulation and the demands by labor that the state deal with the consequences of accumulation on the lives of workers [there] is a systematic tendency for the state sector to expand in the course of capitalist development" (Hodson, 1978:431-432).

The state functions as part of the business sector by producing goods and services for capital and labor, such as education, health and legal services, recreation facilities, and transportation, communications, and other infrastructure. The state also acts as an employer. Though relatively little research exists on employment in the state sector, segmented economy theorists argue that wages should be higher than in the peripheral sector due to the strength of employee organizations (Hodson, 1978) and the state's ability to finance wages and benefits through taxation (Fligstein et al., 1983).

The usefulness of segmented economy theory in explaining local inequality should be seen as historically specific, dependent upon the characteristics of the accumulation process in the wider society. An accumulation strategy involves the mechanisms by which capital accumulates surplus and the social and political conditions, such as the balance of power between capital and labor and relations among segments of capital, which enable this to occur (Wood, 1986:103). The post-World War II period has been termed the fordist regime of accumulation (Noel, 1987; Kenney et al., 1989; Davis, 1978). It is characterized by markets for mass consumption and by mass production techniques that raise the productivity of labor and increase real wages. The economy is dominated by oligopolistic enterprises within which relatively powerful labor organizations are situated. The segmentation of industries into core, peripheral, and state sectors is a reflection of the economy of the fordist era. During the 1970s, however, the fordist regime entered into a period of crisis and, as some have argued (Kenney et al., 1989; Noel, 1987), a new regime of accumulation may be emerging. This has two implications for segmented economy theory. First, the previous advantages of core employment relative to other sectors appear to have changed since the 1970s. Second, the extent to which the segmented approach illuminates post-fordist industrial structure is as yet unclear. These issues are considered in later sections of this chapter.[1]

THE AGRICULTURAL SECTOR AND FARMING

The tendency toward market concentration and increasing firm size, as found in the industrial sector, has also been observed in farming. However, farming has not changed as rapidly or in the same qualitative ways as industry. The growth of large-scale capitalist enterprises employing hired labor has proceeded more slowly. Production units dependent on family labor still characterize the vast majority of farms.

The development of farming, as distinct from other agricultural activities (the provision of agricultural inputs and the processing, transporting, and marketing of farm products), merits special consideration. All these activities were originally performed by the farmer. As the economy expanded, however, agricultural functions not directly associated with the biological nature of farming shifted from the farm enterprise to local nonfarm enterprises and later, to nonlocal enterprises (Goss et al., 1980). Early productive activities transferred to the nonfarm sector involved the transporting, processing, and marketing of farm products. Grist mills and cottage weaving were processing activities long performed off-farm (Swanson, 1982:57). The infrastructure created by the railroad expansion in the latter half of the nineteenth century facilitated the growth of major food processors, wholesalers, and retailers (Chandler, 1977:209–215). Provision of farm inputs by nonfarm firms tended to follow the transfer of output functions. During the post-World War II period, the quantity of purchased inputs provided by nonfarmers increased dramatically, doubling from 1940 to 1977 (Hamm, 1979:218). Fertilizer, machinery, agrochemicals, petroleum, as well as finance became routinely provided by nonfarms firms, with escalating costs for farmers (Havens, 1986:44). By 1979, of the total value of domestically produced and consumed food in the United States, 68 percent went to food processing, distribution, and marketing costs, 26 percent to input suppliers, taxes, interest, and hired labor, and only 4 percent was received as net farm income (de Janvry and LeVeen, 1986:89).

The growth of agribusiness and its centrality to the U.S. economy is reflected in employment and sales. In 1982, about 20 percent of the labor force was employed in nonfarm food and fiber industries compared to only about 3.4 percent in farming. The entire agricultural system thus employed nearly one out of four Americans. Agriculture also contributed over a fifth of the total Gross National Product (The National Commission on Agricultural Trade and Export Policy, 1986:40).

Nonfarm agricultural enterprises developed much as other industries did, as evidenced in the tendency toward market concentration and growth of large firms (Havens, 1986; Goss et al., 1980; Friedland et al., 1981). Concentration in the farm input industries tends to be highest in agricultural chemicals and farm machinery and equipment (Hamm, 1979:221). In 1980, the proportion of market shares of the top four firms exceeded 50 percent for pesticides, tractors, and combines (Tweeten, 1984:29). Food processing and distribution have also become concentrated, with just forty-four companies receiving over two-thirds of all revenues from these industries by 1979 (Havens, 1986:44). The economic concentration of these large firms allows them to exert control over the prices paid and received by farmers, "sandwiching" them between "a monopoly-controlled input sector and a monopoly-controlled output sector" (Havens, 1986:45).

In addition, concentration of production is also occurring in farming itself as agribusiness extends into farm production through vertical integration or through contract farming. Vertically integrated enterprises, such as those in lettuce production, grow in their own right or contract out growing, harvesting, and marketing crops (Friedland et al., 1981). Contract farming involves the vertical coordination of farm production under agreements between farmers and processors. It allows agribusiness to tightly monitor aspects of the production process, such as the time of delivery and production standards (de Janvry and LeVeen, 1986:90). By 1980, all of the sugar cane, sugar beets, vegetables for processing, and citrus fruits, 99 percent of broilers, 95 percent of potatoes, 90 percent of seed crops, 90 percent of turkeys, and 89 percent of eggs were produced under integration or contract (Krause, 1987, Table 9:20). Corporate farms represented only about 2.6 percent of all farms in 1982 and, of these about 90 percent were family-held or owned by ten or fewer shareholders. The vast majority of U.S farms are peripheral enterprises located in competitive markets, such as grain and general farming, dairy, and hog production (Havens, 1986:40). The following section discusses conceptual perspectives on and major structural trends in the evolution of farming as distinct from other agricultural activities.

THE UNEVEN DEVELOPMENT OF THE FARM SECTOR

Conceptual Approaches to the Transformation of Farming

Classical as well as contemporary political economists have explored the development of the farm sector in first world societies.[2] The classical theorists were particularly interested in how the motion of the wider economy affected the shape and structure of farming. Taking England as a model, Marx assumed that industrial capitalism presupposed the destruction of the peasantry and the development of a capitalist agriculture, reflected in a three tiered agrarian structure of landless laborers, tenant farmers, and landowners (Marx, 1967). Marx saw capitalist development in farming as lagging behind that of industry because of the particular dependence of farming upon land. The use of land as a factor of production implies the extraction of ground rent by the landowner and a loss of capital accumulation to the producer. Marx also noted that the biological processes involved in farm production discouraged capitalist investment (Fitz-Simmons, 1986). Despite these barriers, Marx saw the tendencies toward concentration and centralization as so compelling that farming would follow industry, eventually becoming organized along capitalist lines (Goodman and Redclift, 1985).

Marx's model of agrarian change ultimately proved to be unique to the English case. Later, political economists attempted to revise Marx's assumptions by explaining the apparent persistence of independent commodity production and by tracing its evolution under capitalism. For Lenin, the penetration of capitalism into Russian agriculture involved a process of depeasantization in which most peasants were on a path toward proletarianization, while a few emerged as an agrarian bourgeoisie (Lenin, 1974). Extending his analysis to the United States, Lenin (1934) reported a similar disintegration of independent production and growth of capitalist farming. He concludes that a comparison of industry and agriculture "shows that despite the incomparably greater backwardness of the latter, there is a remarkable similarity in the laws of evolution, and that the displacement of small-scale production occurs in both branches of the economy" (Lenin, 1934:69).

Kautsky (1988) also noted a similarity between the development of industry and farming in terms of the concentration and centralization of capital and proletarianization of independent producers. However, Kautsky argues that these general tendencies met resistance in agriculture and attempted to show that agriculture operates according to its own principles of development, which differ from those of industry (Newby, 1986a). As capitalism progresses, nonfarm capital comes to penetrate farming. Simple commodity producers undergo a process of differentiation, whereby some farmers come to increasingly resemble wage-laborers and others, large-scale capitalist producers. Farmers first become dependent on nonfarm sources for inputs, markets for outputs, and subsistence goods. Large producers, increasingly linked to the agribusiness chain, capture advantages resulting from economies of scale in land, labor, and technology, costs in marketing outputs and in purchasing inputs, and in easier access to credit. As holdings become centralized and technology develops, smaller units fail to absorb available household labor. If no supplementary off-farm employment were available, Kautsky argued that these producers' living standards would decline. They would be forced to limit family size or to migrate to other areas. As industry entered rural areas, however, smaller producers would rapidly seek off-farm employment, either engaging in part-time farming or selling off holdings to become fully dependent upon wage work, although Kautsky emphasized the former. Proletarianization was thus seen not so much as a process of dispossession from the means of production but rather as household differentiation and "the emergence of the worker peasant, peasant worker, or part-time farmer" (Newby, 1986a:14).

On balance, Marx, Lenin, and Kautsky were concerned with broad theoretical issues, the integration of agriculture into the larger economy and how the economy transforms agriculture; and with prospective rather than retrospective insights on agricultural change. However, the theories were developed during specific historical periods, focused on particular national examples, and were formed in the context of late nineteenth century political debates and agendas. Capitalism was in its competitive stage, and the role of the state and global accumulation processes were just being understood. As a consequence, the classical theories cannot be used unequivocably to analyze modern U.S. agriculture.

In general, the later twentieth century literature lacks the vision of the early theorists. Recent writers have made less effort to develop a broad, prospective account of agricultural change under advanced capitalism. While large-scale, capitalist enterprises in the nonfarm sector developed rapidly, the persistence of family labor production in farming has continued to be a theoretical problem. One way of addressing this issue has been to compare the nature of farm production with nonfarm, industrial production.

In comparison to industry, farming presents barriers to the penetration of capital (Mann and Dickinson, 1978; Goss et al., 1980). First, the biological nature of farming reduces its attractiveness to capitalist investment. Biological transformations are more vulnerable to changes in production than the physical transformations engendered by industry (Pfeffer, 1983:542; Swanson, 1982:52–53). Biological transformations are difficult to halt in midproduction, should production conditions become unfavorable. The effects of natural conditions such as poor weather, pests, and blight also increase the vulnerability of farming (Swanson, 1982:53).

Another difference between farming and industry concerns the importance of land as a factor of production. Two characteristics set land apart: first, the quantity of land is limited so that it "cannot be produced and reproduced" as can other factors of production; second, land is immobile or unable to "enter and leave different enterprises" (Goss et al., 1980:90). Marx, using the British example, argues that the requirement for land as a factor of production and its limited availability tended to discourage capitalist investment in farming. In contrast, land was historically abundant in the United States and has often been an attractive investment, as it was during the 1970s when it was used as a hedge against inflation (Goss et al., 1980). The dependence of farming upon land, however, adds risks and complexities to production that impede investment (Fitz-Simmons, 1986:337). Land prices are affected by a number of factors in addition to area and location, such as fertility, terrain, and climate. Land markets are localized, complex, and influenced by demands outside agriculture. They are sluggish in response to fluctuations in the wider economy. Farmers cannot rapidly increase or reduce investments in land as production conditions change. Also, farmland's fertility can be exhausted.

Theorists have also delineated other factors that account for the slower development of capitalist enterprises in farming. Mann and Dickinson (1978) argue that in farming, unlike most other industries, there is a major disjuncture between labor time (the amount of time active labor is required) and production time (the amount of time capital is tied up in production). Due to the seasonality of farming, production cycles are discontinuous and involve waiting stages alternated with stages of heavy labor input. The disjuncture between production and labor time results in: lower profits, because capital tied up in production is turned over less frequently; infrequent realization of profits, generally only at harvest time; and labor recruitment problems. On balance, Mann and Dickinson (1978) argue that most farm production is unattractive to capitalist investment, except in those commodities where production and labor time more closely coincide. In contrast, family labor farming predominates in commodities where production time greatly exceeds labor time, such as in annual crop and livestock production. Mann and Dickinson's position has been a source of debate (Mooney, 1982; Singer et al., 1983) and has spurred much related work (see for example, Pfeffer, 1983; FitzSimmons, 1986).

Another set of literature attempts to explain the persistence of simple commodity production by emphasizing its advantages over large-scale, capitalist farming and its functions for larger segments of capital. Friedmann (1981, 1978) argues that family labor farms may be more competitive than capitalist farms because of their capacity to self-exploit, or to adjust consumption levels according to available surplus. Family labor farmers may occupy production niches by specializing in commodities which are not profitable for capital (Mottura and

Pugliese, 1980). Further, this farming serves an industrial reserve function by absorbing labor in time of unemployment. It facilitates state legitimation because it helps quell potential political instability associated with joblessness (Mottura and Pugliese, 1980). Finally, family labor farming provides benefits to agribusiness. According to Davis (1980) family farmers should be viewed as 'propertied laborers' who may own their own means of production but who are 'exploited' in the sphere of circulation or through input and product markets.

While much of the literature on farm structural change centers on the presistence of simple commodity production, a few researchers have focused on broader, external factors that shape the development of farming. De Janvry and LeVeen (1986) argue that farm change is a result of three fundamental processes. The first is the commodification of agriculture, in which factors of production (land, labor, capital, and technology) become commodities that can be bought, sold, and priced. The second process involves the way in which farming becomes integrated into and subject to agribusiness control. Use of purchased inputs increases, specialization of commodities develops, and activities formerly performed on the farm are externalized. The third process involves the position of agriculture in the international division of labor. The increased dependence of U.S. agriculture on markets for exports, for example, has created new sources of uncertainties and risks for farmers.

Kenney et al. (1989) likewise argue that forces outside agriculture, such as change in global and national economy and the role of the state, are important for understanding the structure of agriculture. They tie the configuration of these forces to particular periods of accumulation. According to Kenney et al. (1989), the Great Depression and the New Deal transformed farming from an extensive system of production, dependent on increased land and labor for growth and using relatively low levels of manufactured inputs into a commercial, technologically innovative, profit oriented system. Under fordism, farmers became progressively integrated into circuits of capital both as producers and consumers. In the first instance, farmers responded to an enormous national market by producing masses of commodities at uniform levels of quality. This entailed integration into output industries, such as food processing, wholesaling, and retailing. In the second, farmers became consumers of mass produced farm inputs from petrochemicals to farm machinery as well as nonfarm commodities, notably, processed foods and consumer durables. As a result of these changes, farming became suitably integrated with the industrial system. And as long as fordism was a viable strategy of accumulation, industry and farming could expand and grow. From 1948 to 1972, farm yields rose, government subsidies were manageable, and the cost of food declined as a percentage of workers' income.

The review of the classical and contemporary literature points to shortcomings and new directions for a political economy of agriculture. First, much of the contemporary literature is built upon a narrow theoretical agenda focused on the persistence of family farming rather than its transformation and on the internal dynamics of the farm unit. While the classical theorists examined how the exigencies of wider economic forces were played out in agriculture, current theorists tend to focus on the factors that move agriculture from *within*. The literature also overemphasizes the distinct character of farming as a production system and tends to ignore theoretical developments outside the sociology of agriculture and other social science disciplines related to agriculture. A new political economy of agriculture should return to the broader substantive issues addressed by the early theorists while incorporating an understanding of the present structure and future evolution of capitalism. As Kenney et al. (1989) show, assumptions about the wider economy have implications for the parallel development of agriculture and industry. Dynamic conceptualizations of farm structure based on the variety of ways in which capital penetrates agricultue are also needed. Concepts such as simple commodity production, for example, no longer characterize the farm sector. Finally, the structure of agriculture should be regarded as historically specific, mirroring at any particular point the larger economic environment.

In the context of the previous literature, how then can contemporary agriculture structure be characterized? Several theorists argue that it is important to focus on the ways in which nonfarm capital has penetrated or become linked to the farm economy (Kautsky, 1988; Kenney et al., 1989; de Janvry and LeVeen, 1986). This penetration takes place along the lines of major production factors and acts to stratify the farm sector. Farming becomes characterized by both the concentration and fragmentation of holdings; by units that have either little or extensive need for hired labor; and by units that are increasingly linked to the nonfarm sector for operating capital or household reproduction. The stratification process is evident in a deepening dualism in the farm sector. Small, often part-time farms proliferate. Large-scale industrial farms dependent on hired labor gain increasing shares of market production. Simple commodity production units decline and those remaining take on a modern analogous form—capital-intensive, profit oriented, family operated enterprises whose fortunes are particularly dependent on land, capital, and technology markets.

The Structural Transformation of Farming in the United States

Historical trends in the development of farming are important for understanding the shape and structure of the contemporary farm sector. Farm structure involves "the control and organization of resources needed for farm production" (Rasmussen, 1980:3). It refers to the number and sizes of farms, ownership and control over factors of production, use of technology, and degree of commodity specialization, as well as the social, economic, and political conditions of farmers (Rasmussen, 1980:3).

Goss et al. (1980) note that the institutional requisites for the development of the farm sector under capitalism—the existence of private land ownership and beginnings of production for markets—were formed prior to the Civil War. The war brought the three regional farm economies, "plantation south, yeoman farmer west, and industrial northeast—into full-blown capitalist development" (Goss et al., 1980:94). Western commercial farming became interdependent with the urban, northeast industrial market; and the bonds of slavery were replaced with those of sharecropping and wage labor in the south.

Structural changes occurring from the post-Civil War period to 1940 have often been contrasted with those from 1940–1980 (Goss et al., 1980). Characteristics of farm structure are presented in Table 2.1.[3] From the period following the Civil War until about World War II, family labor farming continued to expand. The number of farms grew from about 2 million in 1860 to about 6.4 million in 1910 then stabilized for the next several decades. The population living on farms steadily declined from about 35 percent of all Americans in 1910 to 23 percent by 1940. The amount of land in farm production showed small increases over this same period. Average farm size grew only slightly, from 153 acres in the post-Civil War period to 174 acres by 1940. Fixed capital in land and buildings per farm actually declined somewhat from 1910 to 1940 while family labor fairly consistently outnumbered hired labor by a ratio of three to one. However, there was no mistaking that farming was becoming progressively market oriented as evidenced by the constant and rapid growth of agricultural sales.

The dramatic changes in agriculture after World War II have their roots in the New Deal and in the technological changes initiated during this period (Kenney et al., 1989). New Deal policy and institutional initiatives embodied in the Agricultural Adjustment Act, Commodity Credit Corporation, Farm Credit Administration, and other institutions tended to regularize farm production and income and to diminish risk. This also ensured a more stable demand for input services as well as relatively stable commodity prices for food processors. Infrastructure such as that provided by the Tennessee Valley Authority and the Rural Electrification Administration enhanced the viability of rural life and integrated farmers into national consumption markets. This further served to diffuse political tension brought about by the Depression and massive dislocation of segments of the farm production. It also legitimated nonradical farm organizations, guaranteeing a more conservative rural population. More intesive cultivation practices were encouraged by acreage set-aside programs combined with high price supports. The development of the tractor and biological and chemical innovations reduced labor demands and enhanced productivity. By World War II, a commercial and innovative agriculture produced relatively low cost food for urban people while ensuring adequate incomes for many farmers (Kenney et al., 1989).

TABLE 2.1

The Historical Structure of U.S. Farming: Selected Characteristics

Year	Farm Numbers (1,000)[a]	Farm Population[b] As % of Total	Land in Farms (100,000 Acres)[a]	Average[a] Farm Size (Acres)	Gross Sales[c] Per Farm (Constant $1982)	Value of[a] Land & Buildings Per Farm (Constant $1982)	Family or[d] Unpaid Workers/ Hired Workers
1850	1,449	—	239	165	—	—	—
1860	2,044	—	407	199	—	—	—
1870	2,660	—	408	153	—	—	—
1880	4,009	—	536	134	—	—	—
1890	4,565	—	623	136	—	—	—
1900	5,737	—	839	146	—	—	—
1910	6,361	34.7	879	138	10,817	63,651	3.00
1920	6,447	30.0	956	148	10,341	54,060	2.96
1930	6,288	24.8	987	157	10,141	51,408	2.92
1940	6,096	23.1	1,061	174	10,577	40,769	3.10
1950	5,648	15.2	1,202	213	21,084	57,322	3.26
1960	3,955	8.7	1,171	296	27,831	111,974	2.74
1970	2,944	4.7	1,098	373	40,849	173,810	2.85
1980	2,428	2.7	1,036	427	67,167	366,861	1.84
1985	2,327	2.2	1,016	437	55,655	266,528	1.84
1989[e]	2,154	—	995	462	58,330	219,236	2.03

[a] Sources for these data are: *Farm Real Estate Historical Series Data: 1850-1970* (ERS-520), Washington, D.C.: USDA, Economic Research Service, June, 1973; *Farm Real Estate Historical Series Data, 1950-1985* (Statistical Bulletin 738), Washington, D.C.: USDA, Economic Research Service, December, 1985. Figures from 1985 have been updated by calculations from data in *Agricultural Resources: Agricultural Land Values and Markets Situation and Outlook* (AR-10), Washington, D.C.: USDA, Economic Research Service, June, 1988.

[b] *Historical Statistics of the United States: Colonial Times to 1970*, Washington, D.C.: U.S. Department of Commerce, Bureau of the Census, 1973; *Estimates of the Population of the United States to August 1, 1987*, Population Estimates and Projections Series P-25, No. 1512, Washington, D.C.: U.S. Department of Commerce, Bureau of the Census, September, 1987; *Current Population Reports*, Series P-27, No. 61, Washington, D.C.: U.S. Department of Commerce, Bureau of the Census and USDA, Economic Research Service, June, 1988. The farm population was not estimated prior to 1910.

[c] Source for 1910-1982 is Gary Lucier, Agnes Chesley, and Mary Ahern, *Farm Income Data: A Historical Perspective* (Statistical Bulletin 740), Washington, D.C.: USDA, Economic Research Service, May 1986. For 1985 and 1989, data have been updated from appropriate volumes of *Agricultural Outlook*, Washington, D.C.: USDA, Economic Research Service. A consistent series of gross sales per farm cannot be generated before 1910.

[d] Sources for these data are the following volumes for the appropriate years: *Agricultural Statistics 1962*, Washington, D.C.: USDA, 1963; *Agricultural Statistics 1972*, Washington, D.C.: USDA, 1972; and *Agricultural Statistics 1987*, Washington, D.C.: USDA, 1987. Family workers include farm operators doing one or more hours of farm work and members of their families working 15 hours or more during the survey week. Hired workers include all persons doing one or more hours of farm work for pay. Unpaid workers include farm operators doing one or more hours of farm work and other unpaid workers working 15 hours or more without cash wages. Due to changes in government data collection, the figures through 1970 reflect the ratio of family to hired workers and those after reflect the ratio of unpaid to hired workers. The change in the ratio from 2.85 in 1970 to 1.84 in 1980 reflects real more than definitional changes in the growth of hired relative to unpaid or family labor over the 1970 decade. For example, in 1972, the ratio of unpaid to hired workers was 2.82, nearly the same as the previous year when family workers were last estimated.

[e] 1989 figures calculated from data in *Agricultural Resources: Agricultural Land Values and Markets Situation and Outlook* (AR-14), Washington, D.C.: USDA, Economic Research Service, June, 1989, and *Agricultural Outlook* (AO-160), Washington, D.C.: USDA, Economic Research Service, January-February, 1990. Gross sales for 1989 are a forecast. Ratio of unpaid to hired workers is an average of April, July, and October surveys from *Farm Labor*, Washington, D.C.: USDA, National Agricultural Statistics Service, August 14 and November 14, 1989.

From 1940 to 1980, the number of farms decreased by more than half and by 1989 had declined to about 2 million. While almost one out of four Americans lived on farms at the start of World War II, only about two out of every hundred did so by 1985. The total amount of land in farming, however, changed relatively little over this period. Average farm size in acres almost tripled from 1940 to 1989. Agricultural sales per farm (in constant dollars) increased from under $11,000 in 1940 to nearly $60,000 by 1989. Farm real estate values grew steadily from the postwar period to the late 1970s, when they surged upward before declining in the face of the farm crisis of the 1980s. The growth in farm size combined with a decline in farm population means that capital has been increasingly substituted for farm labor. In the decades before 1940, labor accounted for about half of all farm inputs but only for 14 percent in 1981 (Tweeten, 1984:7). Operating and physical capital such as machinery and equipment more than doubled as a percent of inputs over the same period (Tweeten, 1984:7).

Farm Scale. Commercial production has tended to become concentrated on a smaller number of large farms.[4] The percent of large farms with 1,000 or more acres increased from 1.7 in 1940 to 7.2 percent in 1982. The amount of farmland held by these large farms nearly doubled over this period and they held 61 percent of all farmland by 1982 (Albrecht and Murdock, 1988:32). Agricultural sales also tend to be concentrated on large farms. Using constant 1960 dollars to classify farms, de Janvry et al. (1987:87) show that farms with sales over $100,000 increased from under 1 percent of all farms in 1960 to over 9 percent in 1985. In 1982, the 1.2 percent of farms with gross sales of $500,000 and over, the 'superfarms' of American agriculture, garnered 32 percent of total agricultural sales (Albrecht and Murdock, 1988:32).

Concomitantly, analysts have noted trends toward declining numbers of medium-size farms and greater numbers of small farms (Albrecht and Murdock, 1988; Goss et al., 1980; Stockdale, 1982; Tweeten, 1984). Medium-size farms or those from 50 to 499 acres held about half of all farmland in 1940 but less than a quarter by 1982 (Albrecht and Murdock, 1988:32). The number of farms in this category likewise declined from 63 percent of all farms to 55 percent from 1969 to 1982. In contrast, the number of very small farms, those under 50 acres, grew slightly during this period. In 1982, about 61 percent of all farms were small, with sales under $20,000 (Albrecht and Murdock, 1988:32). These farms accounted for only about 6 percent of total farm sales. Moderate-size farms with gross farm sales from $20,000 to $100,000 constituted about a quarter of all farms and accounted for about 22 percent of sales.

How did this rapid concentration of capital and expansion of large enterprises and marginalization of smaller producers come about? In the United States, farming has been historically a highly competitive industry (Cochrane, 1979).

In order to increase profits and to gain competitive advantage, farmers have tended to expand production. However, when producers collectively expand (and assuming that demand remains relatively constant) overproduction occurs. This leads to decreased prices and decreasing economic security for most farmers. Overproduction has been endemic to U.S. agriculture for over a century (Goss et al., 1980). Farmers attempt to expand production generally by employing capital in the form of technology as a substitute for land and labor inputs. According to Cochrane (1979), this puts farmers on a relentless "treadmill of technology." They are continually forced to adopt new technologies or be driven out of business by more innovative competitors. Early adopters gain only temporary competitive advantages since other farmers eventually catch up and employ cost cutting technologies themselves. Because of the competitive conditions in farming, lower production costs tend to lead to lower market prices; and since the demand for food is inelastic, farmers' incomes decline as market prices fall. The cycle continues as farmers compensate for shortfalls in income by expanding production which in turn results in overproduction at the aggregate level. Intensified competition and the technological treadmill foster the growth and expansion of large farms. Large producers are also able to 'cannibalize' or purchase the farms of those who can no longer compete on the treadmill.

Other factors have also contributed to greater accumulation of capital in farming. Certain government programs and policies encourage expansion by reducing risk and allowing equity to be leveraged further or by favoring large farmers (Tweeten, 1984; de Janvry et al., 1987). For example, federal crop insurance reduces biologically related risks. Commodity programs and government marketing orders stabilize prices and farm income (Tweeten, 1984:32). Benefits from commodity programs are also greater per producer and per dollar of output on larger farms (because larger farms tend to participate more in these programs, with the exception of superfarms whose payments are limited) (Tweeten, 1984:32). Monetary and technical economies of scale and easier access to credit further benefit larger operators (Strange, 1988). Finally, agricultural experiment station research at land grant colleges and the resources of the Extension Service have been argued to favor larger over smaller producers (Hightower, 1973; de Janvry et al., 1987).

Ownership. Along with changes in the numbers and sizes of farms, ownership, managerial, and labor functions have been transferred increasingly to nonfarm entities. Historically, farms, farmland, and operating capital tended to be owned and managed by households residing on the farm (Goss et al., 1980). From the late 1800s to the post-Depression era, land ownership by farm operators declined while tenant operators increased in numbers and in the amount of land held.[5] In 1935, the Census of Agriculture reported that about 47 percent of farms were operated by full-owners who owned all the land they farmed; 10 percent were operated by part-owners who both owned and rented land; about 42 percent were operted by tenants, of whom about one-half were Southern sharecroppers; and the remaining 1 percent were operated by farm managers. From 1935 to the mid-1950s, the percent of full- and part-owner farms and their acreage increased, while the percent of tenant farms declined. It should be remembered, however, that the total number of farms decreased precipitously during this period, hence the actual number of full-owner operators (as well as tenants) declined.

From the 1950s onward, the amount of farmland held by full-owners has remained relatively constant while that held by part-owners has increased. More recently, the percent of full-owners declined from 62 percent of operators in 1969 to 59 percent in 1982. During this same period, part-owners increased from 25 percent to 29 percent of all operators while tenant operated farms declined only slightly (Albrecht and Murdock, 1988:40). Part-owner farms and tenant farms tend to be larger and more profitable than full-owner farms (Albrecht and Murdock, 1988:39). Both part-ownership and tenancy represent progressive strategies of adapting to farm change (Tweeten, 1984:12; Buttel, 1983a:92). Land rental allows farmers to capture economies of scale, attain a favorable cash flow, and reduce instability and problems of land acquisition. By owning some land, part-owners also gain home security and an outlet for savings and investment. Changes in land ownership are reflected in farm residence patterns. About a quarter of operators reside off the land they operate, a figure that increased slightly over the 1970s (Tweeten, 1984:18).

Goss et al. (1980:105–106) have noted a similar pattern of reduced ownership of nonfarmland capital by operators, including rental of machines, equipment, and buildings and employing machines on a contract or custom basis. Reasons for the lowered land and other capital ownership by operators are many (Goss et al., 1980:106). Over time, farming has required growing capital investments, so that sole ownership of production factors has become increasingly difficult. Nonfarm interests, such as corporations and urban people seeking rural life-styles, have had added incentives for farm ownership, squeezing the market for land in some rural areas.

Organization of the Farm Enterprise. The business organization of farming also has changed. Although the vast majority of farms are individual or family operated (sole proprietorships), incorporated farms have been increasing in numbers and sales. Data on farm organization were not included in the agricultural censuses before 1969, making long-term trends difficult to trace. In 1982, about 87 percent of farms were family organized; 10 percent were partnerships; and about 3 percent were corporations (Albrecht and Murdock, 1988:36). Partnerships generally consist of two or three partners, often from the same family (Tweeten, 1984:15). Family farms accounted for 59 percent of agricultural products sold and averaged 330 acres; partnerships accounted for about 16 percent of sales and averaged 680 acres; and corporations accounted for about 24 percent of sales and averaged 2,087 acres (Albrecht and Murdock, 1988:36; Krause, 1987:2). The number of incorporated farms recorded by the census increased from 21,513 in 1969 to 59,792 in 1982, an increase of 178 percent (Albrecht and Murdock, 1988:37). Corporate farms also account for increasing percentages of all farm sales, from 18 percent in 1974 to 23 percent in 1982 (Krause, 1987:1).

The great majority of incorporated farms (89 percent) are family-held by census definition and have ten or fewer shareholders (Krause, 1987:1). In 1982, these farms had 85 percent of all the acreage in farm corporations and their sales were more than 4½ times greater than those of nonfamily-held corporations (Krause, 1987:3). Almost half of cash receipts received by nonfamily-held corporations are in the marketing of just one commodity, fattened cattle (Albrecht and Murdock, 1988:38). Income tax advantages during the 1970s prompted family farms to incorporate. Incorporating also expedites estate planning and can ease farm ownership and management transfers to the next generation (Krause, 1987:13).

By 1981 ten states responded to the perception that corporations were a threat to family farming and passed legislation restricting the activities of farm corporations, through limiting the size of landholdings, restricting corporate integration into farming, or prohibiting particular types of corporations from farm production altogether (Krause, 1987:2). Concern about corporate farming should be centered more on issues such as scale, concentration, and use of hired labor than on form of business organization. As farm sales increase, the percentage of incorporated farms grows. In 1982, the largest farms with annual sales of over a half million dollars had about 70 percent of commercial vegetable sales, 60 percent of greenhouse and nursery products, and half of the sales of cattle, cotton, fruits and nuts, miscellaneous field crops, and poultry (Krause, 1987:7). However, of these large farms, slightly more (40 percent) were sole proprietorships than corporations (37 percent).

Farm Labor. Another trend in farming is that labor and management functions have been increasingly separated (Goss et al., 1980). Hired farm workers accounted for about a quarter of the farm labor force from the first decades of the twentieth century until the early 1970s (Holt, 1984). Since this period, however, the number of farm operators and unpaid family workers has declined while the absolute number of paid workers has remained relatively stable. As Table 2.1 shows, the number of hired workers relative to unpaid workers rose dramatically during the 1970s. In 1970, unpaid, family workers outnumbered hired workers by nearly three to one but by 1989 they exceeded hired workers by only about two to one. Moreover, the number of workers of longer duration (75 days per year or over) has tended to increase (Goss et al., 1980:109).

Farms relying on hired labor are commodity and spatially specific (Holt, 1984). Midwestern farms hire only about one-fifth of needed labor, the remainder provided by operators and their families. About one-third of the farm labor force is hired in the Northeast and South. And in California, about 75 percent is hired. Florida, Arizona, parts of the Mississippi Delta, and Texas counties of the Rio Grande also have extensive hired farm employment. Migrant farm workers, those who travel overnight to do farm work, comprised only about 6 to 8 percent of the total hired farm labor force in 1975 (Holt, 1984:23). California ranks first in use of migrant labor (about one-quarter of all seasonal migrant workers were employed in the state in 1978) followed by Arizona and Florida (Fritsch, 1984:78). Hired rather than family labor predominates in extensively irrigated areas where fruits and vegetables are grown, near large metropolitan areas that have concentrations of horticultural operations, and in plantation and ranching areas, which historically have had large operations (Holt, 1984:10).

Over the years, hired farm workers have been subject to poor employment conditions: exhausting physical work, poor sanitation and housing, and hazards from machinery and pesticides and other agricultural chemicals (Coye, 1986). Farming ranks with construction and mining as being among the most hazardous industries in terms of injury and death rates. In spite of these dangers, the national income rank of hired farm workers is the second lowest in this country; only domestic household workers fare worse (Tweeten, 1984:19). The low income of hired farm workers is primarily caused by intermittant unemployment (de Janvry et al., 1987:71).

Some improvements in hired farm work were evidenced in the postwar period, although many of these were to be setback during the 1980s. The Fair Labor Standards Act amendments scheduled increases in the minimum wage for farm workers during the 1970s so that the minimum wage for farm and non-farm workers is now the same (Erven, 1984:382). But because of various exemptions of farms of certain sizes as well as evasion by farm owners, it is estimated that only 40 to 50 percent of farm workers are covered by minimum wage legislation (Huffman, 1984:51). Unions have also helped raise farm workers' wages and fringe benefits either directly through collective bargaining or indirectly because of unionization threats (Hayes, 1984). Farm worker unionization, however, has been largely confined to California (Glover, 1984:257). In 1985, only about 2 percent of agricultural wage and salary workers were unionized, compared to almost 15 percent in private, nonagricultural industry (U.S. Bureau of the Census, 1986, Table 693:409). As nonfarm industries have filtered into farming areas, competition for labor drives up farm worker wages and farm workers themselves gain additional sources of employment (Holt, 1984:31). Finally, there is some evidence that jobs on large-scale industrialized farms have become more highly skilled and renumerated over time (Mamer, 1984).

Part-time Farming. As farming operations have grown larger, it has become increasingly difficult for smaller operators to compete. Wage work provides the major vehicle for sustaining operators in farming who would otherwise become fully proletarianized. The percent of operators with 100 or more days of off-farm employment has steadily increased, from only about 15 percent of operators in 1940 to 43 percent in 1982 (Albrecht and Murdock, 1988:34). Off-farm income has consistently increased as a proportion of total household income for smaller farmers (de Janvry et al., 1987). In 1982, the largest farms (annual gross sales over $500,000) accounted for only about 1 percent of off-farm income received by farmers while small operations (sales under $40,000) accounted for 82 percent (Ahern, 1986:81).

The presence of off-farm employment has several implications for the political economy of agriculture. First, Goss et al. (1980:112) note that while part-time farming allows farmers to adapt to fluctuating financial conditions, there may be increased self-exploitation as family members work longer or take additional off-farm employment during periods of low commodity prices. Second, Holland and Carvalho (1985) argue that the presence of part-time farming has disguised capitalist penetration into agriculture: the destruction of family labor farming and increased concentration of production in large units has been obscured by the persistence of masses of small (albeit, part-time) producers. However, as a consequence of the economic downturns of the 1980s, the industrial base of rural areas appears to be deteriorating. If this continues to be the case, opportunities to engage in part-time farming will decrease and control over farm production by large-scale enterprises will be more pronounced (Holland and Carvalho, 1985). Third, part-time farming may provide advantages to capital by serving an industrial reserve function and by underwriting some of the costs of reproducing the labor force. Employers may be able to pay lower wages to rural workers because they have alternative consumption and income sources.

Characteristics of Producers. In addition to changes in control over factors of production, characteristics of producers themselves have changed. The number of black operators has declined dramatically: in 1930, blacks made up about 14 percent of farm operators but only about 2 percent in 1982 (Tweeten, 1984:17; U.S. Bureau of the Census, 1986, Table 1101:622). Much of this change results from the displacement of small black operators, particularly tenant farmers, from Southern agriculture as a consequence of the mechanization of cotton and other commodities. Women operated about 5 percent of farms according to the 1982 Census of Agriculture. However, census data obscure women's real contributions by counting only one operator per farm unit. A national survey of over 2,500 farm women revealed that 55 percent considered themselves to be one of the main operators of their farms (Rosenfeld, 1985). Moreover, women's contributions to farm work appear to have increased in some areas during the 1980s, partly as a consequence of the farm crisis (Gladwin, 1985).

In Summary. Historically, the process of agricultural change has resulted in the separation of factors of production from the control of independent producers (Goss et al., 1980). This process is manifest in the transformation of a relatively homogenous farm sector to a differentiated one in which producers occupy a range of positions from hired labor to capitalist producers. At one end of the continuum are large-scale enterprises structured around and dependent upon wage labor, having substantial market control; at the other are small enterprises dependent on off-farm work. Farmers in the middle generally provide labor and management but are tied to off-farm markets in land and capital. Compared to smaller and larger units, they are particularly vulnerable to economic fluctuations: they lack advantages of larger producers, such as diversified sources of capital and economies of scale in buying and selling, while having fewer opportunities for off-farm income compared to smaller producers. As a consequence, these modern analogs of traditional family labor farming appear to be declining relative to smaller and larger producers.[6] The structure of farming thus reflects a complex articulation of farm enterprises with the nonfarm economy and general development tendency toward the concentration of production in larger and fewer units.

ECONOMIC CRISIS, INEQUALITY, AND RECENT PATTERNS OF RESTRUCTURING

Toward the end of the 1960s, a series of strains erupted in the global economy that have implications for U.S. agriculture and industry as well as general levels of inequality. These strains have been taken as evidence of a crisis in the fordist regime of accumulation. Until this period, the United States had experienced rising prosperity and world trade domination (Gordon et al., 1982:167–168), which was reflected in the economic gains of Americans. Economic strains were becoming apparent on a global level, however, as evidenced by market saturation and industrial overcapacity (Storper and Scott, 1986:4). By the early 1970s, the world economy entered into a period of sustained decline, which was seriously aggravated by the 1973 oil crisis. Growth rates deteriorated, productivity declined, and inflation rose in all the advanced capitalist economies (Gordon et al., 1982:168). In 1971, the United States ran its first trade deficit since 1893 (Blumberg, 1980:111). Rates of U.S. productivity slowed in the early 1970s and then actually declined at the end of the decade (Blumberg, 1980:135–136). Prolonged unemployment at relatively high levels became a general trend (Kolko, 1988: Chapter 22).[7]

As a consequence of the deteriorating economy, "living standards in the U.S. have ceased to grow significantly and the great inequality characteristic of American society continues unchanged" (Blumberg, 1980:66; see also Hoppe, 1987). Real wages began to decline in 1974, falling by 1980 to points attained in the early 1960s, and generally continuing to fall through 1987 (Kolko, 1988:318). Real increases in median family income began to slow in the 1970s. From 1979 to 1980, median family income declined by almost 6 percent, continued to decline through 1982, and only incrementally improved by the end of the decade (U.S. Bureau of the Census, 1986, Table 732:436). This deterioration in income occurred despite the increased employment of working wives and despite the higher educational attainments achieved by Americans in the postwar era (Blumberg, 1980:89; Jacobs, 1985:178). The percentage of the population below the poverty level remained at close to 12 percent throughout the 1970s, increased dramatically to 15 percent in 1982–1983 and remained at 14 percent in 1985 (U.S. Bureau of the Census, 1986, Table 745:442). In the mid-1980s, the poverty population approximated that of two decades earlier—during the Johnson administration's War on Poverty. Further, the poor are actually falling behind the rest of the nation in terms of living standards because the gap between the poverty line and median family income has widened (Blumberg, 1980:99–100). Even for middle income groups, the costs of consumer purchases, such as food, automobiles, and housing are increasingly more difficult to bear (Blumberg, 1980). Many workers have turned to credit. Consumer debt reached a record 19 percent of all take-home pay in 1986 (Kolko, 1988:318).

What are the implications of these changes for workers in the segmented economy? Kolko (1988:309) notes that 2.3 million manufacturing jobs disappeared from 1980 to 1985, nearly all permanently and most in high wage industry. Management has tried to take advantage of this restructuring by demanding concessions and attempting to rollback previous gains, particularly of workers in the core sector (Gordon et al., 1982:218–219). Rates of union membership among American workers have fallen, from about 30 percent in the early 1970s to under 20 percent by 1985 (U.S. Bureau of the Census, 1986, Tables 692, 693:408–409). Management hostility has played a key role in this decline (Goldfield, 1987; Piore, 1985). Production workers in the core sector experienced lower wage gains, increased unemployment and higher accident rates over the 1970s than in previous decades (Gordon et al., 1982, Table 5.9:218). In contrast, working conditions and earnings deteriorated less in the periphery mainly because these never improved as much during the postwar expansionary period (Gordon et al., 1982:225). The fastest growth occupations are now in peripheral, service sector jobs: janitors, fast-food workers, clerical workers, and nurses' aides (Kolko, 1988:310). In 1985, average weekly earnings in the service sector were $256, about two-thirds of those in manufacturing. Weekly earnings in retail trade, another important component of the peripheral sector, were less than half of those in manufacturing (U.S. Bureau of the Census, 1986, Table 676:401). Public sector employment has declined as a consequence of the fiscal contraction of the state (Kolko, 1988:311) and wages have tended to decrease relative to those in manufacturing (U.S. Bureau of the Census, 1986, Table 675:400).

Other changes are also occurring in the industrial sector that portend a radical restructuring of American business. There is a movement away from mass production technologies towards those permiting greater flexibility and diversity of products at similarly low cost in order to cater to specialized consumer markets (Kenney et al., 1989; Piore and Sabel, 1984). Rigid job assignments based on Taylorist methods are increasingly seen as barriers to productivity and are being replaced with flexible work rules to accompany new technologies (Kolko, 1988:322). The use of subcontracting, homework, and temporary and part-time employment in order to lower labor costs is increasing (Kolko, 1988:312). These changes suggest that many of the operating principles of the fordist era have broken down. American industry and workers now appear poised on the edge of a new economic environment and social structure of accumulation (Piore and Sabel, 1984).

Crisis and Change in the Farm Sector

Crisis in U.S agriculture became evident somewhat later than in the industrial sector. Farm income had remained stable from 1960 through the early 1970s but hit record highs from 1972 to 1974, a consequence of weather disturbances and increasing global food demand (Kenney et al., 1989:142). Grain prices and land values climbed during the 1970s. Poverty among farm families declined from 21 percent in 1966 to 13 percent in 1979 (de Janvry et al., 1987:86). By about 1980, however, these signs of prosperity began to disappear. Real farm income declined (Kenney et al., 1989) and poverty among farm families increased sharply to over 20 percent in 1981 before declining to 16 percent in 1986 (de Janvry et al., 1987:86).

The crisis of U.S. agriculture had its origins in both long-term structural trends and in the conjuncture of specific economic events of the early 1980s. The drive for competitiveness involves the expansion of production and hence the need for borrowed capital, which makes farmers more vulnerable to higher interest rates. Increased dependence on purchased inputs also makes farmers more susceptible to low commodity prices. Thus the penetration of market forces increases the competitiveness, but at the same time, vulnerability of farm operations. Historically, U.S agriculture has been characterized by problems of oversupply, fluctuating and often low farm incomes, and high state costs of supporting the farm sector (de Janvry and LeVeen, 1986). Exportation of agricultural commodities was encouraged during the late 1960s as a strategy to deal with these problems. One consequence, however, was to make farming more vulnerable to new sources of price and income instability (de Janvry and LeVeen, 1986). From 1970 to 1980, agricultural exports expanded almost six times due to favorable economic conditions and the declining value of the dollar (Kolko, 1988:171). Farm prices rose and farmers expanded operations by investing in land, machinery and equipment, often borrowing heavily to do so (Leistritz and Murdock, 1988).

By the 1980s, the conditions that fostered agricultural expansion reversed. U.S. farmers were faced with recession, a rise in the value of the dollar, declining world demand for U.S products, and low commodity prices. Meanwhile, the costs of producing farm commodities and interest rates rose. As returns to farmland diminished, land values declined, falling 27 percent nationally from their 1981 peak and almost 60 percent in some of the major farming states by 1986 (Leistritz and Murdock, 1988:17). Declining land values eroded farmers' equity. As a result, some farmers found that:

> asset values dropped below the total of their liabilities, and others found that their diminished farm income was no longer adequate to service (i.e., make interest and principal payments) the massive debts accumulated during the boom period. As lenders refused to further credit to some borrowers who appeared to be insolvent or initiated legal action against those who were delinquent on loan payments, farm liquidations increased. From 1982 to 1986 the percentage of farms going out of business nearly tripled...and the percentage going through bankruptcy more than quadrupled (Leistritz and Murdock, 1988:17).

The types of producers vulnerable to the farm crisis varied by region, commodity, and farm/household characteristics. Midwestern farms, those in the Northern Plains, Great Lakes, and Corn Belt were particularly affected. Cash grain production, found throughout the Midwest, has experienced declining markets for exports. Note also that domestic consumer markets have changed: per capita consumption of beef has dropped since 1976. This has in turn weakened the demand for cattle feed crops such as corn and soybeans. Farms in the South, many of which are involved in cash grain production such as soybeans, also were affected by the crisis (Leistritz and Ekstrom, 1988).

Moderate-size, commercial farms with gross sales from $40,000 to under $250,000 have had the severest financial problems, or higher debts to assets and cash flow problems (Leistritz and Ekstrom, 1988:87). These farms tend to have younger operators, use primarily family rather than hired labor, and may have combined renting and ownership to expand operations. Households on such farms depend mainly on farm income for their livelihood and secure few cost advantages of size. In contrast, smaller farms are less likely to have high debt ratios since they have not needed to borrow extensively to expand operations. They also rely more on alternative income sources, such as off-farm employment. Larger operations also have been less vulnerable because they have cost advantages through inputs and marketing or through their efficiency and they are often engaged in high return enterprises such as specialty crops or feeder cattle

(Leistritz and Ekstrom, 1988:87). Murdock et al. (1988:157–158) estimate that about 50 percent of those who leave farming in agriculturally dependent counties from 1985 to 1995 will be family farmers from medium-size farms. The farm crisis has thus accelerated previous structural trends toward dualism in farming through the elimination of family farms.

The farm crisis parallels the crisis in the wider economy in a number of ways. First, both are consequences of the heightened influence of global trade and financial conditions on the domestic economy. Second, changes in the nature of consumer markets and the development of new technologies are changing the structure of farming as well as industry. Consumer demand for distinct food items, such as ethnic and organic products, are encouraging the production of nontraditional or specialty products: fruits, vegetables, horticultural crops, and animal specialty products over bulk production of corn, wheat, or soybeans (Kenney et al., 1989; Smith et al., 1987). Biotechnologies and information technologies allow greater product diversity while permitting centralized control over operations (Kenney et al., 1989). This may result in the growth of large, diversified farming operations such as those found in California agriculture and alternatively, of smaller, specialty types of farms, which may be operated on a part-time basis (Kenney et al., 1989; Smith et al., 1987). Successful farmers may be those with flexible production routines who can quickly adapt to market changes. Third, as a consequence of the wider economic crisis, government intervention in the privatized economy has become increasingly costly, and conflict over the allocation of state resources may intensify. For example, it is becoming more difficult to support the demands of commodity lobbies for increased farm subsidies (de Janvry et al., 1987). Finally, the economic crisis has eroded previous financial and other employment related gains of industrial and farm workers as well as of many farm operators.[8]

SPATIAL ASPECTS OF THE UNEVEN DEVELOPMENT OF FARMING AND INDUSTRY

The organization of economic production has undergone a process of uneven development, which is reflected in a segmented industry structure and in an increasingly dualistic farm structure. The economic changes of the 1970s and 1980s contributed to further variegation in both sectors. The process of uneven development can be observed geographically as well as temporally.[9] Scott and Storper (1986:302) discuss the inherent tendency for geographic unevenness under capitalism:

Why, we may ask, is the landscape of capitalism characterized not so much by a pattern of widely dispersed production sites and equal levels of income, as it is by a tremendously uneven distribution of economic activity and marked disparities of income and social welfare?...Geographical unevenness is socially and historically produced out of the basic dynamics of commodity production as such. In capitalism, the organization of labor processes, the transactional structure of production, the peculiarities of local labor markets, and the many different external economies that arise out of dense localized forms of development all create pressures that lead to high levels of development in some areas and relative backwardness and stagnation in others.

Over time, capital has become increasingly indifferent toward space: transportation and communication improvements have reduced the importance of location for markets and production inputs; technical changes in automation processes have allowed for smaller production facilities and separate workplaces; locational flexibility has been enhanced through large corporate structure; more industrial sites have become available to industry; and production systems are becoming more globally dispersed (Storper and Walker, 1984). The diminishing importance of location in regard to nonlabor factors of production has made issues of labor sourcing (skill, costs, unionization levels) particularly important locational considerations (Gordon et al., 1982:218–219; Urry, 1984:55). Location and relocation are now essential for "shaping and changing the employment relation in a continuing effort by management to remain competitive and contain class struggle within the workplace. Mobility in space is not a luxury for capital, but a necessity" (Storper and Walker, 1984:41).

Large manufacturing establishments were initially located in cities and in Frost Belt states, due to the proximity and availability of production factors and ready access to markets. For several decades, there has been a shift in population, jobs, and investment capital from older industrial metropolitan areas in the North to the South and Southwestern states and from various regions of the United States to the third world. Since the early 1970s, conditions related to the fordist economic crisis, including postwar labor victories, which constrained management's ability to respond to changing national and global economic demands, accelerated firm closings and relocations (Bluestone and Harrison, 1982:15–19). The response of capital was to disinvest from certain industrial sectors and in the areas where these predominated and to relocate in search of lower wage, unorganized labor—a motive that came to dominate other locational factors including tax and subsidy benefits (Gordon et al., 1982:219). Runaway plants, shutdowns, and permanent physical cutbacks are estimated to have caused the loss of 38 million jobs during the 1970s (Bluestone and Harrison, 1982:35). Plant closings were particularly concentrated in manufacturing industries such as autos, steel, and tires, usually considered providers of core sector jobs and in Northeast and North Central states. There have also been considerable intraregional differences in the process of deindustrialization. For example, the industries upon which the 'New South' was built, textiles, apparel, electronics, and other labor intensive industries that tended to be located in rural areas, have experienced plant shutdowns and relocation to third world countries (Falk and Lyson, 1988). Reindustrialization has also occurred in some areas, such as the expansion of hi-tech industries around urban New England communities in the 1980s.

The organization of farm production also varies spatially. As in nonfarm industry, labor recruitment and control play an important role in the development of different systems of production (Friedland et al., 1981; Pfeffer, 1983; Thomas, 1981). Pfeffer (1983:540) argues that the "interaction of labor management constraints imposed by the natural conditions of production with particular economic, social, and political conditions" have given rise to three major historically and spatially specific farming systems: corporate farming in California, family farming in the Great Plains, and sharecropping in the South. All three regions were initially characterized by a concentration of landholdings. In California, the historical availability of waves of immigrant labor consolidated the pattern of large-scale industrial farming. In the Great Plains, large farmers were unable to secure and maintain needed hired labor and therefore to compete with the family operations, which then came to dominate this area. Sharecropping developed in the South as planters had to devise new methods of labor recruitment and retention after the Civil War.

In brief, social relations characterizing a particular region and the biological exigencies of the commodity (which may be circumvented or diminished through technology) intersect so that the following systems are observable today. The Northeast is characterized by small farms producing for urban markets and a continuing loss of farms and farmland (Buttel et al., 1988). In the Midwest, commercial family farms producing cash grains predominate. The South is more heterogeneous: small, part-time farms are common particularly in tobacco growing areas such as Kentucky and North Carolina while large, industrial type farms still predominate in the old cotton belt and in sugar producing areas (Skees and Swanson, 1988). Agriculture in the West tends to be large-scale and dependent upon irrigation and hired labor.

The spatial intersection of farming and nonfarm industry is another aspect of uneven development. This has two implications for understanding economic structure and local inequality. The first is the nature of the interdependency between farming and the nonfarm economy. This takes a number of forms. For example, nonfarm employment can subsidize farm operations by providing additional income and shelter from economic downturns. By these means it can even encourage new entrants into farming (Beaulieu et al. 1988:217–218; Falk and Lyson, 1988). As noted previously, however, the incidence of self-exploitation in farming may increase because nonfarm employment facilitates adaptation to low farm returns. Incoming industries often contribute to higher land values and taxes particularly when close to metropolitan areas and thereby may make it more difficult for operators to expand operations. Farming also influences local industry. Historically, farming has been a reserve supplier of labor to industry in times of upswings and has absorbed excess labor during downturns.

The second implication is that because farming and industry tend to intersect in rural areas, current restructuring of both economic sectors has tended to evolve into a general rural economic crisis. Labor-intensive, routine, manufacturing industries, such as textiles, apparel, food, and furniture and other traditionally rural industries such as oil, gas, coal, and lumber production have experienced recent downturns as a consequence of rising foreign competition, weak markets, and strong dollar (Henry et al., 1988). As the economy has shifted to services, rural areas have continued to be left behind. Service employment has grown much slower in nonmetropolitan areas and the fastest growing and higher paying services are concentrated in urban areas (Henry et al., 1988). Deregulation has also had an adverse impact on some aspects of the rural economy. Deregulation of the banking industry has tended to raise interest rates to rural borrowers. Transportation deregulation has made prices for airfare and truck hauling comparatively higher in rural than in urban areas (Henry et al., 1988). The farm crisis has also unevenly affected rural areas. Murdock et al. (1988) estimate that by the mid-1990s, agriculturally dependent counties will experience substantial declines of the working age population, losses in wholesale and retail trade, local earnings and tax revenues, reduced trade and service employment, and cuts in public services.

These changes in economic structure have seriously jeopardized the well-being of rural people, undermining more than a decade of gains. Inequality between rural and urban areas, once thought to be closing, is now widening. The net in-migration of residents to nonmetropolitan areas of the 1970s reversed during the 1980s. Between 1986 and 1987, there was a net out-migration of nearly one million people from nonmetropolitan areas (O'Hare, 1988:2). From the 1960s to 1980, metropolitan unemployment exceeded the nonmetropolitan rates. From 1980 onward, however, nonmetropolitan unemployment rose and by 1986 was 26 percent higher in nonmetropolitan areas (O'Hare, 1988:4). Incomes have been lower historically in nonmetropolitan areas, even after cost of living adjustments. During the 1970s, nonmetropolitan income began to catch up with that in metropolitan areas and by 1979, the median income of nonmetropolitan families was 79 percent of that of metropolitan families. During the 1980s, however, nonmetropolitan median family income once again began to fall, declining to 73 percent of that in metropolitan areas by 1986 (O'Hare, 1988:5). The percent of the population in poverty likewise has been greater historically in nonmetropolitan areas, although the gap decreased during the 1970s. The gap began to increase again during the 1980s and by 1986, the poverty rate was 18 percent among the nonmetropolitan population, nearly 50 percent higher than that of the metropolitan population. Nonmetropolitan poverty is concentrated among young adults and children, with the poverty rate for children about one-third higher than in metropolitan areas. One out of four rural children lived in poor households in 1986 (O'Hare, 1988:6–7). The 1980s were thus characterized by a growing inequality between urban and rural areas both in terms of the quantity and quality of employment and in socioeconomic conditions.

IN SUMMARY

The organization of economic production has undergone a process of uneven development over space and time. The development of the industrial sector is largely characterized by the growth and segmentation of capitalist enterprises or those in which the capital-labor relationship exists. In contrast, the biological nature of farm production, dependence upon land, problems of labor recruitment, and other factors add risks and complexities to farming, creating barriers to the growth of large-scale enterprises employing wage-labor. Capital has tended to enter farming via relationships of exchange in which control over factors of production becomes progressively transferred from the farm household to nonfarm entities. The competitive nature of farm production, government programs, technology and other factors have contributed toward the development of a dualistic system based on many small, low-volume, part-time farms and a few large farms which account for ever growing shares of farm sales. Moderate-size family farms have been increasingly edged out of this system.

Farming and nonfarm industry were further transformed by the erosion of the fordist regime of accumulation, which had characterized the U.S. economy since the postwar period. Changes emerged first in the industrial sector in the 1970s. Plant closings and relocations, increases in unemployment, and declining unionization rates deteriorated the power of American workers. In contrast, global economic demands and domestic forces such as interest rates had generally favorable impacts on the farm sector during the 1970s. But by the early 1980s crisis enveloped the farm economy too. Moderate-size family farms experienced the brunt of the crisis, compounding the factors related to their long-term decline. The decline of real wages and the growth of poverty signalled the reversal of postwar gains in living standards and rising inequality in America during the 1980s decade.

The development of economic structure is also spatially uneven as capital continually seeks out ever more profitable sectors and locations. Technology has reduced many former locational barriers, allowing capital to become relatively more mobile than labor. As economic structures come to be spread unevenly across different places, so too are levels of inequality. Capital tends to build upon pre-existing inequalities, leaving persistent historical gaps between regions such as the South and the rest of the nation and between rural and urban areas.

The next chapter extends some of the previous issues about economic structure and inequality by focusing on the effects of farm structure on localities. It centers on the five decades of research which has tested the Goldschmidt hypothesis that large, industrialized farms are related to greater economic inequality and lower quality of life.

—————— Farm Structure and Socioeconomic Inequality

The effects of farm structure and change on localities is a topic of considerable controversy. Most debates revolve around the potential detrimental impacts of large-scale industrialized farming as opposed to family operated farms. Despite decades of research, the controversy continues, enlivened by the recent farm crisis and dramatic transformation of family farming. In this chapter, I evaluate critically previous studies and probe the reasons for the long-standing debate.

GOLDSCHMIDT'S STUDY OF ARVIN AND DINUBA

Of the studies that examine the effects of farm structure on community well-being, none has achieved more recognition than Goldschmidt's 1944 case study of two California communities. Goldschmidt observed that agricultural production was becoming increasingly concentrated in larger farms while the number of full-owners declined. He questioned the impact this trend would have on the future of family farming and on the rural community. His study was a test of the Jeffersonian ideal "that the institution of small independent farms is indeed the agent which creates the homogenous community, both socially and economically democratic" (1968:306).

Goldschmidt (1968; 1978a) tested his hypothesis through a case study of two rural communities in the San Joaquin Valley: Arvin, a community dominated by large farms; and Dinuba, a family farming community. He argued that the two communities were similar on a number of factors, which were important as controls. Agricultural sales were approximately the same. Both communities produced high value, specialized crops, which utilized irrigation and a harvest work force. Both were in the same climatic zone, approximately equidistant from urban centers, and similar in population size. Neither had any "significant advantages from nonagricultural resources or from manufacturing or processing" (Goldschmidt, 1968:308). There were important differences between these two communities in terms of farm scale and organization, however. Dinuba supported 722 farm operators, with an average farm size of 57 acres. In contrast, Arvin supported only 133 farm operators, with an average farm size of 497 acres, nine times as large as that of Dinuba. More than three-quarters of Dinuba farms were operated by full-owners, in contrast to about one-third in Arvin.

In comparing the two communities, Goldschmidt noted varying socio-economic differences which he attributed to farming patterns, particularly the scale of operations. An important difference involved the stratification structure (1968:346). About two-thirds of major household income earners were farm laborers in Arvin compared to under one-third in Dinuba. Farmers and white-collar workers made up only a fifth of the major household income earners in Arvin but half of those in Dinuba. Sustenance and living conditions were higher in Dinuba. The town supported a larger population per volume of agricultural sales and there was greater availability of running water, electricity, radio and telephones. Schools and parks were numerous and of higher quality. Paved streets, sidewalks, and garbage and sewage services were provided more frequently. Government decision-making was more democratic in that residents had an impact on community welfare issues through local popular elections while in Arvin, much decision making was left in the hands of community officials. Social participation was greater in Dinuba, as indicated by the number of civic and social organizations, community newspapers, and churches. Finally, Dinuba supported a more varied nonfarm economy than Arvin, with more than double the number of retail business establishments and a greater volume of retail trade.

According to Goldschmidt (1968:308), small-scale farming produces a community of middle class individuals, with a high stability in income and tenure, and "a strong economic and social interest in their community. Differences in wealth among them are not great, and the people generally associate in those organizations which serve the community." In the large farm community, however, relatively few people have economic stability and wealth, with large numbers, "whose only tie to the community is their uncertain and relatively low-income jobs" (Goldschmidt, 1968:308).

Goldschmidt (1968) outlined a casual explanation of the differences between the two communities. A juncture of historical and environmental factors produced the initial differences in farm scale between Arvin and Dinuba. The scale of operations, in turn, influenced class structure, resulting in a large group of wage-laborers and a small group of independent producers in Arvin, with no such major differences in Dinuba. Finally, the greater number of lower class individuals in Arvin was the major factor related to its "poverty of social institutions, lower level of living, lower education, lower community loyalty and higher population turnover" (Goldschmidt, 1968:308).[1]

The Small Farm Viability Project (1977), as part of a state-wide effort to assess the status of small farms in central California, revisited Arvin and Dinuba three decades later. Its report (1977:229–230) reaffirmed Goldschmidt's findings:

The disparity in local economic activity, civic participation, and quality of life between Arvin and Dinuba...remains today. In fact, the disparity is greater. The economic and social gaps have widened. There can be little doubt about the relative effects of farm size and farm ownership on the communities of Arvin and Dinuba.

FURTHER STUDIES ON THE EFFECTS OF INDUSTRIALIZED AND FAMILY FARMING

Since Goldschmidt's seminal work, a number of studies have examined the relationship between farm structure and socioeconomic well-being. Chronologically, these studies were conducted first during the Depression era, as social scientists observed the decline of family farms and trends toward large-scale farming. But nearly three decades passed before the issue entered the forefront of concern again in the early 1970s. This long neglect, particularly by rural sociologists, resulted from disciplinary organization and dominant theoretical perspectives, which diverted attention from the analysis of economic structure and social conflict (Newby, 1983; Friedland, 1982). Goldschmidt (1978a) also argues that large farmers and political authorities made attempts to suppress information about the effects of industrialized farming, ranging from book burnings of John Steinbeck's *The Grapes of Wrath*, to Goldschmidt's termination from the USDA's Bureau of Agricultural Economics and the eventual demise of the Bureau itself.

By the mid-1970s, postwar changes in farming and their effects on communities could no longer be ignored. Social scientists were struck by a new rural environment that failed to resemble the bucolic descriptions of the past. Political unrest as evidenced in the growth of the American Agricultural Movement and tractorcade protests of Washington, D.C. centered attention on the farm sector. Moreover, the dominant sociological paradigm, functionalism, with its stress on consensus and social equilibrium, was increasingly subject to criticism and replacement by conflict theories, such as perspectives from the new structuralism and political economy. Because these new theories focused on social change, competition, and coercion, they could more systematically deal with the upheavals occurring in the farm sector. Thus dramatic changes in farming coupled with developments in sociological theory fostered a renewed focus on the Goldschmidt issue.

Although studies in the Goldschmidt tradition employ various analytical frameworks, regional locations, and methods of data collection, they share certain characteristics. Most research is based upon testing aspects of the following relationships. Communities are interrelated with their farming hinterlands; changes in farm structure produce changes in the community. Two major changes in farm structure have had great community impact (Swanson, 1982:103). First, as production has tended to become concentrated into larger farms, the total number of farms and the size of the farm workforce have both decreased. Second, the farm workforce has become more like the industrial workforce: the number of hired laborers and managers has increased while the number of traditional family farmers has decreased.

The decline in farm numbers and workforce implies that individuals involved in farming will be forced to out-migrate from their communities unless nonfarm employment can be secured. Because out-migration results in a decline of total community population (assuming no new in-migration), economic and social institutions dependent on the local population are likely to decline (Buttel, 1980a). The qualitative changes in class structure accompanying the concentration of production imply that simple commodity producers become less politically and economically dominant, while the political and economic dominance of large-scale producers increase. An increase in hired farm workers and managers further signals the growth of a subordinate population.

Does Industrialized Farming Jeopardize the Locality? The Evidence

Although studies in the Goldschmidt tradition do not unequivocally demonstrate that industrialized farming jeopardizes its immediate locality, much empirical evidence does support this hypothesis. In summarizing the findings of this research, a couple of remarks are in order. First, the purpose of most studies is to examine the impact of indicators of one or both farm concepts—farm scale and organizational characteristics—on socioeconomic well-being. Farm scale is generally considered in terms of sales or acreage and is the concept used by nearly all studies. Other organizational characteristics are usually conceptualized as the extent of off-farm dependence on production factors, such as land, labor, mangement, and capital. Thus, the studies focus on concepts such as land tenure, extent of hired labor use, control over farm operations, and use of capital for farm inputs. Organizational characteristics tend to be analyzed less frequently than scale. Second, in examining relationships between farm scale/organization and socioeconomic well-being, most studies have taken a linear approach: they hypothesize that the larger the farm or the greater the organizational dependence on off-farm inputs, particularly labor, the more negative the impact on socio-economic well-being (Tweeten, 1981; Skees and Swanson, 1986). As a consequence, researchers tend to present findings that contrast small and medium size farms and/or farms dependent on family supplied production factors with large farms and/or those dependent upon hired labor. The few studies examining other aspects of the farm/well-being relationship, such as the impact of part-time and contract farming are considered separately from those that specifically focus on the Goldschmidt hypothesis.

With the above limitations in mind, the studies point to a generally consistent relationship. They find that large-scale and/or hired labor farming is related to worse socioeconomic conditions (and concomitantly, that smaller, particularly family labor farming is related to better conditions) as evidenced by the following impacts:

(1)   a decline in or smaller local population (Goldschmidt, 1968; Heady and Sonka, 1974; Rodefeld, 1974; Wheelock, 1979; Swanson, 1980).
(2)   lower incomes for certain segments of the population, such as hired laborers, increases in income inequality, or increases in poverty (Tetreau, 1940; Goldschmidt, 1968; Heady and Sonka, 1974; Rodefeld, 1974; Flora et al., 1977; Wheelock, 1979).
(3)   lower levels of living (Goldschmidt, 1968; Rodefeld, 1974).
(4)   lower numbers or quality of community services (Tetreau, 1940; Goldschmidt, 1968; Raup, 1973; Fujimoto, 1977; Swanson, 1980).
(5)   less democratic political participation (Tetreau, 1940; Raup, 1973; Goldschmidt, 1968; Rodefeld, 1974).
(6)   lower community social participation and integration, greater social-psychological problems for hired farm workers (Goldschmidt, 1968; Heffernan, 1972; Rodefeld, 1974; Martinson et al., 1976; Poole, 1981).
(7)   decreased retail trade and fewer, less diverse retail outlets (Goldschmidt, 1968; Heady and Sonka, 1974; Rodefeld, 1974; Fujimoto, 1977; Marousek, 1979; Swanson, 1980; Skees and Swanson, 1986).
(8)   environmental pollution, depletion of energy resources (Tetreau, 1940; Raup, 1973; Buttel and Larson, 1979).
(9)   greater unemployment (Marousek, 1979).

Further, in accordance with Goldschmidt, the previous studies tend to find that farm scale and organization impact upon the stratification system: local society reflects the statuses imposed by the economic system. Thus an agricultural system of large-scale farms dependent upon hired labor, as opposed to family labor farming, produces a local social structure composed mainly of hired workers (assuming agricultural dependence) (Flora et al., 1977; Goldschmidt, 1968; Tetreau, 1940; Rodefeld, 1974; Wheelock, 1979).

While a number of studies support Goldschmidt, others draw conclusions that do not endorse his thesis. These divergent findings happen for various reasons. First, findings are affected by the researchers concept of farm structure and the types of indicators examined. Consequently, some studies find that the scale of operations, measured in acreage or sales, does not affect socioeconomic conditions in the way hypothesized by Goldschmidt. For example, Skees and Swanson (1986) find that increases in farm scale are related to increases in property taxes, indicating the availability, though not necessarily the use of, greater public revenue for community services in large farm areas. Harris and Gilbert (1982) report the total effects of large scale farms on rural income to be moderately positive. Heaton and Brown (1982) conclude that large farms conserve more energy per dollar value of agricultural products sold and have lower rates of energy usage; therefore they may offer environmental advantages.

In contrast to the effects of scale, dependency on hired farm labor appears to have a more consistent, negative relationship to well-being. Gilles and Dalecki (1988) for example, find that in two Midwestern areas, increases in the numbers of workers per farm are related to poorer socioeconomic conditions, while increases in farm scale tend to be related to better conditions. Wimberley and Reif (1988) have systematically investigated whether the results of the Goldschmidt hypothesis depend upon the indicators of farm structure utilized. They also find that hired labor dependency tends to be related to worse socioeconomic conditions but that other relationships, such as those involving scale and ownership, do not follow directions outlined by Goldschmidt.

Second, the time period during which the study is conducted may affect results. As economic development progresses, off-farm factors may come to mediate potential detrimental effects of large, industrialized farms. Finding little relationship between population decline and growth in farm scale in Pennsylvania communities over a thirty year period, Swanson (1982) concludes that communities tend to become less agriculturally dependent over time so that nonfarm factors, particularly off-farm employment opportunities, play a greater part in determining community well-being. Wheelock (1979) makes a similar argument. He reports that counties with relatively larger farms in 1960 had growth in population and median income in the 1970s and suggests that negative consequences of rapid farm change (also found in his study) may be offset by other community factors.

Third, the effects of farm structure may vary by the type of socioeconomic conditions considered. Agricultural economists have argued that specific costs and benefits are associated with both large and small farms. Heady and Sonka (1974) report that smaller farms have positive socioeconomic effects for farmers and their communities but lead to higher food costs for consumers. Marousek (1979) found a trade-off between smaller and larger farms: small farms provide greater employment while large farms produce greater area income. A related issue is whether the dependent variable of concern is an economic one. The few studies that examine noneconomic impacts such as health, education, and other social variables seem to report more divergences (see Green, 1985; Eberts, 1979b).

Fourth, the effects of farm structure may vary by regional location, an issue I discuss more extensively in Chapter 7. A series of studies sponsored by the Office of Technology Assessment provide valuable evidence on regional variations (Swanson, 1988). Findings for agriculturally dependent counties in California, Texas, Arizona, Florida, other parts of the West, and the Great Plains tend to support aspects of Goldschmidt's hypothesis. However, for other regions—the South, Northeast, and Corn Belt—results are more mixed or less supportive.

Fifth, the unit of analysis or type of geographic entity analyzed may affect results (Wimberley, 1987). Though Goldschmidt compared townships, subsequent studies generally examined larger area units such as states or counties. These more highly aggregated units may obscure relationships occurring at lower levels, such as within a particular community.

Finally, differential findings may result because of the nature of the relationships specified. According to Skees and Swanson (1986), studies in the Goldschmidt tradition may require reconceptualization. They note that such studies possibly misspecify the relationship between farm scale and well-being by examining only linear rather than curvilinear relationships. Virtually all studies assume that smaller farms result in better conditions. In constrast, Skees and Swanson (1986) find that counties with either smaller or very large farms are more likely to have high levels of unemployment.

Divergences also exist in that relationships extended from the Goldschmidt hypothesis are not always supported. Studies that analyze the effects of modern farm types that vary from the traditional family farm ideal, such as contract farming and part-time farming, have generally not found negative community impacts. Heffernan et al. (1981) find few differences between part-time and full-time farmers regarding their perceived attachment to community social activities, reasons for living in rural areas and perception of community goals. Skees and Swanson (1986) report that part-time farming tends to be associated with higher standards of living. Heffernan (1982b:340) notes that the "research that has been done finds little alteration in the quality of life in rural communities that can be attributed to a trend toward vertical integration." Heffernan's (1972) own study of contract poultry operations supports this contention.

Summary of Studies in the Goldschmidt Tradition

Studies examining the impacts of farming on socioeconomic conditions are summarized in Table 3.1. While these represent much of the major research in the Goldschmidt tradition, they by no means reflect an exhaustive account of the literature.[2] The studies are classified by the method of data collection, the sample analyzed, and regional location. The studies followed several methodological approaches. The case studies of Goldschmidt (1968, 1978a) and the Small Farm Viability Project (1977) compared individual communities with different agricultural structures. Surveys of farmers and/or their households were employed by Tetreau (1940), Heffernan (1972), Rodefeld (1974), Martinson et al. (1976), Heffernan and Lasley (1978), Heffernan et al. (1981), and Poole (1981). Secondary data, from population, business and agricultural censuses, government reports, and business listings allowed analyses of entire communities, counties, or states. This was the most common method of assessing the farm/socioeconomic structure relationship. The type of independent variable used to represent farm structure is also delineated. As noted previously, most analysts use measures of

TABLE 3.1

Summary of Studies Examining Farming and Socioeconomic Conditions

Study	Methodology	Region	Independent Variables	Dependent Variables	Results
Goldschmidt (1968, 1978a)	case study of two communities	California	scale/organization	socioeconomic indicators/class structure/services/population/social participation/politics/retail trade	support
Tetreau (1938, 1940)	survey, 2700 households	Arizona	scale/organization	socioeconomic indicators/class structure	support
Heffernan (1972)	survey, 138 broiler producers	Louisiana	organization	social psychological indicators/community involvement	support
Heady and Sonka (1974)	linear programming model of 150 producing areas	continental U.S.	scale	socioeconomic indicators/income, employment generation	mixed: large farms lower food costs but generate less services and total community income
Rodefeld (1974)	survey, 180 producers from 110 farms	Wisconsin	scale/organization	socioeconomic indicators/class structure/services/population	support
Martinson et al. (1976)	survey, 180 producers	Wisconsin	organization	social psychological indicators	support

TABLE 3.1 *continued*

Study	Methodology	Region	Independent Variables	Dependent Variables	Results
Fujimoto (1977)	secondary data for 130 towns	California	scale	community services	support
Flora et al. (1977)	secondary data for 105 counties	Kansas	scale/ organization	socioeconomic indicators/class structure/services	mixed: industrialized farming contributes to income inequality but other relationships not clearly supported
Small Farm Viability Project (1977)	reanalysis of Arvin and Dinuba	California	scale/ organization	socioeconomic indicators/class structure/services	support
Goldschmidt (1978b)	secondary state-level data	entire U.S. except Alaska	scale	agrarian class structure	support
Heffernan and Lasley (1978)	survey, 36 grape producers	Missouri	organization	community social and economic involvement	mixed: operators of nonfamily farms less involved in social activities but little support for other relationships

TABLE 3.1 *continued*

Study	Methodology	Region	Independent Variables	Dependent Variables	Results
Wheelock (1979)	secondary data for 61 counties	Alabama	scale	socioeconomic indicators/class structure/population	mixed: destabilizing effects of large farms may be mitigated by nonfarm factors
Marousek (1979)	economic projection modeling, one community	Idaho	scale	socioeconomic indicators/income, employment generation	mixed: large farms result in greater regional income but small farms result in greater employment
Buttel and Larson (1979)	secondary state-level data	entire U.S.	scale/organization	energy usage	support
Heaton and Brown (1982)	secondary county-level data	continental U.S.	scale/organization	energy usage	did not support
Swanson (1980)	secondary data for 27 counties	Nebraska	scale	socioeconomic indicators/population	support
Poole (1981)	survey, 78 farmers	Maryland	scale	involvement in community organizations	support

TABLE 3.1 *continued*

Study	Methodology	Region	Independent Variables	Dependent Variables	Results
Harris and Gilbert (1982)	secondary state-level data	continental U.S.	scale/organization	socioeconomic indicators/class structure	mixed: large farms result in more lower class farm personnel but have positive total effects on rural income
Swanson (1982)	secondary data for 520 communities	Pennsylvania	scale/number of farms	population	did not support
Green (1985)	secondary data for 109 counties	Missouri	scale/organization	socioeconomic indicators/services	mixed: large farms have few significant community impacts
Skees and Swanson (1986)	secondary data for 706 counties	Southern U.S., excluding Florida, Texas	scale/organization	socioeconomic indicators/services	mixed: both large and small farms related to higher unemployment; other relationships mixed
MacCannell and Dolber-Smith (1986)	secondary data for 98 counties	Arizona, California, Florida, Texas	scale/organization/capital intensity	socioeconomic indicators/population/retail trade/local government taxation and expenditures	support

TABLE 3.1 *continued*

Study	Methodology	Region	Independent Variables	Dependent Variables	Results
Flora and Flora (1986)	secondary data for 234 counties	Great Plains and West	scale	socioeconomic indicators/retail trade/population	support in that medium-sized farms enhance community well-being
Buttel et al. (1986)	secondary data for 105 counties	Northeast	organization	socioeconomic indicators/ population/retail trade	do not support
van Es et al. (1986)	secondary data for 331 counties	Corn Belt	scale/ organization	socioeconomic indicators/ population	do not support
Gilles and Dalecki (1988)	secondary data for 346 counties	Corn Belt and Central Plains	scale/ organization	socioeconomic status	mixed: counties with greater numbers of hired laborers tend to have lower socio-economic status; other relationships not supported

scale and/or other organizational features of the farm enterprise. The studies examined a wide variety of dependent variables. Most dependent variables could be classified as to whether they were socioeconomic indicators or measures of income and quality of life; indicators of socioeconomic class, such as percent of wage laborers; indicators of quality and types of community services and trade; measures of population; and social-psychological indicators, including measures of powerlessness and alienation.

Finally, the results of the study are presented in the context of a test of the Goldschmidt hypothesis that large-scale, industrial farming has negative impacts in regard to the dependent variables examined. While most studies test a number of relationships, the researcher's overall estimation as to the extent of support is presented. The results of the studies were thus classified as supporting, failing to support, or as having mixed findings. As indicated in Table 3.1, the Goldschmidt hypothesis has received more support than disconfirmation by the previous studies: about half of the twenty-six studies support Goldschmidt and another nine have mixed findings.

The conclusions of studies examining the impact of farm structure on socioeconomic conditions summarized by Heffernan (1982b:340–342):

> All relevant research to date suggests that a corporate type of agriculture results in a reduction in the quality of life for at least some people, especially the hired workers in rural communities. No single study or set of studies can answer all of the research questions, but it seems significant that a dozen studies, spanning four decades and all regions of the nation, and performed by different researchers using different methodologies, have rather consistently shown that a change toward corporate agriculture produces social consequences that reduce the quality of life in rural communities.

While Heffernan is correct that most studies prior to the early 1980s supported Goldschmidt, more recent findings have been mixed. The following section examines the problems of research on the impact of farming on socioeconomic conditions.

Criticisms and Limitations of the Previous Studies

The research on the Goldschmidt hypothesis still remains vulnerable to a number of criticisms that limit closure on the debate. One set of criticisms is centered at the methodological level. In regard to his own study, Goldschmidt (1968:392) asserted that "Nobody [has] pointed to inaccuracies in the data, to failure of analysis, or to the evidence that I was said to disregard." Criticism of the study, he argued, was not methodological but rather directed at the study's implications, by agribusiness supporters. More recently, however, Goldschmidt's study has been challenged on a methodological level. Using a variety of pre-collected data sources, Hayes and Olmstead (1984) argue that Arvin and Dinuba were not closely matched areas and differed on variables that were supposed to be controlled, such as population size, crop mix, community age, and absence of extraneous economic advantages. They (1984:433) maintain, that although Goldschmidt's hypothesis may indeed be correct, "Arvin and Dinuba were too dissimilar to warrant the type of comparative analysis that he attempted." While their retrospective analysis merits consideration, it does not refute the basic relationship postulated by Goldschmidt. Furthermore, the Small Farm Viability Project's (1977) findings of persistent differences between Arvin and Dinuba lend continued support to Goldschmidt.

However, the issue raised by Hayes and Olmstead—the adequacy of control variables—is important and concerns not only Goldschmidt's study but other studies that examine farm/socioeconomic relationships as well. Control variables are needed to specify the conditions under which farm types have various effects and to discern possible spurious relationships. The delineation of these variables and the method by which they are held constant have been problematic. Some researchers have confined their studies to only nonmetropolitan areas in order to limit the influence of nonfarm factors. However, this itself does not control fully for agricultural dependency, urbanization, or industrial activity. In most rural areas, manufacturing and service industries are economically more important than farming; consequently, they have greater effect on quality of life. When nonfarm factors have been held constant, as in a few recent studies, the relationship between large-scale farming and community well-being has not completely supported Goldschmidt (Swanson, 1982; Skees and Swanson, 1986). Further studies that delineate and control for nonfarm factors are needed to more rigorously test the impact of farm structure.

Studies employing linear programming and other modelling techniques (Heady and Sonka, 1974; Marousek, 1979) in order to predict the impact of large scale agriculture have related limitations. The acceptance of outcomes is contingent upon accepting the assumptions of the model, such as the inclusion of all relevant variables (or factors that may intervene), which may be untenable.

An additional methodological criticism is that most studies, including Goldschmidt's, have been cross-sectional and thus "fail to provide the longitudinal evidence which is needed to investigate the social consequences of agricultural structural change" (Korsching and Stofferahn, 1985b:1). Longitudinal analyses are important because they more closely reflect the empirical realities of changing agricultural structure and, hence, can offer more direct evidence of the impact of these changes. They can also indicate whether farm changes create permanent or only temporary imbalances in the community.

A further methodological criticism raised by Swanson (1982) and Korsching and Stofferahn (1985,a,b) involves the scope of the studies. Most have been confined to areas with specific types of agriculture, which limits the generalizability of findings. Only a few studies have examined the effects of farm structure for the entire United States. These include: state level analyses by Buttel and Larson (1979), Harris and Gilbert (1982), and Goldschmidt (1978b), and a county level analysis by Heaton and Brown (1982).

There are also a number of conceptual limitations with studies in the Goldschmidt tradition, some of which were touched upon in previous sections. The first problem concerns the conceptualization and measurement of farm structure. Researchers are often unclear about what aspects of farm structure are relevant for assessing socioeconomic impacts. There has been a general tendency to conflate farm scale with organizational characteristics such as ownership, managerial control, and hired labor dependency, which seems to have stemmed from Goldschmidt himself (Green, 1985). Scale is often used as a proxy for other concepts, creating several problems. First, scale and organizational form do not always coincide (Goss, 1979). Second, the focus on scale has fostered a tendency to examine only linear relationships between farm structure and socioeconomic conditions. Finally, attention is directed to a concept that may have less causal importance to community well-being. Green (1985:264) notes that organizational factors, particularly the use of hired (nonfamily) workers and type of ownership, rather than scale per se, may be more relevant determinants. Such factors directly reflect social relations while scale is only a descriptive, production-related concept.

Even those researchers who carefully distinguish the conceptual dimensions of farm structure relevant to socioeconomic conditions have difficulty measuring their concepts. For example, political economists have developed no systematic, generalizable measures of farm structure corresponding to producers' class positions or that categorize units into differentiated forms of production. Despite focus on a particular farm structure concept, researchers tend to be eclectic in their choice of measures. Most use single item measures of farm scale or organization which are often assumed to be representative of a complex farm type. A serious problem in the development of measures has been the availability of appropriate data. The Census of Agriculture, our major source of national data, does not permit examination of individual farm units and reflects mainly data of interest to production scientists.

Another conceptual problem with studies in the Goldschmidt tradition has been the uncritical tendency to view interrelationships between farm and nonfarm variables linearly. As noted previously, researchers generally hypothesize that the larger the farm, the more negative the impact on socioeconomic well-being. This implies that small farms should have a more positive impact, an observation not always borne out empirically. For example, Tweeten (1981:140) states that researchers have failed to realize that:

Dinuba was a town surrounded by family-sized farms (slightly larger than average size), not by small farms. Many towns in the South are surrounded by small, low-income farms. These communities are characterized by an egregious lack of economic and social vitality and are hardly models to be emulated. Given the importance of income and employment to well-being, the farm of optimal size from the standpoint of the community is not a small, low-income farm.

Assuming the unavailability of off-farm employment, small, low-income farms would logically be expected to reduce well-being for farmers and their localities. The assumption of a linear relationship between farm structure and well-being, however, has prevented most researchers from testing such relationships.

The one-way causality implied in most studies is a further limitation (Swanson, 1990; Beaulieu and Molnar, 1984; Korsching and Stofferahn, 1985a,b; Moxley, 1986). Changes in farm structure tend to be examined as causes rather than effects of changes in nonfarm community structure. Researchers have neglected that farming is impacted "by growth or decline of the local population, by community economic development activities, by competing demands for land and water resources, and by cries for environmental controls" (Beaulieu and Molnar, 1984:1).

Researchers have also neglected to go beyond the original relationships set forth by Goldschmidt involving comparisons between large, industrialized farming and smaller scale, traditional family farming. Little attention has been given to the impacts of more recent and increasing farm types, such as part-time and contract farming, part-ownership and renting.

Finally, there are limitations at the theoretical level. Few researchers tie tests of the farm/socioeconomic well-being relationship to a larger body of theoretical knowledge, particularly that outside rural sociology. Most view the problem of economic structure and socioeconomic outcomes as unique to the farm sector. This inhibits the development of a broader theoretical explanation for the impact of farm and other structural changes and does little to illuminate existing social science theory.[3]

RECENT EXTENSIONS OF RESEARCH ON FARM STRUCTURE AND THE LOCALITY: FARM CRISIS STUDIES

Studies on the farm crisis represent another approach to the analysis of farm-community relationships (Brooks et al., 1986; Bultena et al., 1986; Murdock et al., 1986; Heffernan and Heffernan, 1986; Murdock et al., 1988). They consider structural trends similar to the ones Goldschmidt examined but they emphasize the decline of midsize, commercially oriented, family farms rather than the growth of industrialized farming. The decline of these farms is seen in terms of a loss of middle class independent producers who sustain community institutions and businesses. Although most studies focus only on farm families, their implications extend to the entire community. For example, Heffernan and Heffernan (1986) studied stress and social-psychological depression among farmers who lost their farms for financial reasons. They argue that communities may undergo a similar collective depression, which inhibits new economic investment and the vitality of social life. Murdock et al. (1988) discuss the long-term effects of the farm crisis for 472 agriculturally dependent counties over the 1985–1995 period. They project serious declines in population, personal earnings, trade and service industries and other rural businesses, and increasing fiscal problems for local governments. As a consequence, local social organization and community solidarity will be strained and social-psychological problems will likely increase.

Analyses of the farm crisis tend to have the same limitations as the Goldschmidt studies. For example, they tend to be confined to certain areas and to be cross-sectional rather than longitudinal. The studies are also not linked to theoretical perspectives on the organization of economic production and they tend to view the farm crisis in isolation from changes in the wider economy. However, such studies are important to the farm/local well-being debate because they focus on recent farm structural patterns and trends, such as indebtedness, part-ownership, renting, and capital investments and to the middle sector of farmers rather than to the small/large farm dichotomy presupposed by many of the Goldschmidt studies.

REFORMULATING THE DEBATE

A major factor limiting resolution of the Goldschmidt debate is that many of the assumptions underlying the previous studies, particularly less recent ones, reflect a populist perception of the political economy. First, the literature tends to be premised on the bucolic ideal that simple commodity production units should be the normal form of farming. Yet it is questionable to what extent such units ever existed outside regions such as the North and beyond the early part of the twentieth century. Traditional family labor farms have not been able to reproduce themselves under the onslaught of the market economy. In their place, we find moderate-size operations with varying tenure arrangements and links to outside capital, dependent upon and supporting the consumption needs of household labor. Small operations which cannot provide for total household subsistence have also emerged. Relatedly, the studies tend to view the growth of industrialized farming as an aberration, facilitated by urban financiers and a detached or unscrupulous political bureaucracy. Analysts seem to neglect the fact that the centralization and concentration of production has occurred throughout the economy. Moreover, when considering nonfarm enterprises employing wage-labor, larger scale is generally associated with better working conditions and higher wages. Instead of stressing the uniqueness of industrialized farming, researchers should focus on the social processes that have led to or inhibited the growth of large firms in both the farm and nonfarm industrial sectors.

The implicit populism of many studies has a number of consequences. Development and change in the farm sector have been overlooked or have not been regarded as resulting from the normal operation of the economic system. Researchers have neglected modern farming patterns that vary from the simple commodity ideal. Long-standing assumptions about the nature and impacts of different farm types go unchallenged instead of questioning their relevance under present societal conditions. The Goldschmidt studies also tend to take an all-or-nothing approach in which declines in farming are seen to irrevocably damage local economies. While farm decline may result in population displacement and out-migration in some areas, others gain new employment. Rural communities have been particularly attractive sites for routine manufacturing and other, often peripheral, industries.

Finally, the structural approach taken by the studies leaves little room for human action. That is, researchers tend to treat farm workers and family farmers, at least implicitly, as passive victims of economic circumstances. Rather, it is important to achnowledge and explore how these groups have resisted the power of large capital and the imposition of lower living standards.

The Goldschmidt debate should be reformulated to reflect the contemporary structure of farming and wider political economy. Like the nonfarm sector, class position, firm, and industry circumscribe the organization of production in farming. Thus the location of farmers in the agrarian class structure, the position of specific farm units among other units of surplus accumulation, and the position of farming itself in the segmented economy are the relevant lines for assessing farm impacts on communities. Farm operators should be viewed as occupying a range of positions from semi-proletarianized, part-time farmers to capitalist producers. Farm enterprises take a variety of organizational forms and extend from small to large units of surplus accumulation. And, as noted previously, farming has many of the characteristics of peripheral industry. Changes in farm structure become important in understanding local inequality because of their qualitative impacts on community class structure and therefore on the social, political, and economic character of community life (Holland and Carvalho, 1985). Finally, the effects of any type of farm structure on localities must be seen as historically specific and capable of being modified by popular action.

Given these points, it is possible to note some general tendencies about the effects of farming on localities. The presence of large, industrialized farms, as Goldschmidt and others have noted, implies a two-tiered class structure consisting of a few owners and many hired workers. Associated with these class positions are income and consumption levels, political power, and numerous related life chances that unequally benefit farm owners. In general, industrialized farming will offer seasonal, low-wage, peripheral employment. However, the actual conditions on large farms may vary as production becomes more rationalized and as fewer unskilled positions are needed; as unions empower farm workers; and as state income guarantees and nonfarm employment opportunities allow farm workers to withhold their labor or to demand higher wages. Hired farm laborers can be expected, on the basis of their class position and situation in low quality, peripheral employment, to have poorer socioeconomic conditions than independent family producers.

Neglected by the Goldschmidt studies are variations within the family labor production units that constitute the bulk of the farm sector. Like simple commodity producers, most farmers today are dependent upon family rather than hired labor; however, other characteristics, such as dependencies on off-farm capital for operating expenses and ownership strategies tend to vary from this ideal type. As a consequence, while simple commodity producers could be considered part of the petite bourgeoisie, most current producers are said to occupy contradictory class locations (Mooney, 1983). Producers who are closer to proletarianization (in that off-farm work is necessary because holdings are too small to sustain the family) should be expected to have lower socioeconomic conditions than those with larger holdings, or who are closer to the petite bourgeoisie.

However, variations among individual producers and historically specific economic conditions preclude simple generalization. For example, Kautsky (1988) argued that industrialization of the countryside in Germany and other areas of Europe contributed to the impoverishment of part-time farmers due to low industrial wages, exhaustion of labor power from both farm and off-farm work, and because holdings had become too small to sustain family consumption. In the contemporary U.S., motivations for part-time farming vary from supplementing low nonfarm wages and consumption levels to a hobby or tax write-off. The quality of nonfarm employment occupied by producers more directly determines their well-being than does their farming status. While research generally shows that part-time farming is not associated with a deterioration in living standards (although small scale farming appears to be), the political economic implications of part-time farming can be detrimental. As noted previously, part-time farming disguises the decline of family farming, helping to legitimate the myth of Jeffersonian democracy in the farm sector. It may also increase farmers' self-exploitation and serve various economic interests of capital over labor.

On the basis of farmers' proximate class locations and scale of operations, midsize, family operated farms should be associated with better socioeconomic conditions, as the Goldschmidt studies suggest. However, moderate-size family farms tend to be particularly vulnerable in the sphere of exchange. As smaller units of surplus accumulation in a competitive industry, they lack the market power of large, industrialized farms. In the agribusiness chain, they are sandwiched in between price-setting input, marketing, and processing firms. Macroeconomic changes, such as in export markets and interest rates, also eroded their positions in the land and credit markets during the 1980s. While in the past family producers could limit consumption to withstand economic downturns, this strategy is ineffective with today's highly leveraged farms. In other words, although these farms should offer better socioeconomic conditions, their stability is historically specific and recently, precarious.

The effects of farm structure and change extend beyond the farm gate, reverberating across localities to the extent they depend upon this economic activity. For example, operators of industrialized farms may exert political control over community development, such as their control of water rights in some areas of California. Family operated farms tend to purchase input and consumption goods locally, thereby sustaining retail trade (Murdock et al., 1988). The decline of these farms may send a series of secondary shock waves throughout the community, reducing employment and wages in local suppliers. Tertiary effects may include greater demand for public assistance and social services, a reduction of the tax base, and unemployment in other industries and services (Murdock et al., 1988). The growth of large, industrialized farms has been associated with similar detrimental impacts, such as reduction of local employment and income generating capabilities.

In conclusion, generalizing from a political economy perspective, large, industrialized farms should lower socioeconomic conditions and lead to greater inequality in localities. Family farms should have differential effects on inequality: those sustaining independent producers through farming alone should benefit localities; those that do not may have adverse impacts. As noted previously, however, these relationships are not immutable but depend on wider social and historical conditions, including popular action.

IN SUMMARY

Although many studies support the Goldschmidt hypothesis, they cannot be accepted unequivocally. First, on the theoretical level, researchers have neglected to link analyses with broader theoretical perspectives and research traditions. Comprehensive explanations of the impact of farming on socioeconomic welfare have not been developed. Second, the conceptualization of farm structure and farm-community relationships needs broadening and clarification as studies have tended to: conflate farm scale with other organizational characteristics; examine only linear, one-way causal relationships; and neglect examination of recent, increasing farm types, such as part-time farming.

Methodologically, the studies also have a number of weaknesses. These include the dearth of longitudinal analyses; the inadequacies of delineating and controlling for relevant variables; and limited geographic scope. Recent studies have been more conceptually and methodologically sophisticated but have also turned up more divergences (e.g., Flora et al., 1977; Swanson, 1982; Skees and Swanson, 1986; Green, 1985). It is unclear if these result more from conceptual and methodological applications or whether farm/well-being relationships have changed over time, as nonfarm factors have achieved greater community impact. The Goldschmidt debate cannot be resolved until researchers begin to seriously address the previous issues.

A key point of this study is that the effects of farm structure should be viewed in context with other factors affecting localities, particularly, industrial structure, worker power, and spatial characteristics. The following chapter continues with a discussion about why these factors are central to understanding the patterns and levels of local inequality.

Industry Structure, Worker Power, Spatial Characteristics, and Socioeconomic Inequality

Structural perspectives have been used by agricultural and industrial social scientists to explore the ways in which the economic system generates inequality. This chapter continues to discuss the effects of economic structure by focusing on industry. In developed economies, farming has a very limited impact on local inequality, even in areas that depend economically upon farming. Nearly 70 percent of the earnings of laborers and proprietors in nonmetropolitan U.S. counties dependent on farming are from nonfarm sources (Bender et al., 1985). A study of the farm sector must be supplemented with an understanding of industry, because local inequality is particularly a function of the latter sector. Moreover, failure to incorporate industrial structure into analyses of farm structure has been a limitation of studies addressing the Goldschmidt debate. Although structural perspectives represent an improvement over conventional, neoclassical approaches, they too have certain shortcomings. Such studies often neglect the impact of geography on life chances and ignore the ways in which human agency can modify structural constraints. The second part of this chapter considers these issues by focusing on how the power of workers (vis-à-vis employers) and spatial characteristics shape local levels of inequality.

INDUSTRIAL STRUCTURE AND INEQUALITY

Studies documenting the effects of industrial structure on socioeconomic conditions generally take one of three major approaches. Some focus on new, incoming industry and tend to be more concerned with incremental employment than with industrial quality impacts on localities. Others are those grounded in economic segmentation theory that examine qualitative differences among industries and their implications for workers. Finally, a more recent set of studies focuses on the consequences of industrial segmentation for localities.

Industrializing the Locality

National and local industrial policies as well as popular perception generally assume that the recruitment of new industry benefits communities. As a consequence, in the attempt to attract industry, communities may gamble away scarce resources that could be allocated to local welfare or become locked in bidding wars so that any advantages of the incoming industry are lost (Falk and Lyson, 1988). That new industry entails costs as well as benefits is demonstrated by Summers et al. (1976). They reviewed 186 studies conducted between 1945 and 1973 that examined the effects of incoming manufacturing plants, predominantly in metal production and fabrication, chemicals, and clothing, on nonmetropolitan communities. Plant size ranged from fewer than 10 to more than 4,000 workers. Their conclusions included the following: (1) The host community experienced population growth in a clear majority of plant locations; this growth was likely due to increased in-migration with unchanged or decreased out-migration. (2) Employers tended to prefer younger workers. (3) New jobs often did not go to the local unemployed, underemployed, minorities, or to the marginally employable close to the poverty level. (4) High-skill, high-wage industries were less likely to hire local disadvantaged persons while low-skill, low-wage industries were more likely to do so. (5) Any increase in the fiscal resource base of the local community was often outweighed by the increased costs of services provided to the new industry or the community. (6) There was some evidence that incoming industries increased labor demand directly and indirectly by stimulating other local economic sectors which, in turn, led to small increases in per capita income and decreases in unemployment. Although changes in income distribution were generally not examined, the studies suggest that the relative income status of some groups, such as the elderly and minorities, may be lowered as costs of living and taxes rise.

A more recent perspective on the uneven effects of industrialization is presented by Falk and Lyson (1988). They evaluate critically the types of employment generated by new industries in the South during the 1970s. They show that while new, technologically sophisticated industries moved to the South, they located mainly in metropolitan areas. In contrast, rural areas, particularly those with a high concentration of blacks, remain characterized by low-wage, peripheral, often declining industries and marginalized from the benefits of Sun Belt development.

In sum, incoming industries do not have uniform effects on localities and their residents (see also Shaffer, 1979). Within the locality, groups with the least socioeconomic resources, the elderly, poor, less educated, or minorities may become relatively worse off. Regional unevenness also may occur as some localities experience industrial growth while others stagnate. As competition for new avenues of employment heightens under deindustrialization, incoming industries are also likely to provide fewer local benefits.

Industrial Segmentation and Workers' Economic Attainments

The consequences of industrial segmentation for workers' earnings and poverty levels have been explored in numerous studies. Research based on national samples and data over at least two decades, 1960–1980, has tended to find higher earnings for workers in the core sector (Beck et al., 1978; Fligstein et al., 1983; Hodson, 1978; Gordon et al., 1982; Tigges, 1988). Workers in peripheral industries have been shown to have about twice the likelihood of falling below the poverty level, compared to core workers (Beck et al., 1978; Hodson, 1983). Most of the studies on economic segmentation argue that larger firms with higher productivity and greater control over their markets have more ability to pay higher wages. Higher wages minimize turnover and help retain a stable workforce, possibly trained at company expense. The development of core industries went hand in hand with unionization, further ensuring higher wages and a steady supply of trained workers. Indeed, postwar economic growth was premised upon a social contract between big capital and big labor that guaranteed industrial peace as a trade-off for raising workers' standard of living (Bluestone and Harrison, 1982).

While most studies focus on the privatized sectors, a few have examined the consequences of state sector employment. Hodson (1978) examined average earned income by economic sector using 1973 data. Income was highest in the core and lowest in the periphery. Income from state employment fell between these two sectors. Hodson (1978:437) argues that state-sector wages should be "relatively high because of the political clout of organized state employees." As compared to the core sector, however, wages should be somewhat lower due to lower productivity per worker and taxpayer resistance. Fligstein et al. (1983:298) likewise argue that state sector employees should receive wages at levels close to those of the core because the state can finance higher wages through taxation. However, using a national sample of 1,399 employees for 1969, they find that core sector employment produces significantly higher earnings than the state or periphery and no significant differences between the latter two sectors.

Although segmented economy theory assumes that a variety of job conditions are associated differentially with core and peripheral employment, nearly all research has focused on earnings. As a consequence, nonmonetary aspects of segmentation and potentially inconsistent findings have been neglected. For example, the relationship between segmentation and unemployment has been assumed but relatively untested despite anomalous findings that peripheral sector workers did not experience more frequent unemployment than those in the core (Schervish, 1983:33). Such findings conflicted with "one of the explicit hypotheses of the dual economy perspective" (Beck et al., 1978:711).

Schervish (1983) examined the employment status of male workers from the Current Population Surveys conducted over the 1969–1978 period. The odds of being unemployed were lowest for workers in the state sector; workers in the core were slightly more prone to unemployment than those in the periphery. According to Schervish (1983:145), the state sector experiences low unemployment due to its "ability to generate constant revenues and to execute deficit spending. This combines with a growing secular demand for services and a further increase in this demand when other sectors create unemployment." Core industries are more vulnerable to fluctuations in consumer demand and when confronted by decreased demand, adjust output (and the number of workers) rather than prices. In contrast, peripheral industries tend to respond to decreased demand by lowering prices; real wages are decreased in order to lower production costs and workers may quit. Schervish (1983) shows that over the business cycle, the core sector is more variable in its employment patterns. During recession, core sector workers experience more unemployment than those in the periphery, while the state sector may expand due to increased need for public services.

Industrial Segmentation and the Locale

A more recent set of studies focuses on the effects of industrial segmentation on local inequality. These studies postulate that industrial structure influences economic well-being through direct creation of job positions and associated earnings (Bloomquist and Summers, 1982; Tomaskovic-Devey, 1988c). In addition, industrial structure is argued to have other, less direct effects on well-being (Jacobs, 1982; McGranahan, 1980). Wage spillovers may occur: the presence of high wage firms in the core sector may increase wages paid in other sectors as employers compete in the labor market. Further, local suppliers to core firms can demand higher prices and consequently pay better wages. High wage industry thus "not only affects incomes for those employed in these plants but also induces an area wage 'roll-out', which drives up the wages in the rest of the economy" and creates a higher and more equal distribution of local income (McGranahan, 1980:316). In a broader sense, core employers need a stable, reliable workforce and to this end may actively support the social reproduction process by paying higher wages and sponsoring progressive state interventions.

Nearly all research on industrial segmentation in localities focuses on economic outcomes, such as earnings, income levels and distribution, and poverty. Bloomquist and Summers (1982) show that industry affects local inequality directly as well as indirectly, through occupational structure. They found that counties with a growth in concentrated (types of core) sector employment had higher and more equitably distributed income levels and distribution. Growth in state sector employment had negligible impacts. Industrial structure was also shown to affect occupational structure: core sector employment generated more skilled manual occupations which in turn were related to less income inequality while peripheral employment was associated negatively with these occupations and thereby to greater income inequality. Horan and Tolbert (1984) found a dimension of high-wage manufacturing and an urban trade dimension, both reflecting core industry types, positively related to earnings and median income for fifty-one Southern labor markets. Jacobs (1982) examined the effects of segmentation across states for the 1960–1970 period. States with more concentrated or core types of industry had more equal household income distributions, while states having a greater proportion of their labor force in small establishments had more unequal distributions.

Tomaskovic-Devey (1988a, 1988c, 1987) has documented the consequences of industrial segmentation on poverty rates. In a study of 100 SMSAs for 1979, Tomaskovic-Devey (1988a) found that core employment was significantly related to higher mean earnings for workers and a lower labor force poverty rate and indirectly related to lower SMSA poverty rates. Using data for all U.S. counties for the 1960–1980 period, Tomaskovic-Devey (1988c) found that counties with a greater proportion of their labor force in core employment had significantly lower poverty, while those with a greater proportion in the extractive sector (forestry, fishing, farming, and mining) had greater poverty. In contrast to expectations, a growth in state sector employment was positively associated with poverty. An issue involved in this later finding is whether state employment actually heightens poverty through its earnings structure or whether state employment represents service allocations which may be greater in high poverty localities. Tomaskovic-Devey argues in favor of the former explanation. A third study by Tomaskovic-Devey (1987) reported that South Carolina counties having a higher proportion of their labor force in service (peripheral) employment had higher poverty rates.

Sheets et al. (1987) examine segmentation in service industries and its effects upon underemployment (defined as poverty level, full-time, part-time, or intermittent employment) for the 100 largest SMSAs. They report that SMSAs with a larger proportion of their labor force in consumer services (personal services and retail trade) have higher underemployment. This is particularly true for retail trade, where a 1 percent increase results in an almost equivalent rise in the number of part-time, year-round workers with earnings below poverty. Employment in government and nonprofit social services is also related to higher underemployment.

The previous studies thus show that the effects of economic segmentation extend beyond the workplace and into the community. They also suggest that some revision of segmented economy theory may be needed. First, although it has been rather consistently established that earnings are higher in the core, earnings in the state and periphery may not differ substantially from each other. Second, the effects of segmentation on unemployment vary in ways not initially predicted by theory. This implies that segmentation may have other unanticipated effects, particularly on nonmonetary variables that have yet gone unstudied.

PERSPECTIVES ON WORKER POWER

The labor market matches the supply and demand for labor, connecting households to firms and employers through jobs and earnings (Schervish, 1983:13). From the demand side, the labor market involves the action of employers and

firms in generating differential levels of employment, unemployment, and earnings. From the supply side, it involves the processes by which workers are willing
to exchange their labor power for earnings or to withhold labor power altogether.
Structural perspectives on industry as well as on farming have tended to focus
on the demand aspect of labor market relationships, that is, on the opportunities
or lack thereof created by economic structure. In attempting to explain local inequality, such a focus in incomplete because it neglects the action of labor. In
this section, I examine worker and household characteristics and resources that
allow people to resist the earnings and employment structures imposed by capital.

Neoclassical economic and functionalist perspectives tend to assume, for-
mally or implicitly, that exchange relationships occur in a free competitive market
where parties share relatively equal bargaining power and access to full information. This contrasts with the basic political economy assumption that market
exchanges among firms, between firms and workers and their communities, and
between firms and the state are inherently unequal relationships in which big
capital dominates (Bluestone and Harrison, 1982; Schervish, 1983). Although
the exigencies of capital necessarily prevail in the market place, they are limited
by the power of workers and by the mediation of the state. Worker power can
manifest itself as factors that enable labor to exact market rewards from capital
or, alternatively, to resist demands that serve capital's interests. These factors may
be resources gained through working class struggle, such as labor organizations
and state social welfare; they may be local labor market conditions, such as
unemployment or extent of racial or gender discrimination; they may reflect
ascribed or achieved traits of labor market participants.[1] Worker power is unevenly
distributed over individuals, particular class segments and places.

From the Marxian perspective, workers struggle over the production and
distribution of surplus value; this is manifest in conflict over wages and the conditions of work. In the contest between capital and labor, the power of capital
is strengthened, if for instance:

> workers compete among themselves (along racial lines, to pick one possi-
> ble dimension), rather than presenting united demands of the capitalists;
> if the state refuses to provide a decent income maintenance program so
> that some workers are still driven by what Weber called "whip of hunger";
> or if state-supported schools instill all workers with an orientation toward
> monetary rewards and with some general "productive" skills required in
> employment (Gordon, 1972: 65–66).

Conceptualizations of worker power have been incorporated into new structuralist approaches and applied to the behavior of labor both at the point of production and in the locality. While many conceptualizations use human capital
attributes, such as education, race, and gender, these are interpreted differently

from conventional, individually based factors: they are seen as collective properties of workers which enhance power vis-à-vis employers (Tigges, 1988). Most research examines worker power from the vantage of the point of production. Within the firm, labor's bargaining power is increased by the presence of collective organizations among employees, by resources embodied in work positions, including employer investment in training, skill level, and workplace autonomy, and by group attributes conferring higher production statuses, such as age, gender, race, and job tenure (Tigges, 1988; Schervish, 1983; Kalleberg et al., 1981; Beck et al., 1978). Less frequently, worker power has been viewed as a local resource. For example, recent British perspectives consider the mechanisms by which workers shape local labor market conditions, through the use of labor law, trade union membership, domestic and community organization, and state welfare (see Fine, 1987). Jacobs (1982) argues that political resources differentially possessed by capital and labor affect local socioeconomic conditions. He shows that greater democratic participaton, as measured by voting levels, reduces income inequality among states. Tomaskovic-Devey (1988a,c) systematically outlines the factors contributing to the power of workers and their households in a locality. He argues that where this power is strong, the population will have greater ability to exact better quality jobs, income, and living standards. These factors, which give conceptual definition to the term worker power, are market security, labor force characteristics, and local unemployment levels.

Market Security

Market security involves the resources possessed by the working class (or by segments of this class) that reduce dependence on employers and can be used to demand better quality jobs (Tomaskovic-Devey, 1988c:109). Such resources include what is termed the social wage: "that amalgam of benefits, worker protections, and legal rights that acts to generally increase the social security of the working class" as well as the labor organizations and professional associations protected by social legislation (Bluestone and Harrison, 1982:133). Much of the legislation establishing the social wage (or social safety net), such as that for workmen's compensation, unemployment insurance, and public welfare, was instituted first at the state and local levels and later by the national government under Wilson and Roosevelt (Bluestone and Harrison, 1982:134). These represent hard-won gains born out of working class struggle, consolidated and extended during the post World War II period. Until the 1970s, they would be at least grudgingly supported by employers in order to ensure the industrial peace necessary for pursuing global opportunities for profit. I focus on two key components of market security, labor unions and social welfare programs.

Unions. Political economists have taken contrary positions about the role of unions under advanced capitalism. On one hand, unions are seen to mediate the relationship between capital and labor: they remove conflict from the shop floor so that production is not disrupted and encourage a common interest between labor and management on which enterprise growth and survival hinge (Aronowitz, 1973; Braverman, 1974). This position is akin to that taken by liberal industrial relations analysts who emphasize the benefits of unionization for capital (e.g., a stable disciplined workforce) and labor (higher wages and benefits) (Freeman and Medoff, 1984). However, while liberal industrial relations analysts take pleasure in this industrial harmony, the previous political economy perspective views it as a danger: unions undermine class conflict, fragment the labor force, and inhibit unified working class action. Although recognizing the constraints of unionism under capitalism, an alternative political economy position argues that unions are fundamentally organizations of working class struggle.[2] Unions give collective voice to employee demands and protect workers against employers' attempts to extract greater surplus through lowering labor costs and altering the labor process. This position has gained greater acceptance under the erosion of the postwar accord between big capital and big labor: the goals of unions have come to increasingly conflict with those of management (Piore, 1985).

Unions have been shown to alter power arrangements in terms of economic gains and working conditions. Hall (1986:307) argues that historically unions have had a greater influence on improving work conditions, such as through employment security, benefits, and job control. Comparisons of wage rates between unionized and nonunionized employees show that unions raise wage rates for the former, even when worker, job, and industrial characteristics are held constant (Helfgott, 1980; Kalleberg and Berg, 1987; Fligstein et al., 1983; Kalleberg et al., 1981). The ability of unions to raise wages, however, depends in part upon the industry in which they are located and tends to be greater in concentrated sectors (Helfgott, 1980). For example, apparel manufacturing is a relatively well organized but low-wage industry; this stems from its competitive nature.

Schervish (1983) argues that although unionized jobs are higher paying, they also tend to be subject to greater employment instability. This is because most unionized employment is in concentrated industries that tend to lay off employees in economic downturns rather than raise prices. Indeed, formalized procedures for laying off workers are generally a part of union contracts. Workers in unionized industries also traditionally have had greater resources, such as skills and job contact networks, which would allow them to quit with another job in hand. However, as job opportunities have become increasingly closed in unionized industries, unionized workers are often left with a choice between chronic unemployment or employment in low-wage, low-skill, unorganized industries.

Unions also have effects that extend beyond particular workplaces and industries (Helfgott, 1980). Historically, unions have prompted the state to assume responsibility for destabilizing economic outcomes, such as through unemployment, retirement benefits, and worker health legislation. The presence of unions may also raise wages among nonunionized workers in the same labor market. Unorganized firms may pay higher wages to circumvent unionization and even without the fear of unionization, nonunion firms may have to pay higher labor costs in order to compete with unionized firms for local labor. Unionization levels are also related to various aspects of local inequality. Tomaskovic-Devey (1988a) reports that although the percent unionized production workers slightly lowers the employment rate, its total effect is to reduce poverty within SMSAs.

Programs of the Welfare State. The programs and policies enacted by the state also strengthen the security of labor. In order to counteract imbalances resulting from the operation of the privatized economy, such as unemployment and poverty, which might undermine societal legitimation and the accumulation process, the state provides various social expenses, such as public assistance AFDC (Aid to Families with Dependent Children) and other income or in-kind transfers as well as protective legislation, such as the minimum wage.[3] These are representative of the power of the working class both in a historical and immediate sense. As Block et al. (1987:ix–x) note:

> Capitalism from the beginning has confronted people with the continual threat of economic dislocation. . . The only sure 'logic' of the market is change and disruption; and for many of us, the only protection lies in the programs of the welfare state . . . for example, unemployment insurance and other income maintenance programs mitigate the impact of the business cycle. Medicare and Social Security help the elderly survive in an economy that has little use for them. A host of special programs protect children and single mothers from destitution. Whatever its shortcomings, the American welfare state has blunted the most damaging effects of the market economy; and this alone represents an enormous human achievement. . . the modern welfare state is the product of decades of political effort by ordinary Americans to gain some control over their lives in the face of massive economic disruptions.

The programs of the welfare state that involve income transfers, particularly means-tested public assistance, strengthen the power of labor because they provide a nonmarket source of income, thus offering shelter from the exigencies of the local economy.[4] Almost one out of four Americans would have been in poverty in 1983 had it not been for cash public transfers, which lowered the official rate to 15.2 percent (Danziger et al., 1986:56–57). The largest, both in expenditure and recipients, and most controversial of public assistance programs is AFDC, Aid to Families with Dependent Children. The level of benefits and eligiblity requirements of AFDC are set by the individual states. AFDC benefits lowered the poverty rate among recipients by some 15 percent in 1983 (Morris and Williamson, 1986:66). However, for the same year more than three-quarters of families still remained below the poverty level even after receiving AFDC and other public assistance cash payments. The effect of AFDC is more to reduce the degree of a family's poverty rather than to raise them above the poverty line, making it a subpoverty income support program (Block et al., 1987). But as the real value of AFDC benefits has not been increased to keep up with inflation, the poverty lessening ability of AFDC has declined, particularly during the Reagan years (Morris and Williamson, 1986).

Public assistance strategies have been surrounded with controversy over their effects on welfare dependency and work incentive. The role of AFDC in increasing intergenerational welfare dependency and in altering family composition (such as the ability of single parents to set up independent households) appears limited. AFDC also does not seem to account for unmarried female recipients' decisions to have children (Morris and Williamson, 1986). Teenage pregnancy and family dissolution have continued to rise despite declining real values of welfare benefits (Danziger and Weinberg, 1986).

A voluminous literature has addressed the effects of welfare on the work incentive. Piven and Cloward (1987:22) summarize the conclusions of these studies. They note that the major effect of income transfer programs, including those for the elderly such as social security, is to reduce the total annual hours of work in the economy from about 5 to 7 percent. If such programs were eliminated and if employment did not increase more rapidly than the labor force, unemployment would rise similarly by 5 to 7 percent as former beneficiaries searched for jobs. In contrast to popular and governmental opinion, Block et al. (1987) view the work disincentive as beneficial for withholding the least productive labor from an already overcrowded labor market and from further weakening the economic position of American workers, particularly the lowest paid. Relatedly, they note that current workfare programs, which move welfare recipients into available (generally low paid) employment, undercut the power of labor.

At the local level, higher income transfers should improve economic well-being by reducing the extent of poverty and enhancing the ability of labor to bargain for better jobs (Tomaskovic-Devey, 1988a,c). In a study of the 100 largest SMSAs, Tomaskovic-Devey (1988a) found that higher AFDC payments were associated with higher earnings but slightly lower employment rates. The total effect of AFDC, however, was to reduce the SMSA poverty rate. A state level study by Sanders (1988) reports that a rise of $50 in average monthly AFDC payments reduces the family poverty rate by about .33 percent. Finally, in a study of all U.S. counties, Tomaskovic-Devey (1988c) found that higher AFDC and social security payments reduced the amount of household poverty, although the effects of these programs were stronger during the 1960s than the 1970s.

This suggests that poverty has become more irradicable in the face of recent economic changes and the declining real value of transfer payments.

The effects of AFDC as a work disincentive across individual states has been examined by Kodras (1986). She argues that while benefit levels influence the choice between work and welfare, this choice is further constrained by local employment barriers and by obstacles to welfare assistance. Kodras (1986) measures the work disincentive by the ratio of mean AFDC payments over the mean earned income of poverty families. Large values of this measure indicate high welfare payments relative to employment earnings and thus represent an economic incentive to replace work with welfare. Kodras (1986) finds that the work disincentive is lowest in states with high poverty and a punitive welfare system (where welfare services and benefits are low); and highest where jobs are difficult to get or nonremunerative. Thus, the disincentive is highest on the West coast, upper Midwest and lower New England—areas with less poverty—and lowest in the South, particularly the Southeast. These findings support much of the previous discussion that higher income transfers serve to withhold low-wage, redundant labor. Kodras (1986) also notes that welfare need and benefits are mismatched, with poorer states having the lowest benefits. She attributes this to three factors: (1) the state may decide to support capital and provide a labor force willing to work at any cost; (2) fiscal resources may be lacking; (3) public political persuasion may support the dominant ideology.

Structural Characteristics of the Labor Force

Social structural characteristics of a particular labor force, particularly race, gender, and educational level also affects its bargaining position with respect to capital. Conventional neoclassical economic theory and functionalist sociology assume that women and minorities tend to receive lower earnings because they are less productive—either that they lack human capital skills or investments (such as education) or in the case of women, that their family commitments make them unstable workers. In effect, these perspectives blame the victim for possessing the wrong mix of human capital characteristics. In contrast, political economists argue that social structural processes create differentials in the value of wages for different groups of workers. Historically, because of racism and sexism, capital has been able to assume that the costs of the social reproduction of minorities and women are lower, which has been reflected in lower wage rates. In the workplace, hiring practices and previous channelling through education and training relegate minorities and women to the lowest rungs of working class jobs. There, high job turnover and limited training ensure that these groups emerge relatively unskilled with unstable work histories, fit to be rehired only by other low-wage firms. The process represents a vicious circle or self-fulfilling prophecy in which minorities and women face revolving barriers to better employment (Sheets et al., 1987).

Ethnic minorities, especially blacks, and women have historically faced discrimination through the personal tastes of individual employers or in a statistical sense, in which employers apply generalized attributes to members of the group at large, such as assuming that women do not make good workers due to family commitment (Tomaskovic-Devey, 1988c). Race and gender are thus said to be a screening device to allocate or withhold jobs. Tomaskovic-Devey (1988c) observes that discrimination not only lowers the earnings of those who face discrimination but can undercut working class solidarity in general, heightening inequality among labor force segments and reducing the bargaining power of the working class. Indeed, it is often argued that the internal stratification of the working class along the lines of race, gender, education, and occupation is created and maintained to diffuse cohesive class action (Gordon, 1972).

Research on the segmented economy has long noted the tendency for women and minorities to be crowded into low-wage, peripheral industries (Hodson, 1978; O'Connor, 1973). The state sector (public administration) and related non-profit services, such as health and education, are also composed of large numbers of women and minorities (Sheets et al., 1987:42). However, even when industry of employment, education, and other relevant variables are taken into account, race and gender are still predictive of earnings in national studies of workers (Fligstein, 1983; Beck et al., 1978; Tigges, 1988). The wage gap between men and women and between blacks and whites in the same occupation also expanded during the 1980s (Kolko, 1988:318). In 1985, full-time female workers earned about 66 cents for every dollar male full-time workers earned and black full-time workers, about 78 cents for every dollar earned by whites (U.S. Bureau of the Census, 1986, Table 680:402). These earnings disparities are reflected in family well-being, through the feminization of poverty and the growing household income gap between blacks and whites.

Discrimination across labor markets takes differing forms depending upon whether it involves gender or race (Tomaskovic-Devey, 1988c). Discrimination by gender is structurally perpetuated through the chanelling of women into a narrow range of low-wage, sex segregated occupations and industries and through the domestic division of labor which assigns women responsibility for household reproductive activities. Tomaskovic-Devey (1988c) argues that while gender discrimination is pervasive, it can be assumed to be relatively constant across labor markets and is reflected in the structure of employment. On the other hand, racial discrimination is not only evident in the structure of employment but takes a qualitatively different form which is manifest over space. Historically, there have been limited educational and capital investment and high degrees of direct discrimination in localities with large minority populations. In such localities, the bargaining power of all workers, even the white working class, is low as a consequence of these racially based social structural patterns.

Research on the effects of race over areal units generally shows that higher black and other ethnic minority populations are associated with poorer economic conditions, such as greater poverty and poverty-level employment (Tomaskovic-Devey, 1988a; Sheets et al., 1987). In contrast, the proportion of women in the labor force has been reported to have no effect on poverty level employment (Sheets et al., 1987) and only indirectly affects the poverty rate, notably through the extent to which households are headed by women (Tomaskovic-Devey, 1988a). The latter study, in fact, reports a positive relationship between the percentage of male workers and labor force poverty. In sum, the empirical research likewise tends to confirm a more even spatial distribution of gender as compared to racial discrimination.

In addition to race and gender, other local group stratification characteristics, such as education, affect the power of workers vis-à-vis employers. That schooling increases individuals' opportunities for better jobs and income is recognized by structural as well as conventional perspectives and has been verified in numerous empirical studies (e.g., Blau and Duncan, 1967; Sewell and Hauser, 1975). However, structural and conventional perspectives differ in regard to the causal primacy accorded schooling and in the reasoning for its effect on economic achievement. As noted previously, the latter perspectives emphasize education and other individual investments in creating higher productivity or job contributions which are then rewarded through higher earnings. In contrast, political economy and other structural perspectives argue that beyond the baseline education required, job performance and productivity are only remotely related to schooling and are more a function of job than individual attributes. Jacobs (1982) for example, notes that on-the-job training rather than formal education has been shown to be more predictive of workers' productivity. Other studies show that returns to education are not constant as conventional perspectives would suggest but vary across structural locations such as industrial sector and class and occupational position (Stolzenberg, 1978; Wright, 1979; Beck et al., 1978; Kalleberg et al., 1981). Structuralists also contend that educational criteria are not neutrally applied to allocate individuals to positions but serve employers' interests in a variety of ways. Like race and gender, education is used as a screening device in hiring and to balkanize and co-opt segments of the labor force. Educational credentialism is also a way to exclude minorities and others with limited educational access (Hall, 1986).

Rather than emphasizing the role of education in expanding economic opportunities, political economy and other structural perspectives argue that the educational system serves to reproduce the class structure (Bowles and Gintis, 1976). While this process is usually viewed as an aspatial one, it is particularly evident over areal units. Because administrative bodies largely composed of the nonpoor determine and allocate school expenditures, lower income areas are likely to obtain worse facilities (Schiller, 1980). Unequal education is also perpetuated in the ways schools are financed. About half of all elementary and secondary school expenditures are financed by local property taxes and most of the remainder by state revenues, with only about 10 percent financed by the federal government (Schiller, 1980:139). Children in poorer states and localities are thus limited by lower educational expenditures. At the local level, educational inequality is intertwined with economic inequality so that the educational attainments are in part a function of a population's income levels.

A related issue concerns the role of educational strategies in improving local economic well-being. Educational upgrading allows an individual to jump ahead in the labor market queue, enhancing his/her job opportunities, but it does nothing about enlarging the job queue itself. Thus, at the aggregate level, attempts to reduce poverty by upgrading a labor force through education, while politically palatable, are useless unless coupled with an expansion of better employment opportunities.

Education however, can be considered a group resource that affects the ability of a labor force to demand better employment conditions. Areas with lower education are vulnerable to low-wage employment for reasons suggested above: because employers use education as a screening device, indicator of job capability and productivity, for credentialist purposes and so forth. While analysts generally posit a link between local educational levels and employment quality and economic well-being, the strength of this link appears varied. Jacobs (1985) reports that dispersion in schooling is the strongest predictor of income inequality among states. Skees and Swanson (1988) find that educational level is the most important determinant of well-being for Southern nonmetropolitan counties. In contrast, Tomaskovic-Devey (1988c:28) reports that education as measured by the percentage of adults who finished high school has only a small affect on county poverty rates which "makes a direct human capital explanation of this relationship . . . implausible." Sheets et al. (1987) similarly find little relationship between education as measured by median years of schooling and poverty level employment for SMSAs when characteristics of local industrial structure and other relevant variables have been held constant. In sum, structural perspectives as well as empirical research question the extent to which education is a direct cause of local economic conditions.

Unemployment

Determinants of unemployment at the aggregate level have been little addressed in the sociological literature (Ashton, 1986; Schervish, 1983). Neoclassical economic as well as Keynesian perspectives, while differing on the causes of unemployment, tend to see it as a correctable, temporary or cyclical imbalance, with a relatively even effect across groups of workers and industrual sectors. In contrast, structural theorists and political economists emphasize that unemployment varies rather systematically by type of industrial sector and worker with, for example, race, gender, and educational level affecting the likelihood of unemployment. Political economists are particularly concerned with how unemployment increases the bargaining power of capital in the labor market, and on how the needs of specific firms and systematic requirements for profitability create fluctuations in unemployment (Schervish, 1983). Maintaining a reserve army of unemployed workers depresses the level of wages and contains job turnover and the demands of labor. It also provides a malleable, surplus population that can be paid at low wages should demands for labor arise.

Unemployment or the tightness of the relationship between the number of jobs and job seekers is the final indicator of worker power delineated by Tomaskovic-Devey (1987, 1988c). When available employment exceeds the number of job seekers, the power of the local labor force increases as employers compete among one another for labor. Wages rise and local economic well-being generally increases, assuming the costs of living remain relatively stable. Tomaskovic-Devey (1988c) notes that levels of unemployment have both cyclic and secular effects on local well-being: current unemployment levels denote the availability of jobs and long-term unemployment rates can affect general earnings levels of the local job structure. Blank and Blinder (1986) show that rising unemployment was the major contributor to the increase in national poverty during the 1973–1983 period, with effects of about seven times those of inflation.

Research across various areal units confirms a relationship between unemployment and other types of socioeconomic well-being. In a national, county level study, Tomaskovic-Devey (1988c) finds that counties with higher unemployment have higher poverty. Skees and Swanson (1986) report strong relationships between unemployment and poverty and income levels for nonmetropolitan, Southern counties. Sheets et al. (1987) find that unemployment is related to greater numbers of poverty-level jobs in SMSAs. Another study of SMSAs finds that higher unemployent rates result in lower average job earnings and that both higher unemployment and longer unemployment duration lead to higher poverty (Tomaskovic-Devey, 1988a).

SPATIAL STRUCTURE AND INEQUALITY

Geographical space is the final factor important in understanding inequality in socioeconomic conditions. As discussed previously, most economic and sociological theory on inequality is constructed aspatially. That is, space is assumed away as uninteresting and inconsequential; or processes based on individuals or groups without any particular spatial referent are assumed directly transferable to aggregate spatial units.[5] Focusing on the forces that create socioeconomic inequality at the local rather than the individual level can clarify and extend existing theoretical perspectives. Moreover, this focus makes it easier to analyze inequality in household consumption and in the labor force's collective ability to reproduce itself.

Space plays an important role in creating inequality because it indicates location in the wider system of social relations. Location affects the level of socioeconomic well-being within a particular locality for several reasons. First, the organization of farming and industry and the resources and structural characteristics which constitute worker power are unevenly distributed over space. In this case, space is not significant in and of itself, but because of the social forces embodied in different locations. Spatial characteristics also reflect distinct historical patterns of social relations, which influence the subsequent development of an area. Initial regional inequalities, such as differences between rural and urban areas or between the South and the rest of the nation, tend to be compounded over time. For example, the USDA delineates 242 nonmetropolitan counties as persistently impoverished, having per capita incomes in the bottom quintile of all U.S. counties for at least the past three decades (Bender et al., 1985). Nearly all of these poor counties are located in Appalachia, the Ozarks, and Mississippi Delta—areas where prior historical disadvantages (as a consequence of internal social relations and/or unequal exchange relations with outside capital) continue to have a marginalizing effect. Finally, spatial location reflects ecological factors such as population dispersal, agglomeration tendencies, or physical landscape, which (in addition to attracting and repelling segments of capital and labor) may present real barriers to the circulation of goods and services. However, ecological factors should not be overemphasized. The impermeability of certain areas, such as rural Appalachia, has often been invoked to explain low levels of development and standards of living, thereby downplaying the role of social structural factors. Further, as capitalism has evolved, physical barriers have become less significant, being transcended by technology and new methods of business and service organization.

Spatial characteristics that affect local inequality include the region of the country, rurality, urban proximity, and particularly for this study, agrarian dependence. Regional differences between the South and the rest of the nation are well known and documented. Historical analyses have traced how social relations under the plantation economy set the stage for subsequent patterns of low-wage employment, extensive poverty, weak power of labor, coercive state, and institutionalized discrimination (Wood, 1986; Mandle, 1978). While the industrial restructuring of the late 1960s through the 1970s was credited with altering some of these patterns, rural areas, particularly those with a significant black population continued to fall behind (Falk and Lyson, 1988). Most of the 20 states having right-to-work laws that discourage union security are located in the South and Southwest (Hall, 1986:303). Levels of state income transfers continue to be set low in Southern states, encouraging employment in poverty level positions (Kodras, 1986). Southern as well as Appalachain mountain states still rank low on nearly all indicators of socioeconomic well-being, such as income, health, and educational levels (Smith, 1982).

Rural areas have been historically associated with primary sector employment, lower worker power, and generally lower socioeconomic conditions. Declines in the farm population coupled with the need for low-wage, unorganized labor, made some rural areas attractive sites for peripheral manufacturing, particularly after World War II. As discussed in previous chapters, however, the farm crisis and restructuring of manufacturing heightened inequality in rural America in the 1980s, altering trends such as the population turnaround and poverty reduction of the previous decade. Rural areas have also experienced perennial problems of service provision, which have been exacerbated by recent employment changes (Lewis, 1983). The more isolated and dispersed nature of rural populations makes the circulation of commodities and service provisions costlier. Rural people have been faced with continuing declines of such services as schools, retailing, churches, and a shortage of health professionals. Services have tended to become consolidated into fewer and larger units located in urban centers, which makes them less accessible to rural residents.

Related to rurality is the dependence of the local population on farming. Areas with large populations on farms are generally situated "on the periphery of the capitalist state...[and] have been traditionally associated with lack of development and incomplete penetration by outside capital" (Winter, 1984:125). Farm communities tend to be particularly distant from population centers and have generally experienced decades of population loss; many have a high proportion of elderly residents (Bender et al., 1985). Local populations that depend on farming for subsistence, residence, or both tend to have lower levels of living and income as compared to the general population (Seninger and Smeeding, 1981).

In addition to the extent of farming dependence in an area, the previous chapter shows that qualitative differences in farm structure affect local well-being. These differences can also influence the power of the local labor force to extract wages and benefits from employers. The costs of reproducing a labor force and therefore wages can be lowered where workers underwrite part of their own subsistence through part-time farming. On the other hand, where full-time farming can be viably pursued, the population gains an alternative to paid employment and a bargaining chip for higher wages from employers (Schulman and Lobao, 1989).

ECONOMIC STRUCTURE, WORKER POWER, AND SPATIAL CHARACTERISTICS: THEORETICAL RELATIONSHIPS AND EMPIRICAL EXPECTATIONS

This study addresses a long-standing debate about the effects of farm structure on socioeconomic conditions but it differs conceptually from other literature in this area. It starts from the premise that the Goldschmidt hypothesis involves an underlying set of assumptions about how the local economy generates socioeconomic inequality and, even more fundamentally, about the origins of inequality itself. Broadening the Goldschmidt debate in this way shows that it is part of the traditional social science concern with inequality. It opens up the various perspectives that have been used to account for inequality and situates the Goldschmidt studies in the context of these perspectives, that is, in the structuralist tradition; it allows linkages to be drawn from other literatures and disciplines outside those which have conventionally addressed the topic. Most importantly, it permits the development of a conceptual framework that links economic structure and other structural factors to inequalities in local socioeconomic conditions. By proceeding backward, that is by focusing on inequality and the forces that create it (rather than focusing singly upon farm structure), this study also responds to previous critiques of the Goldschmidt literature concerning the adequacy of controls and potential intervening factors that can alter the relationship between farm structure and the local community.

The organization of production in farming and industry, the balance of power between labor and capital, and spatial characteristics provide the framework for understanding the uneven distribution of resources and life chances across localities. From the literature on the Goldschmidt hypothesis, I expect that localities dominated by large-scale, industrialized farming will have relatively low socioeconomic conditions. The complex internal stratification and changing dynamics of the family farm sector (as well as the theoretical underdevelopment of these topics) make its difficult to predict the relationship between family farming and socioeconomic conditions. Studies in the Goldschmidt tradition long posited that localities with family farming had better socioeconomic conditions. However, recent work suggests that moderate to larger family units are associated with better conditions, but that the smallest family units may have adverse community impacts. For the purposes of testing the Goldschmidt hypothesis, I will follow the traditional studies in expecting that both smaller and larger family units are associated with better conditions, while realizing this may not hold empirically.

In a market economy, the economic attainments of most people come mainly from their own or household members' participation in paid employment. The literature on industrial segmentation shows that segments of capital have differential stakes in supporting the consumption of levels of particular workers. In the core sector, higher profits, market control, labor organizing efforts, and the nature of labor control combine to raise wages and to make capital more progressive in its support of workers' consumption levels. The generally converse situation in the peripheral sector leads to lower wages and consumption levels. The state sector has been linked at least conceptually to relatively high wages, close to those of the core. However, recent empirical research has challenged various segmented economy assumptions, such as the level of wages in the state sector and the relationship between unemployment and segmentation. I will follow the traditional research in expecting that localities with a greater extent of core employment will have better socioeconomic conditions. State sector employment should result in only slightly less beneficial impacts than the core, followed by peripheral sector, which should reduce socioeconomic conditions relative to the two other sectors.

Economic structure alone provides an incomplete view of how inequality is created because it neglects the population's capacity to modify local conditions. Labor forces are unevenly endowed with resources, such as unions and state welfare, which provide shelter from the exigencies of capital and advance workers' interests; they are characterized by educational levels and racial compositions that heighten or weaken their power to demand better employment; and they confront macroeconomic forces such as unemployment that have cyclical and long-term effects on their market security. The ability of a population to take advantage of these resources and social forces allows it to offset the control of capital, thereby creating greater equality within workplace and locale. Localities with a greater unionized workforce, higher levels of income transfers, a more highly educated population, lower unemployment, and a lower minority population should have better socioeconomic conditions.

Spatial characteristics of the locality are the final set of characteristics expected to influence inequality. These circumscribe the location of economic structure and worker power and reflect historical and ecological conditions. Localities situated in regions such as the South and Appalachia, in rural areas with high farm populations, and more distant from large metropolitan centers should have lower socioeconomic conditions.

Finally, it should be noted that the time period may affect the impacts of economic structure, worker power, and spatial characteristics. As the fordist economy has entered into crisis, previous advantages that accrued to each of these factors may be altered. For example, the advantages of industrialized northern locations have declined; unions have been forced to make wage concessions to capital; and returns to traditional human capital factors, such as education, appear to be diminishing.

The Design of the Study:
Data, Measurement of Variables,
and Methods of Analysis

This chapter discusses the methodological aspects of the study. The first section describes the units of analysis and sources of data. The second section explains the measurement of the independent variables (indicators of farm structure, industry structure, worker power, and spatial characteristics) and the dependent variables (indicators of inequality). The third section outlines the statistical procedures and models used for testing the effects of the independent variables upon local inequality.

THE DATA UNITS

The changes in farming, industry, and socioeconomic conditions addressed in this study are a result of broad, historical trends. Because these trends are national in scope and temporally varied, it is appropriate to employ longitudinal data encompassing the entire United States. Socioeconomic inequality can be explored at any conceptually significant aggregate level (Tomaskovic-Devey, 1988c) and researchers have studied it across various ecological units, across nations as well as within the U.S. across states (Jacobs, 1982, 1985), empirically constructed labor markets (Horan et al., 1984), metropolitan areas (Tomaskovic-Devey, 1988a; Sheets et al., 1987), and counties (Bloomquist and Summers, 1982; Tomaskovic-Devey, 1987).

This study is centered on the forces that differentially allocate inequality across localities or locally defined social systems. As an ideal analytical constrct, the locality should confine the major social structural processes of interest within its geographic boundaries. However, in actual localities, some processes will be nonexistent (e.g. there may be no employment in mining or fishing). Further, as geographic boundaries are nearly always permeable, structural processes are unlikely ever to be complete or totally confined to a specific locality (Bradley and Lowe, 1984).[1] For Goldschmidt, the rural community reflected the concept of the local social system. While data at this level would be useful in testing the relationships that were specifically derived from the Goldschmidt study, they are not available for most U.S. communities, particularly over time. Community boundaries also tend to be more geographically unstable than other units of analysis such as states or counties. The large number of data collected at the county level, available for the entire United States and for multiple time periods, make the county a useful unit of analysis. Consistent findings across various areal units lend credibility to empirical generalizations (Heaton and Brown, 1982) such as Goldschmidt's, developed at somewhat different levels of analysis.

Data at the county level offer a number of advantages for this study in addition to availability and coverage. First, because counties encompass both urban and rural locations, they provide a more comprehensive view of social life than would less aggregated units (Eberts, 1979a).

Second, counties approximate local labor markets in that most people work in their county of residence (Tomaskovic-Devey, 1988c). Moreover, the permeability of county boundaries (as measured by the percentage of people who do not work in their home counties and by net migration) does not appear to bias relative socioeconomic levels (Tomaskovic-Devey, 1988c).

Third, the social expenses of federal and state governments are often directly implemented at the county level. Daily administration of social service programs such as AFDC and food stamps takes place through county offices. Local attitudes about such programs have been shown to affect administrative procedures and thereby influence program provisions (Kodras, 1982). For example, county welfare offices may be located in less accessible areas or administrators may informally discourage certain clients. Because counties can be the state-wide administrative unit for social and other community services, studies of counties have a direct bearing on local policy (Christenson, 1976).

Fourth, the county is considered a superior unit for statistical analyses of socioeconomic conditions. Foley (1977) notes that counties are large enough to encompass variations in social, political, and economic structure but not large enough to obscure differences between areas. The use of counties also allows for larger sample sizes than, for example, the use of states.

Finally, studies replicating or extending Goldschmidt's work have already been conducted at the county level (Buttel et al., 1986; Flora and Flora, 1986; Green, 1985; MacCannell and Dolber-Smith, 1986; Skees and Swanson, 1986; van Es et al., 1986; Wheelock, 1979; Swanson, 1980) indicating that scholars have found the county an appropriate level at which to conduct such research. It also means that more specific comparisons can be drawn between this study and others using the same unit of analysis.

Drawbacks of using counties as a unit of analysis include their wide variation in area and in population. Counties also vary by the extent to which they are political units of their respective areas (Foley, 1977:443). As any unit of higher aggregation, county data may even out internal variations found among less aggregated units and so obscure relationships occurring at the community, neighborhood, or other lower analytical levels.

The data examined approximate two points in time: 1970 and 1980. I have several reasons for selecting these years. First, as discussed in previous chapters, changes in economic structure and levels of well-being during this period are historically significant, for they signalled a major transition in fordism. In addition to serving as base points from which to gauge change occurring within the decade, each time point has cross-sectional significance. Recessionary periods occurred in both 1970 and 1980 (Litan, 1988:69). Although they were not identical in intensity and duration, they provide a similar business cycle environment during which much of the data were collected. An eleven month recession from December 1969 to November 1970 was triggered by auto and General Electric strikes and a restrictive monetary policy aimed at stemming rising inflation resulting from the Vietnam war. Real GNP declined slightly by .1 percent over this period. A half year recession characterized the economy from January 1980 to July, 1980. This was sparked by a shock in oil prices and credit controls to restrain the resulting 14 percent annual inflation rate. During this period, real GNP suffered a more significant decline of 3 percent. The availability of data was another consideration in selecting these two years for study. Although agricultural data are available after 1980, the major source of the remaining variables, particularly the indicators of socioeconomic inequality is the decennial census. Since data from the 1990 census will not be available for public use for several years into the decade, this study must rely on earlier censuses.

This study has a major focus on farming. As a consequence, the selection of counties to be included in the analysis was based upon those for which farming, as defined by the Census of Agriculture, was reported. The census generally reports data for counties with ten or more farms. Farming is present in and reported for the vast majority of U.S. counties with the exception of ecologically unsuitable areas including heavily metropolitanized areas such as Manhattan and environmental exceptions such as Los Alamos, New Mexico. The censuses that most closely correspond to the time periods in this study were conducted in 1969 and 1978.[2] Combining the number of counties reported in the 1969 census with those in the 1978 census results in 3,046 counties with farming data for both time periods. From these, nine counties whose division status was altered or whose boundaries changed from 1970 to 1980 were deleted. These included the few Alaskan and Hawaiian counties reported in the Census of Agriculture. It has also been argued that because these states represent atypical agricultural production systems, they merit exclusion from national studies of farm structure (Gilles, 1980). The number of counties employed in this study thus totalled 3,037.

THE MEASUREMENT OF CONCEPTS

This section explains the methods by which the concepts of economic structure, worker power, and spatial characteristics are measured. In addition, the concept of inequality and its specific measures are outlined.

Patterns of Farm Structure

As noted in the review of studies on the Goldschmidt hypothesis, measuring farm structure has been difficult because there is a lack of appropriate national data and because researchers have not defined farm structure clearly and consistently. Single indicator measures, particularly those of scale, are often used to represent conceptually complex farm types. There have been few attempts to develop multiple indicator measures that could tap the more complex and recent dimensions of farm structure (Wimberley, 1987). Researchers also emphasize conceptually different aspects of farm structure that should affect socioeconomic conditions; however, their choice of measures often deviates from these concepts.[3]

The development of measures reflecting the political economic transformations experienced by the farm sector is particularly problematic. As noted previously, there is no encompassing theory of farm change that explains the development or delineates the structure of the various social formations that have emerged in the farm sector under advanced capitalism. The difficulties in characterizing the farm unit are mirrored by a similar difficulty in characterizing the farm producer in class analytical terms: few farmers occupy pure class positions, with most amorphously situated in contradictory class locations.

A key observation in political economy perspectives is that farming has become transformed by the ways in which nonfarm capital has penetrated or become linked to the farm sector. This penetration has taken place along the lines of major production factors and it has acted to differentiate or internally stratify both producer and unit. Differentiation may be said to occur in the organization of farm production, such as land and capital ownership, management of farm operations, and labor inputs, and in farm scale. In addition, operator/household characteristics may reflect off-farm work or demographic adjustments made as the market economy penetrates farming.

In order to operationalize farm structure, measures reflecting the dynamics of differentiation were needed. These measures also had to have the county as a geographical referent and had to be comparable over time. Farm structure is operationalized through indexes developed by Wimberley (1983a, 1985, 1987). The indexes describe differentiation in farm organization, scale, and operator characteristics at the county level. Unlike most previous measures of farm structure, which are single indicator items, each index is composed of multiple items. The indexes measure three patterns of farm structure found in U.S. counties at four points in time, 1969, 1974, 1978, and 1982, and are based on data from the Census of Agriculture conducted in each of these years. This study utilizes the indexes for 1969 and 1978. A detailed description of the indexes, which were developed through factor analysis is presented in the Appendix.

Industrialized Farming. The first pattern, termed "industrialized farming," reflects many of the characteristics the literature attributes to large-scale, industrial style capitalist farming. Farm labor dependency, as indicated by the number of hired workers and expenses for contract labor, is high and county farm structure is organized along corporate lines. This farming pattern is also somewhat capital intensive, with high expenses for custom work and machine hire and rental. As would be expected, this pattern results in high gross sales and hence can be considered large scale in terms of sales. Farm production thus mirrors industrial production through the presence of capital-labor relationships, high volume sales, capital intensity, and organizational structure.

The following census items are used in constructing the farming pattern index for industrialized farming: the total dollar value of annual, gross agricultural sales in the county; the number of corporate farms in the county; the number of hired farm workers; expenses for contract labor incurred by county farms; and expenses for custom work, machine hire, and rental of machinery and equipment. Cronbach's alpha coefficient for this index is .924 for 1969 and .935 for 1978, indicating a high degree of internal consistency among the index items.

Larger Family Farming. This farming pattern reflects an organizational structure of part-ownership and tenant operations and predominates in counties where much of the land is farmed. Larger family farming tends to be particularly capital intensive as investment in farm machinery and equipment are high. Hired labor dependency is low, suggesting dependency upon family labor and nonlabor inputs. The term "family" is included in the index name in order to highlight the absence of hired labor dependency. This farming pattern also generates substantial farm sales but not to the degree of industrialized farming (Wimberley, 1987). Wimberley (1984:4) surmises that such farming is performed by second generation, younger operators who "could be in partnership with the preceding generation and who often rent or lease some of the land they farm." Larger family farming reflects the consequences of differentiation in simple commodity production and may be considered a modern analog of this form of production. Producers are not marginalized in the course of economic development but rather become increasingly integrated into land and capital markets in the attempt to stay in farming.

The census items used in constructing the index for larger family farming are: the proportion of county land in farming, number of county farms operated by part-owners, number of farms operated by tenants, and the estimated market

value of farm machinery and equipment. Cronbach's alpha coefficient is .876
for 1969 and .890 for 1978.

Smaller Family Farming. This farming pattern is distinguished from the
previous one by scale and the related capacity of units to occupy household labor
resources. Smaller family farming describes a county farm structure composed
of many small farms or those with low volume sales. Farms tend to be operated
entirely by the owners who reside on them and by part-time operators who work
off the farm for most of the year. This pattern thus reflects the differentiation
of family labor producers into marginalized farmers via off-farm labor
opportunities.

The index for smaller family farming is constructed from the following
census items: the total number of farms in a county, the number of small farms
(annual gross sales less than $2,500), the number of full-owner operated farms,
the number of resident farm operators, and the number of operators working
200 or more days off the farm. Cronbach's alpha coefficient is .965 for 1969
and .963 for 1978.

To create the farm pattern indexes, each variable was standardized. The
variables for each index were then summed and each index itself standardized
to a mean of 50 and standard deviation of 10. As described in the Appendix, the
standardization procedures and construction of additive indexes were necessary
to develop index scores comparable across time and among the dimensions.

The use of the indexes has several advantages. First, the differentiation
of the farm sector as described in much of the conceptual literature is captured
empirically in national patterns as well as over time. Second, the indexes show
that farm structure is not a "single continuum with gradations from small to large
or corporate farms" but rather a qualitative construct in which differences in
kind must be analyzed in addition to "differences in degree" (Wimberley,
1987:459-460). Third, the indexes empirically establish whether the use of farm
structural variables as proxies for other variables is reasonable: for example, while
hired labor dependent farms are strongly associated with high gross sales, such
farms are not necessarily large scale in terms of acreage. Finally, use of the indexes permits this study to go beyond the conventional examination of single
indicators and linear relationships that have characterized previous tests of the
Goldschmidt hypothesis.

National Patterns of Farm Structure. The geographic distribution of the
three patterns of farm structure is shown in Figures 5.1 through 5.3. County index
scores on each pattern for 1978 are trichotomized based on national rankings
following Wimberley (1987). Counties in the upper 33% of the national distribution are shown as having high levels of a particular pattern and are represented
with a solid shade. Counties with moderate (middle 33%) and low (lower 33%)
rankings are also indicated. Counties with high national rankings on industrialized

FIGURE 5.1

Industrialized Farming

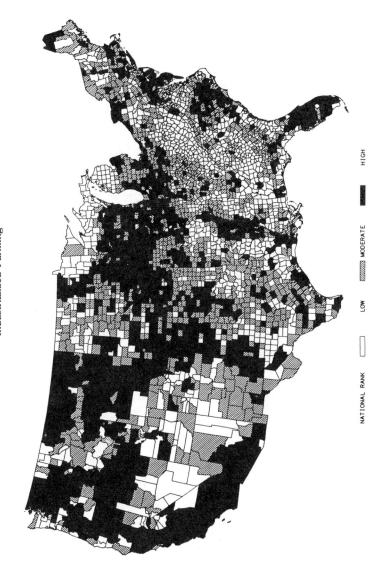

NATIONAL RANK ☐ LOW   ▨ MODERATE   ■ HIGH

FIGURE 5.2

Larger Family Farming

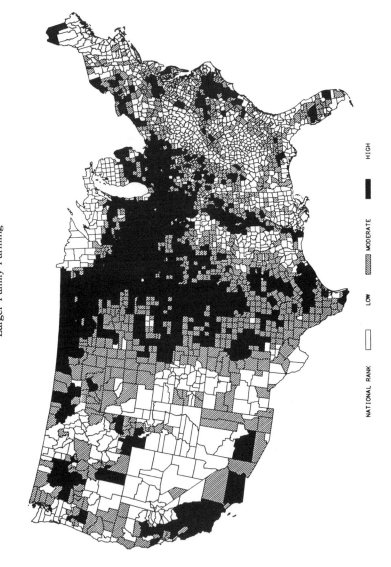

NATIONAL RANK ☐ LOW ▨ MODERATE ■ HIGH

FIGURE 5.3

Smaller Family Farming

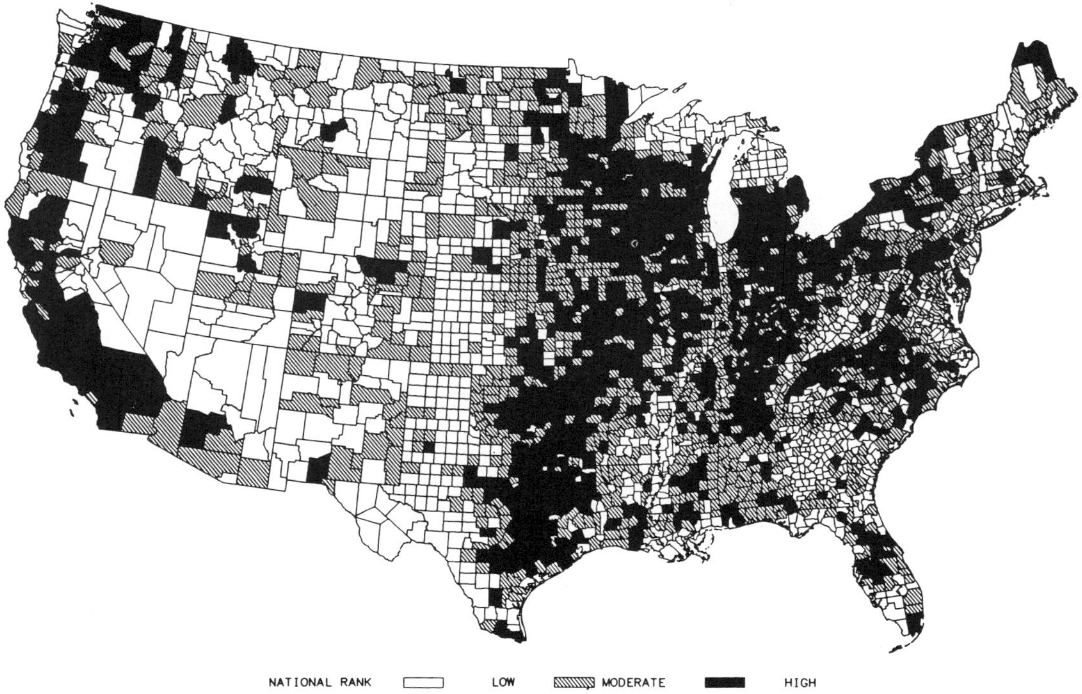

NATIONAL RANK   LOW   MODERATE   HIGH

farming (Figure 5.1) are situated on the Pacific Coast and lower Southwest, parts of Texas, the Midwest and Great Plains, throughout Florida, and along some areas of the Atlantic Coast. Figure 5.2 shows that while larger family farming occurs in many of the same areas, it predominates more in the Midwest and Plains. Counties with a high degree of smaller family farming, as indicated in Figure 5.3, are situated mainly in the eastern mountains, southern Plains, Great Lakes area, and along some parts of the Pacific Coast. It should be noted that although levels of each index may be reflective of the greater number of farms in a county, only the index for smaller family farming contains this variable. The number of farms in a county is also essentially unrelated to county size, as indicated by a near zero correlation between the two variables across U.S. counties (Wimberley, 1987).

The maps show that many counties notably those of the Midwest, parts of Texas, and the Pacific Coast are characterized by high national rankings on all three patterns. When the predominate pattern for each county (the pattern with the highest value) is delineated in another series of maps (not shown), however, regional differences are brought particularly into focus. Larger family farming is the predominate pattern through most of the Midwest and Great Plains; smaller family farming is clearly an eastern and southeastern pattern, predominating in a diagonal from New York through the eastern mountains to the Delta states and also in parts of the southern Plains and the Great Lakes states. Industrialized farming predominates in Florida, parts of the Delta, and from west Texas up the California coast.

As would be expected from these regional differences, the farming patterns are also associated with the production of certain agricultural commodities (Reif, 1986). Larger family farming is highly related to the production of cash grains such as corn, soybeans, and wheat. It is also prevalent where county farms are involved in general, primarily crop operations and in mixed livestock production. Industrialized farming predominates where farms specialize in fruits and nuts, vegetables, and cotton. Smaller family farming is associated with a broader range of commodities, particularly the production of mixed livestock and crops, field crops such as tobacco, dairying, vegetables, fruits and nuts, and poultry. Although the farming patterns tend to be differentially associated with various commodities, the production of many commodities including cash grains, fruit and nuts, and livesock appears evident across all three patterns.

Local Industrial Structure

Segmented economy theorists delineate three ways of organizing production that affects workers' economic gains: production organized by large, monopoly capital; by small, competitive capital; and by the state or government. The industrial structure of a locality can be considered in terms of the proportion of employment generated by each sector (Bloomquist and Summers, 1982;

Tomaskovic-Devey, 1987). In order to operationalize the industrial sectors, this study uses data that apply to a county labor force's industry of employment. These data are available from the Census of Population. Data on employment by industry refer to the type of business or industry in which the employed person spent the most hours during the census reference week or the week prior to enumeration, generally at the end of March or early April. The 1970 and 1980 Census of Population classify employment into forty-one and forty-nine industrial categories, respectively.

Industries were assigned to the core, periphery, or state sector based upon Hodson's (1978) and Bloomquist and Summers's (1982) classifications. Hodson uses key political economic factors, the size of capital, the amount of economic centralization, and the amount of state contracting, as bases for allocating industries to each sector. Because Hosdon's classification scheme utilizes industrial data which are more detailed than that available for counties, it was further modified by Bloomquist and Summers. Their classification is particularly useful because it classifies county employment by the industrial categories available from the Census of Population. Differences in the levels of aggregation lead Bloomquist and Summers to place all utilities, sanitary services, and educational services run by the government in the state sector, while Hodson assigned the latter two services to the periphery. Subsequent revisions of Hodson's scheme by other analysts also lead Bloomquist and Summers to classify four industries differently: food and kindred products are assigned to the periphery, while construction, trucking and warehousing, and other transportation services are assigned to the core. The classification scheme used in this study follows Bloomquist and Summers with the exception of my assignment of both private and government run schools to the state sector because I could not disaggregate two. Most school employment is government supported.

The core, state, and peripheral sectors are defined as the proportion of the employed county labor force in the following industries:

Core Employment

mining
construction
printing, publishing, and allied products
chemicals and allied products
primary metals
fabricated metals
machinery, except electrical
electrical machinery, equipment, and supplies
transportation vehicles and equipment
miscellaneous durable manufacturing

railroad service
trucking service and warehousing
other transportation services
communications services
banking and credit agencies

Peripheral Employment

agriculture, forestry, and fisheries
food and kindred products
textile mill products
apparel
other and miscellaneous nondurable manufacturing
furniture, lumber, and wood products
wholesale trade
retail trade, general merchandise stores
retail trade, food, bakery, and dairy stores
retail trade, motor vehicles and automotive products
eating and drinking places
other retail trade
insurance, real estate, and other finance services
business services
repair services
private household services
other personal services
entertainment and recreation services
hospital services
other health services
educational services other than schools
welfare, religious and nonprofit organizations
legal, engineering, and other professional services

State Employment

elementary and secondary schools and colleges
public administration
utilities and sanitary services

Although I follow much of the literature in using the three sector classification, it should be recognized that actual industrial differences cannot be captured unambiguously in a simple model. Rather, the classification is valuable for shifting emphasis to the role of structural rather than individual attributes in determining employment outcomes and for describing basic divisions in the organization of the fordist economy that contribute to local inequality.[4]

Another methodological issue concerns the use of measures based on industrial rather than firm level employment. Researchers have argued that measures based on the firm of employment are also important for understanding the implications of economic segmentation, since industries may be crosscut by varying corporate structures (Baron and Bielby, 1980; Wallace and Kalleberg, 1981). However, examining employment by industry rather than by firm has been justified for a number of reasons. First, firms operate within the context of an industrial structure, which defines the parameters of firm operating characteristics (Wallace and Kalleberg, 1981). Second, the types and completeness of data collected on industries are generally greater than those collected on firms. Government agencies, social scientists, and business organizations typically aggregate data on firms to the industry level and national data sets generally include respondents' industry but not firm of employment (Wallace and Kalleberg, 1981). Third, firms and their industrial locations often coincide. For example, many industries such as electronics, aerospace, and automotives are accessible exclusively to monopoly firms (Hodson, 1978). Finally, government policy is often aimed at or evident across the industry level. For example, both trade union and minimum wage legislation have industry specific effects: they similarly impact firms in the same industry and exacerbate segmentation among industrial sectors (Hodson, 1978).

In order to address potential intraindustry effects and to broaden the indicators of economic structure, however, I include a variable for the average size of a county's business establishments. This is measured as the number of all service, manufacturing, retail, and wholesale establishments in a county divided by the number of paid employees in such establishments. The sources for these data are the Censuses of Manufacturers, Wholesale and Retail Trade, and Service Industries from the U.S. Bureau of the Census and reported in the *County and City Data Books* (1978, 1983a). The years closest to this study for which such data are available are 1967 and 1977. An 'establishment' refers to a single physical location of business operations. It is not necessarily identical to the firm, which may be composed of more than one establishment. Stolzenberg (1978) found that even when characteristics of employees are held constant, the size of the establishment has a significant effect on employee earnings. This relationship has been linked to firm size and profitability. Larger establishments tend to be operated by large firms with fewer competitors than small firms; they therefore tend to be more profitable and can pay higher wages. Counties with much core employment are likely to have larger business establishments. However, the average size of establishments might also influence local inequality, particularly since the metric and the year of this measure varies from the other industrial indicators. Including this variable thus extends the analysis of economic structure, allowing the scale effects of establishments to be assessed independently of the industry within which establishments are located.

Worker Power

The bargaining power of workers vis-à-vis their employers is conceptually represented following Tomaskovic-Devey (1988a,c) as three factors: market security, labor force characteristics, and local unemployment levels.

Market Security: Union Membership and Public Assistance Levels. Market security refers to resources possessed by workers that provide shelter from the demands of capital. Unions and state public assistance, particularly in the form of income transfers, increase workers' ability to secure better quality employment. The concept of market control is operationalized, following Tomaskovic-Devey (1988a,c) by two variables, union membership and the level of public assistance transfers.

Data on union membership are reported at the state level but are unavailable by county for the entire United States. However, as right-to-work laws are legislated on a state basis, this level should have an important influence on county membership rates. Because of these considerations and its conceptual importance as an indicator of worker power, union membership is measured by the state rates. Data on union membership refer to the employed nonagricultural labor force and include unions directly affiliated with the AFL-CIO, unaffiliated national unions, unaffiliated unions that have collective bargaining agreements with different employers in more than one state, and recognized unions of federal government employees. Unionization rates for 1970 and 1980 were compiled by the Bureau of Labor Statistics (BLS) and collected from the Curent Populaton Survey. They are reported in *The Statistical Abstract of the United States: 1984* (U.S. Bureau of the Census, 1983b, Table 728:440).

AFDC is the largest of the cash income transfer public assistance programs and also the most controversial. The level of state income transfers is measured by the average per capita AFDC payments to recipients, calculated as the total county AFDC payments divided by the number of AFDC recipients. The data sources for this variable are the Social Security Administration for 1980 and the National Center of Social Statistics for earlier years. These data are reported in the Area Resource File, U.S. Department of Health and Human Services. While data on the number of AFDC recipients were available by county for 1970, total county AFDC payments were available for only 1974 and later years. As a consequence, I employ the per capita AFDC payments calculated for 1974 (the data closest to 1970 available) and for 1980.

Labor Force Characteristics: Race and Education. The bargaining position of a labor force is also affected by characteristics of its internal composition, notably race and educational level. Race is measured by the percent nonwhite in a county. It consists of those who defined themselves as being in a nonwhite racial category in the 1970 and 1980 Census of Population and includes blacks, American Indians, Asian and Pacific Islanders, and those of Spanish origin. Blacks are the largest ethnic group, making up about 12 percent of the population in 1980 according to the Census. Hispanics comprised about 6 percent of the population and the remaining groups about 2 percent. Education is measured by the median years of schooling for persons 25 years old and over in a county. The source of these data is the Census of Population. Although gender plays a role in the ability to demand better quality employment, there were several reasons for not employing such a variable in the analysis. As noted in the previous chapter, gender discrimination should be relatively constant across labor markets and should be reflected in the distribution of employment sectors. Finally, a variable measuring the percent of females in the labor force was initially included in the analysis but later deleted because it did not show a consistent or significant relationahip to local inequality.

Unemployment. When the number of available jobs is relatively large compared to the number of job seekers, the power of labor increases as employers compete with one another for labor. Data for unemployment are from the 1970 and 1980 Census of Population. The census definition measures unemployment by the proportion of the civilian labor force 16 years and older who were: (a) neither at work nor "with a job but not at work" during the week prior to enumeration; (b) looking for work during the previous four weeks; (c) available to accept a job; and (d) those who were laid off and waiting to be called back to a job (U.S. Bureau of the Census, 1978:xxxi).

Unemployment has been a problematic concept for researchers both in terms of measurement and causal delineation. As commonly noted, the census definition of unemployment does not include those who have given up looking for a job nor those who work only a few hours a week at a temporary job, and thus underestimates the extent of local unemployment. In nonmetropolitan areas, unemployment is obscured by involuntary part-time and seasonal employment which results from the sensitivity of rural industries to unfavorable weather conditions and to the disproportionate location of industries with unstable labor requirements (Briggs, 1981). Types of unemployment such as temporary layoffs, indefinte layoffs, and those resulting from firing and resignations are indistinguishable. Unemployment is thus not a unidimensional indicator. Rather the causes and consequences of unemployment for different segments of the labor force vary widely and depend upon such factors as the period in the business cycle, industry type, and labor market characteristics (Schervish, 1983).

Spatial Structure

The spatial characteristics of a locality are important for understanding inequality because they indicate historical and present location with respect to national patterns of social relations. This study employs four measures of spatial structure: urbanization, metropolitan adjacency, the extent of farm residence, and regional location.

Urbanization. This variable is measured by the percentage of a county's population living in urban areas as reported in the 1970 and 1980 Census of Population. The urban population includes all those living in places of 2,500 or more inhabitants. The population not classified as urban constitutes the rural population.

Urbanization can be expected to effect local inequality because the organization of economic sectors varies between urban and rural areas. This difference is reflected, for example, in the greater concentration of peripheral and extractive industries in rural areas and greater concentration of state and types of core industries (such as banking and credit) in urban areas (Horan and Tolbert, 1984; Bender et al., 1985; Menchik, 1981). Urban areas also have historically tended to have less poverty and unemployment as well as higher quality of life than rural areas (Morrill and Wohlenberg, 1971).

Proximity to Metropolitan Areas. In addition to urbanization, the extent of metropolitan spread into a county should affect the location of economic structure as well as local inequality. Metropolitan counties refer to those having a large population center (a city of 50,000 or more inhabitants) and any contiguous or outlying counties integrated economically and socially with this population center. Heaton (1980) compared the effects of metropolitan, nonmetropolitan adjacent, and nonmetropolitan nonadjacent location on farm structure, controlling for the level of urbanization as well. He found that centrally located counties were more likely to have capital intensive types of farming and highly intensive land use. These differentials were reported to result from a number of factors. Farmers may produce high return commodities as a response to urban demand. In order to turn a profit on higher cost land closer to urban markets, farming must have greater returns per land unit. New machinery and techniques are developed, promoted and spread outward from urban centers. Distance to metropolitan areas has been a key determinant of industrial location (Massey, 1984). Finally, the effect of metropolitan spread "has been reflected in lower median incomes and lower absolute growth in incomes over time as one moves away from metropolitan centers" (McGranahan, 1980:315).

Metropolitan proximity is a measure developed from the 1970 and 1980 Census of Population. It ranges from 1, a county with low metropolitan spread (a nonmetropolitan county with a largest place of less than 2,500 in population), to 17, a county with high metropolitan spread (a core metropolitan county with a population of one more than one million). More than three-quarters of the counties in this study were nonmetropolitan in 1980 and these had index scores of 6 or less.[5]

Farm Population. Areas where large populations still reside on farms tend to be particularly distant from metropolitan influences, including product and labor markets. A population's dependence on farming for residence, subsistence, or both reflects an incomplete penetration by outside capital and has been associated historically with a lack of development and low socioeconomic well-being. In addition to its spatial significance, another reason for including a measure of the farm population concerns the test of the Goldschimdt hypothesis: researchers have argued that the impact of farm structure is clearer when farming dependency is controlled (Skees and Swanson, 1986). The farm population is measured, using the standard census definition, as the percentage of a county's rural population who reside on farms. This variable is reported in the 1970 and 1980 Census of Population.

Regional Location. Regions embody historical and contemporary social forces that determine levels of inequality among their component localities. Farming and industry structures, worker power characteristics, and agglomeration tendencies vary across regions of the nation. Socioeconomic conditions have been poorer historically in areas such as the South and Appalachia.

Regional differences in social processes have been given little attention by social scientists outside geography and related disciplines. As a consequence, there is an absence of criteria by which regions should be defined and delimited. Such criteria might include, for example, policy relevance and the scale at which regions should be considered (such as a large portion of the country or small local labor market districts). The general lack of agreement or even dialogue about what areas constitute a region often reqires analysts to employ methodologically convenient (rather than conceptually appropriate) definitions, such as U.S. Census regions, which were developed for administrative and data gathering purposes. This study is also constrained by the need to characterize the United States into a limited number of regions, while ensuring that enough interregional variation remains to illuminate the processes of interest.

In a study of regional disparities, Markusen (1987:16) proposes the following definition: "A region is an historically evolved, contiguous territorial society that possesses a physical environment, a socioeconomic, political, and cultural milieu, and a spatial structure distinct from other regions and from other major territorial units, city and nation." The definition of a region used in this study reflects the mix of social and spatial forces advocated by Markusen (1987). Counties in the continental United States were grouped into five major regions based upon a classification scheme developed by Carlin and Green (1988) from the earlier work of Fuguitt and Beale (1978). Fuguitt and Beale (1978) delineated subregional groupings, which conceptually reflect "rather homogeneous combinations of counties having similar economic activity, history, geography, settlement patterns and culture" (Carlin and Green, 1988:17). Carlin and Green (1988) used the subregional groupings to create five major regions for purpose of analyzing farm structure.

These five regions are shown in Figure 5.4. The urban Northeast comprises the metropolitan area from Boston to Washington, D.C. and the manufacturing and metropolitan belt extending from New York to Wisconsin. It is the most populous of the five regions, with many small farms (or two-thirds of farms reporting sales less than $40,000 in 1982). The Eastern Mountains and uplands, or the Appalachian area has historically contained pockets of rural poverty and many small farms (over 87 percent with sales under $40,000 in 1982). The Southeast Coastal Plains, or the area from Virginia to the Mississippi Delta and Florida to Texas, includes the cotton, peanut, and tobacco belts and extensive semitropical agriculture. This region has a large rural black population, many small farms (over 80 percent had sales less than $40,000), and some large farms particularly in former sites of plantation agriculture. Central U.S. agriculture contains the major agricultural producing areas of the Mississippi Delta, the Corn Belt, and the Great Plains. It has the lowest concentration of small farms, with less than 60 percent reporting sales under $40,000. The West, or the area extending in a diagonal from southern Texas across the Rocky Mountains up through the Pacific Northwest contains the fewest counties of all five regions despite its surface size. The southern parts of the region are often characterized by large farms dependent upon irrigated agriculture, while the western mountain counties have extensive Federal lands and limited farming potential.

Carlin and Green's (1988) scheme offers advantages over the use of standard census regions in that similarity among criteria other than location are used to classify counties by region. It also offers advantages over classifications based mainly upon farm criteria (such as the USDA's farm production regions and other agroclimactic or commodity based schemes) because it considers the similarity of nonfarm structural factors present in a region as well. For example, geography affects farm structure through factors such as terrain, soil quality, and rainfall. Settlement patterns such as urbanization levels "affect the set of options a farm family has for dividing its labor between farm and nonfarm activities" (Carlin and Green, 1988:17). Nonfarm industry affects farmland value and employment options. In addition to reflecting similar locational and other structural patterns, each of the regions can be considered as embodying unique historical factors and positions in the national economy. Given the history of inequality and low bargaining power of labor in the South and Appalachian mountains, I expect

FIGURE 5.4

U.S. Regions

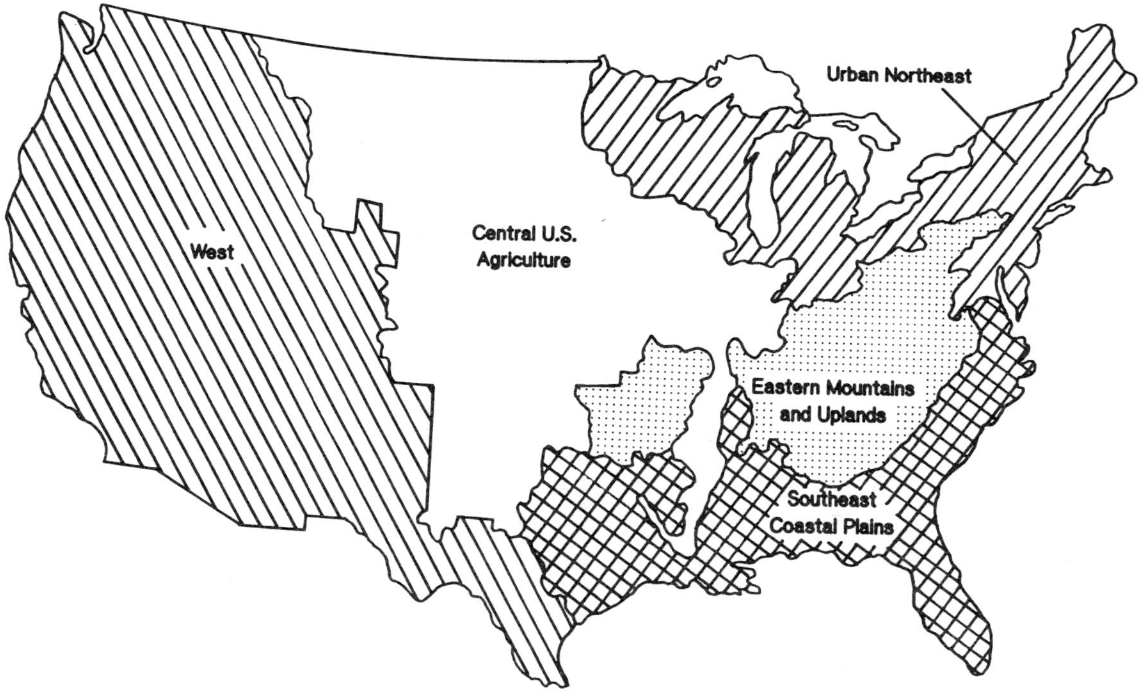

that localities in both regions should have poorer socioeconomic conditions relative to those in other regions.

Although Carlin and Green's (1988) scheme should be particulary useful in a study concerned with farm and nonfarm impacts, some limitations may be noted. First, as any typology that attempts to classify diverse observations, the regions should be regarded as broadly defined and as internally varied. Second, while the regions generally reflect common distinctions, such as differences between the Northeast, North Central area, South, and West, as used in the census, they are somewhat more detailed and not entirely comparable. For instance, the Eastern Mountain area spreads over parts of the North Central, Northeast, and Southern census regions.

Socioeconomic Inequality

Inequality refers to differences in socioeconomic resources and positions in the social order. The spatial distribution of inequality is succinctly expressed as an issue of "who gets what where" (Smith, 1982:19).

What types of inequality are relevant for understanding human life conditions? This question has been addressed in a variety of theoretical literature by psychologists, philosophers, and others who have developed abstract conceptualizations of human needs. These conceptualizations include, for example, Maslow's (1954) hierarchy as well as Marx's assumption about human fulfillment through unalienated labor. Another set of literature has approached the question through the subjective perceptions of the group of interest (e.g., Campbell et al., 1976; Andrews and Withey, 1976). The assumption here is that social groups vary in the kinds of conditions they consider acceptable or desirable. Although this approach has been advocated as an alternative or adjunct to those using objective measures of inequality, subjective rationalizations may be used to justify the status quo: if some people can be defined as content with poor schooling or homelessness, there is less need to eliminate such problems. A third approach, concerned with quality of life or social well-being is empirically based: it focuses on the development of objective indicators through which various social units can be monitored over time (Liu, 1976; Ross et al., 1979). An issue here, in turn, is that outside standards are imposed upon a group's ways of life. However many objective measures of deprivation are so abhorrent (e.g., infant mortality, poverty) that there would seem to be much consensus about their social undesirability.[6]

In this study, inequality is viewed in terms of the distribution of socioeconomic resources important for the reproduction of the local labor force. In a market economy, most individuals' (including about half of all farmers') means of subsistence comes through participation in paid labor. The outcome of competition between capital and labor and the configuration of various forms of capital (both in the farm and nonfarm sector) in a particular locality will be reflected in economic returns to labor and in general socioeconomic levels. The state also intervenes in this process to ensure that socioeconomic levels are aligned with normative expectations of labor and with the interests of capital. Put another way, capital has differential stakes and ability to support workers and their households, workers possess different resources, and the state varies in intensity of support for the interests of capital, all of which translate to variations in the socioeconomic levels at which a particular workforce can reproduce itself. The accumulation process structures the ways in which the labor force is reproduced while accumulation, in turn, depends upon the continual renewal of labor resources.

I measure inequality through several socioeconomic indicators. The first are income levels, including poverty and income distribution. Income levels of a population reflect integration into networks of consumption or ability to purchase needed goods and services in the sphere of circulation. Income also serves as an indicator of position in the stratification system. It therefore determines innumerable life chances beyond the economic arena, for example, in health, education, and social and political participation (Blau and Blau, 1982).

Family income rather than individual and earnings based measures are relevant indicators for this study for several reasons. First, the family unit mediates the relationship between the external economy and individual consumption. It allocates individuals to the market and in turn, distributes market rewards to family members. Local socioeconomic conditions are more appropriately reflected and have the most policy relevance when examined by the actual sociodemographic units in which most people live. Second, family income levels are outcomes of local employment stuctures and state intervention. The operation of both of these social forces can be asessed using family income measures. Income is closely related to earnings, with earnings comprising about four-fifths of workers' incomes (Levy, 1988:112). Third, under advanced capitalism, political struggles have tended to move from the arena of production to that of consumption, involving issues of family survival (such as the quanity and quality of goods and services and environmental quality). Family socioeconomic indicators thus have increasing political relevance. Finally, family measures are particularly appropriate for this study as the farm family is both a unit of production and consumption.

Median Family Income. Family income measures the total money income received by all family members covering the calendar years 1969 and 1979, respectively, as reported by the 1970 and 1980 Census of Population. The money income reported by the census includes cash government transfers such as AFDC, General Relief, and Social Security payments. Median income is the dollar amount that divides the income distribution into two equal groups with incomes above and below this amount.

Poverty. Poverty can be considered as "a social position in which income is insufficient to met some basic social...or physical need" (Tomaskovic-Devey, 1988c:2). The official U.S. poverty income level was originally defined by the Social Security Administration in 1964. It is a measure of absolute deprivation in that below this income level an individual is deprived of the basic necessities of life. The poverty level is based upon the costs of adequate nutrition under emergency or temporary conditions. These costs are then trebled to cover costs of other necessities, such as clothing and shelter, and adjusted by family size and costs of living to determine poverty income thresholds. Data for poverty are reported by the 1970 and 1980 Census of Population and refer to the percent of families in a county whose incomes fell below the poverty threshold for 1969 and 1979, respectively. This threshold for a nonfarm family of four was $3,721 in 1969 and $7,412 in 1979 (U.S. Bureau of the Census, 1978:xxxv, 1983a:xxxvii).

Several points should be mentioned regarding the use of poverty as an indicator of inequality. The poverty level is based upon money income but does not include noncash government supports such as food stamps, rent supplements, and Medicare and Medicaid payments. Pretransfer poverty (which excludes cash income transfers) stood at 24.2 percent in 1983 (Danziger et al., 1986:54). This indicator in general reflects the amount of poverty generated by the economic system, prior to state intervention. Interestingly, pretransfer poverty has remained relatively constant (at about 20 percent of the population) over time, suggesting that this is the 'normal' amount of poverty produced by the economy (Tomaskovic-Devey, 1988a). When cash income transfers are included, this results in the official 1983 poverty rate of 15.2 percent; including in-kind transfers further reduces poverty to 13 percent. State welfare programs thus play an important role in poverty reduction.

Another point is that official poverty thresholds reflect only absolute deprivation. Relative deprivation is said to better reflect poverty in advanced societies in which basic subsistence is met for most people (Tomaskovic-Devey, 1988c). Relative differences exclude individuals from fully participating in social life, isolating them from culture, life-styles, and social institutions and heightening social disorganization among family and community. The gap between poverty and average income has grown continually since 1965, indicating that those in poverty have become relatively worse off compared to the average American.

Income Inequality. Areas where incomes are high should have relatively lower income inequality (Betz, 1974). The Gini coefficient is a frequently used general measure of inequality in distribution. This study employs the Gini coefficient calculated on the basis of grouped family income data for 1969 and 1979 reported in the Census of Population. Procedures for calculating the coefficient are found in Kendall and Stuart (1961). The Gini coefficient has a range of 0 to 1 indicating a progression from perfect equality to perfect inequality.[7] Although various measures of inequality are available, the Gini coefficient is employed because it meets a number of important measurement requirements as a result of its derivation from the Lorenz curve. In addition, its wide use and intuitive appeal make it a commonly understood indicator in the social sciences. For a critique of the Gini coefficient and other measures of inequality see Allison (1978).

Unemployment and Education. The percentage of the population unemployed and median schooling are used both as indicators of worker power and of inequality. The measurement of these variables has been previously described. Economic structures can be expected to have their most direct impact on local economic levels, such as income and income distribution. The use of unemployment and education allow the potential nonmonetary effects of economic structure to be examined. Employment opportunities and educational attainments are unevenly distributed socioeconomic resources necessary for survival in a market economy and they are indicators common to most conceptualizations of social well-being (Smith, 1977; Ross et al., 1979). Few studies have focused on the relationship between segmented economy structures and unemployment, particularly outside the point of production, and few studies have examined farm structure and unemployment. The effects of industry and farm structure on local educational levels generally remain unaddressed. The use of educational level as a dependent variable assumes that populations with certain educational levels are attracted to and maintained in localities because of employment requirements.

Infant Mortality and Related Indicators. Although researchers generally assume that economic well-being translates directly to social well-being, few studies have examined noneconomic quality of life outcomes and virtually none focus on community health conditions (Ross et al., 1979; Smith, 1977). This study attempts to broaden the research on industry, agriculture, and community health by examining an important indicator of health status, infant mortality. The infant mortality rate commonly is used as a surrogate measure of health status because it tends to be more sensitive to change than other mortality indicators and is more reflective of health resource interventions. It also provides a simple, uniform standard that is recognized throughout the health policy area and health-related social science disciplines (Farmer et al., 1984; Rosenblatt and Moscovice, 1982).

In addition to being an important health status indicator, infant mortality is a critical national problem. Although the United States has one of the highest per capita incomes in the world, and despite national declines in infant mortality throughout the 1970s, the nation ranks fifteenth or lower on international comparisons of infant mortality (Pampel and Pillai, 1986:525). The anomalous case of the United States suggests that research must delve deeper into conventional explanations that development and accompanying demographic changes reduce infant mortality. Infant mortality is a reflection of inequities in the opportunity structure or quite literally in the life chances associated with one's position in the social order. As the deteriorating economic conditions of the post-fordist era and federal budget cutbacks have altered the life quality of many, infant mortality has become a significant policy and academic issue (Miller, 1985; Pampel and Pillai, 1986).

This study employs the three-year average county infant mortality rate for 1978, 1979, and 1980 available from the National Center for Health Statistics and compiled by the Area Resource File, U.S. Department of Health and Human Services. The general infant mortality rate refers to number of deaths to infants age one and under per live births. The effects of economic structure on infant mortality are not assumed to be as direct as for the other socioeconomic well-being indicators. This issue is explained further in the following chapter. In addition to income and educational levels, two mortality related factors, teenage fertility and the number of active, nonfederal physicians per capita, an indicator of access to the medical system (Farmer et al., 1984), are expected to mediate the relationship between economic structure and infant mortality. The latter two variables are complied by the Area Resource File, U.S. Department of Health and Human Services. Data for physicians per capita are for 1980. The teenage fertility rate reflects births to mothers aged thirteen through seventeen and is based on five-year county averages for 1973 through 1977. Data for the later 1970s through 1980 were not available. Because most births to teenagers occur outside marriage (Wilson and Neckerman, 1986), this variable can be considered an indicator of family instability associated with early parenthood.

In sum, the previous measures should be useful indicators of inequality. First, they represent important socioeconomic attributes essential for the reproduction of the labor force. Income and employment indicate access to consumption goods, define position in the social order, and are related to a variety of nonmonetary opportunities, in education, health, politics and other areas of social life. Education, in turn, affects access to income and employment and other social rewards. Infant mortality is an important health issue and a literal indicator of the level at which a labor force reproduces itself. Second, the measures represent commonly used and understood quality of life indicators. Third, as tests of the Goldschmidt hypothesis and studies on the segmented economy employ some of the economic indicators, the findings are more comparable to those of other studies. Finally, this study expands previous research by focusing on noneconomic aspects of inequality.[8]

METHODS OF ANALYSIS

This study has three general analytical stages, each of which is described in the separate chapters which follow. Chapter 6 focuses on the effects of farming and industry structure, worker power and spatial characteristics on the indicators of socioeconomic inequality. The analysis shows the results of these relationships at the national level. Chapter 7 is a comparative study of the relationships by region. Chapter 8 examines the linkages between farming and local nonfarm characteristics, particularly industry.

The study includes both cross-sectional and longitudinal, panel analyses of data. Cross-sectional designs examine variables measured at one point in time. Longitudinal designs involve two or more time points. Variables at the earlier point in time are hypothesized to affect those at the later time point, and earlier measures of the dependent variable are hypothesized to have 'lagged' effects on the dependent variable as well. Longitudinal analyses provide stronger tests of causal relationships than cross-sectional designs as they permit examination of the effects of the independent variables on changes in the dependent variable.

Several statistical techniques are employed. The descriptive statistics, the mean and standard deviation, are presented for each variable at the two time points. Multiple regression analysis, which allows for the determination of one variable's net contribution to variation in the dependent variable while holding potential confounding variables constant, is employed in order to test the relationships. Multiple regression is also useful in evaluating and measuring the overall dependence of one dependent variable on a set of predictors. Multiple regression thus permits controlled examination of particular relationships, such as those between farm structure and inequality, and allows assessment of how well inequality is predicted by the proposed model.[9]

A consideration in employing multiple regression analysis concerns the use of statistical tests of significance. Since nearly all U.S. counties are analyzed, statistical tests of significance are not relevant as an inferential tool, that is, for drawing generalizations about an existing larger universe. The statistical coefficients represent the strength and direction of actual relationships existing among U.S. counties. In interpreting the findings, I therefore focus on the consistency of the direction of the relationships and on the magnitude of the coefficients. While significance levels are reported for the reader's interest, the major concern is with the substantive (rather than the statistical) significance of the relationships.

——————————————— Local Inequality: National Patterns

   This chapter presents the analysis of the effects of farm and industry structure and other county characteristics on socioeconomic inequality.[1] It is expected that counties with a greater extent of larger family farming and core employment should have better conditions, while poorer conditions are expected in counties with a greater extent of industrialized farming and peripheral employment. Although analysts have presented conceptual arguments that state employment and smaller family farming should also improve socioeconomic conditions, recent empirical studies show otherwise; testing these relationships contributes to structuralist debates in agriculture and industry. Counties where the bargaining power of workers vis-à-vis their employers is greater and counties with more favorable geographic locations in the national political economy should have better socioeconomic conditions. It is expected that the relationships will hold cross-sectionally for both 1970 and 1980 as well as longitudinally, across these time points.

   Changes in industrial structure, labor power, and indicators of inequality are evident over the 1970-1980 period (Table 6.1). As the farm structure indicators are standardized, their values remain constant over time. Of the industrial sectors, the state experienced the relatively largest growth with the percentage of the employed labor force in this sector expanding from 14 percent in 1970 to 16 percent by 1980. Peripheral employment declined slightly (which appears mainly due to declines in extractive, textiles, and apparel employment). Core employment and mean establishment size increased slightly. There is some evidence of a weakening of labor power over time, as indicated by declines in the percent unionized and growth in unemployment. The nonwhite population expanded. Median education increased from 10.9 to 11.5 years. Per capita AFDC payments increased, largely as a consequence of inflation. The indicators of economic inequality show slight improvement. Increases in median family income reflect mainly inflation. Poverty declined from 17 percent in 1970 to about 13 percent in 1980, although, as noted in Chapter 2, it was to rise again in the early 1980s. Spatial characteristics reflect long-term trends toward a growing urban, nonfarm, metropolitan population.

   The effects of farm and industry structure, worker power, and spatial characteristics on each indicator of inequality are now examined using multiple

TABLE 6.1

Means and Standard Deviations for Major Variables

Variables	Means	Standard Deviations
Economic Inequality		
Median Family Income, 1980	$16,688.07	$3,495.56
Median Family Income, 1970	$ 7,450.64	$1,850.11
Family Poverty, 1980	.125	.063
Family Poverty, 1970	.173	.099
Income Inequality, 1980	.364	.033
Income Inequality, 1970	.386	.042
Industry Structure		
Percent in Core Employment, 1980	.265	.090
Percent in Core Employment, 1970	.245	.102
Percent in State Employment, 1980	.159	.051
Percent in State Employment, 1970	.140	.053
Percent in Peripheral Employment, 1980	.576	.091
Percent in Peripheral Employment, 1970	.615	.109
Establishment Size, 1977	7.067	3.100
Establishment Size, 1967	6.252	3.556
Farm Structure		
Smaller Family Farming, 1978	50.000	10.000
Smaller Family Farming, 1969	50.000	10.000
Larger Family Farming, 1978	50.000	10.000
Larger Family Farming, 1969	50.000	10.000
Industrialized Farming, 1978	50.000	10.000
Industrialized Farming, 1969	50.000	10.000
Worker Power Characteristics		
Percent Unionized, 1980	.212	.079
Percent Unionized, 1970	.259	.098
Per Capita AFDC Payments, 1980	$74.73	$29.31
Per Capita AFDC Payments, 1974	$45.76	$17.04
Percent Nonwhite, 1980	.114	.149
Percent Nonwhite, 1970	.101	.152
Median Education, 1980	11.540	.962
Median Education, 1970	10.893	1.385
Percent Unemployed, 1980	.068	.033
Percent Unemployed, 1970	.045	.023

TABLE 6.1 *continued*

Variables	Means	Standard Deviations
Spatial Characteristics		
Percent Farm to Rural Population, 1980	.142	.120
Percent Farm to Rural Population, 1970	.218	.158
Percent Urban, 1980	.354	.286
Percent Urban, 1970	.343	.283
Metro Proximity, 1980	5.251	4.181
Metro Proximity, 1970	4.857	4.161
Northeast	.168	.374
Eastern Mountains	.229	.420
Southeast Plains	.179	.383
Central U.S.	.296	.456
West	.129	.269

regression analysis. Two types of analyses are performed. First, cross-sectional analyses are presented for each of the study years, which essentially reflect and will be referred to as the 1970 and 1980 time points. Then, the longitudinal analyses are presented. In the latter analysis, the independent variables at the 1970 points are tested for their effects on 1980 socioeconomic inequality indicators and an additional control, the 1970 value of the dependent variable, is included. This analysis is a stronger test of the hypothesized relationships. It permits examination of the effects of farming and industry structure and other county characteristics on changes in socioeconomic levels; and it indicates whether or not the dependent variables have continuing effects over and above initial socioeconomic levels. For examples of other studies that employ lagged values of the dependent and independent variables in order to measure change in the dependent variable, see Farmer et al. (1984), Jacobs (1985), and Cutright (1987).[2]

Several points should be mentioned regarding the specification of the regression models. In the analyses for the income related measures of inequality, unemployment and education are included as independent variables because they are indicators of worker power and because they have conceptual and empirical associations with poverty, income, and income inequality, as described in the previous chapter. Because unemployment and education also signify socioeconomic conditions which are in part created by local economic structure, they are examined separately as dependent variables. Finally, it should be noted that all three industrial structures and all five regions cannot be included in each model as they would result in orthogonality. The core sector is the exluded reference category for interpreting the effects of industrial structure and the Southeast Coastal Plain is the excluded regional category.[3]

The regression coefficients represent the relationship between each respective independent variable and dependent variable while holding constant the effects of the other variables. Both the standardized and unstandardized regression coefficients are reported. The unstandardized coefficients represent the expected average change in the dependent variable associated with a one unit change in the independent variable after the other independent variables have been held constant. For example, the coefficients reported in Table 6.2 indicate that a one percent increase in the unionized workforce would increase median family income by an additional $34.55 in 1980. The standardized regression coefficients are also referred to as beta weights or betas. While the betas do not allow for the estimation of the original units of the dependent variable, they simplify comparisons among variables measured in different units. The analysis focuses upon interpretation of the betas in testing the hypothesized relationships. Unstandardized regression coefficients are generally employed in comparing variables across different populations and over time so that these are useful in cross-sectional comparisons.

A final statistic presented in the regression analyses tables is the coefficient of determination (R^2) which indicates the proportion of variance in the dependent variable explained by the independent variable. As such, it is a summary measure of how well the model predicts local inequality.

As previously discussed, levels of statistical significance do not have customary inferential meaning in the context of an entire population. In testing the hypothesized relationships, attention is directed to the size of the betas and their consistency in direction. Relationships that do not meet the accepted .05 significance level are also reported.[4] Also, because this study employs two different models, one cross-sectional and the other longitudinal with a dependent lag, the independent variables are subject to different controls that influence the magnitude of the betas. Specifically, for cross-sectional models, the variables can explain more variance in the dependent variable because they are not constrained by the dependent lag. The lag represents a county's prior history with respect to the dependent variable, which obviously has an enormous effect on the future potentials of a county. As a consequence, the betas will be smaller and less frequently meet the significance criterion in the lagged models.[5]

THE EFFECTS OF FARM AND INDUSTRY STRUCTURE ON ECONOMIC INEQUALITY AMONG COUNTIES

The first set of analyses focuses on income-related economic well-being among counties. I analyze the relationship between the indicators of farm and industry structure, worker power, and spatial characteristics and the indicators of family income, poverty, and income inequality. In addition to presenting an overview of the general relationships, I show how local characteristics differentially alter or mediate the effects of farm structure.

Median Family Income

The cross-sectional model for 1970 explains about 81 percent of the variance in median family income, indicating a substantial amount of predictive accuracy (Table 6.2). Counties with greater proportions of their labor force in the peripheral and state sector, as opposed to the core sector (the reference category), have lower median family income. This supports the hypothesis that core employment improves socioeconomic conditions. In contrast, the hypothesis that state employment has positive socioeconomic benefits similar to those of the core is not supported. Rather, state employment (beta= $-.109$) lowers income only slightly less than the periphery (beta= $-.123$). Counties with larger business establishments have higher incomes as expected. Counties with a greater extent of larger family farming have significantly higher (beta=.102) income, which supports an aspect of the Goldschmidt hypothesis. Contrary to the findings of earlier literature, counties with a greater extent of smaller family farming have lower (beta= $-.103$) income. Industrialized farming has a negligible effect on income, in contrast to the negative relationship expected from the Goldschmidt hypothesis.

The indicators of worker power and spatial characteristics have impacts on median family income that are generally consistent with previous conceptual arguments and empirical research. Counties with a more highly educated population, lower unemployment, greater unionization, and higher AFDC payments have higher income; the strongest relationship is between income and education. When these variables are controlled, the percent nonwhite population has no relationship to income. Higher income levels are also evident in counties: closer to metro areas; located outside the Southeast; with higher urban populations; and with lower farm populations.

The cross-sectional model for 1980 explains somewhat less of the variance in median family income than the 1970 model. With a few exceptions, the relationships for both time periods follow similar patterns, indicating their rather stable nature over time. While in 1970 the size of the nonwhite population had essentially no relationship to income, the 1980 relationship is negative. This indicates that racial differences in income levels have become more important: counties with a higher white population have higher median family income. In contrast, educational impacts seem to have declined in importance relative to other worker power indicators, particularly unemployment. Regional variations have become less pronounced, with only the West significantly different from the Southeast. This is consistent with observations about the deterioration of the Rust Belt economy and rise of Sun Belt areas over the 1970s decade.

The longitudinal analysis reveals the effects that the 1970 variables have on income levels a decade later. The explained variance of the longitudinal model is about 83 percent with the lagged, dependent variable accounting for the greatest share. Prior income levels, coupled with the effects of the independent variables,

TABLE 6.2

Regressions of Median Family Income on Farm and Industry Structure and Other County Characteristics[a]

Independent Variables	1970 Cross Section	1980 Cross Section	1980 with 1970 Independent & Lagged
Industry Structure			
Percent in Peripheral Employment	−.123 (−20.89)	−.245 (−93.72)	−.170 (−54.67)
Percent in State Employment	−.109 (−38.00)	−.137 (−93.14)	−.069 (−45.54)
Establishment Size	.169 (87.75)	.125 (141.11)	−.063 (−61.51)
Farm Structure			
Smaller Family Farming	−.103 (−19.07)	−.172 (−60.06)	−.048 (−16.95)
Larger Family Farming	.102 (18.82)	.204 (71.22)	.126 (43.99)
Industrialized Farming	−.004 (−0.81)*	−.021 (−7.35)*	−.038 (−13.12)
Worker Power Characteristics			
Percent Unionized	.062 (11.57)	.079 (34.55)	−.036 (−12.82)
Per Capita AFDC Payments	.191 (20.73)	.192 (22.83)	.019 (3.86)*
Percent Nonwhite	−.009 (−1.08)*	−.077 (−18.11)	−.001 (−0.33)*
Median Education	.381 (508.51)	.206 (746.64)	.020 (50.91)*
Percent Unemployed	−.119 (−95.61)	−.235 (−247.73)	−.047 (−71.43)

TABLE 6.2 *continued*

Independent Variables	1970 Cross Section	1980 Cross Section	1980 with 1970 Independent & Lagged
Spatial Characteristics			
Percent Farm to Rural Population	-.108 (-12.60)	-.147 (-42.65)	-.023 (-5.13)*
Percent Urban	.089 (5.80)	.117 (14.40)	-.016 (-2.04)*
Metro Proximity	.241 (107.14)	.330 (275.98)	.139 (117.29)
Northeast	.112 (554.36)	.019 (178.34)*	-.118 (-1,104.02)
Eastern Mountains	.045 (195.71)	-.025 (-205.15)*	-.040 (-334.38)
Central U.S.	.060 (243.87)	.001 (11.27)*	-.055 (-423.30)
West	.122 (671.47)	.075 (783.15)	-.027 (-285.80)
Median Family Income	NA	NA	.796 (1.50)
Intercept	.000 (1,683.44)	.000 (11,764.57)	.000 (9,127.04)
R^2	.807	.739	.829

[a]Unstandardized coefficients are in parentheses.

*Not significant at p ≤ .05.

thus largely explain the median family income of counties in 1980. Counties with greater core employment in 1970 had significant increases in median family income. In contrast, greater state and peripheral employment resulted in lower income than did core employment, although these differences were least for state employment. Counties with larger business establishments in the 1970s also had income losses. Counties having a greater extent of larger family farming in 1970 had significantly higher median income in 1980. Counties with a greater extent of industrialized farming and smaller family farming, however, had small dereases in median family income over this period. The former relationship supports the Goldschmidt hypothesis, in that industrialized farming appears to limit future county socioeconomic gains.

The worker power and spatial indicators have somewhat different patterns of relationships once the prior effects of median family income are controlled. This is not unexpected because median income is interrelated (from low to moderate degrees) with all of these variables. Per capita AFDC payments, percent nonwhite, farm to rural population, and percent urban become nonsignificant. Counties having higher educational attainments in 1970 also had no significant income gains, which appears to counter conventional human capital and functionalist assumptions that higher education in and of itself increases income levels. Rather, this finding suggests that factors beyond educational human capital shape county income levels and, moreover, that returns to education may have declined in the changing economic environment of the decade. Counties that had greater unionization and higher unemployment and that were more distant from metropolitan centers had income losses. Median family income also decreased in all regions outside the Southeast, but especially in the Northeast. The relationships seem to reflect commonly noted patterns of industrial restructuring of the 1970s in which highly industrialized and unionized counties with larger business estabishments and counties in Frost Belt states lost previous advantageous employment opportunities (Bluestone and Harrison, 1982). The findings also suggest that unionization, income transfers, and education had diminished capacity to shelter workers over this period.

Family Poverty

The findings for family poverty (Table 6.3) are similar to those for median family income. For 1970, counties with greater proportions of their labor force in state employment (beta=.133) as compared to core employment have significantly higher poverty rates. In contrast to earlier segmented economy assumptions, poverty is also more strongly related to state than to peripheral employment. Counties with larger business establishments have lower poverty. Smaller and larger family farming exhibit small but significant relationships in the same direction as with median family income: smaller family farming is positively and larger family farming, negatively related to poverty. Industrialized farming has little impact on poverty. The relationships between poverty and the economic structure variables remain essentially the same for the 1980 model.

Similar relationships are also found for both time periods for the worker power and spatial characteristics. Counties with lower education, less remunerable welfare benefits and larger nonwhite and unemployed populations have higher levels of poverty. Unionization, in contrast, has little effect on poverty. Poverty is also higher in counties with larger farm and smaller urban populations and in counties distant from metropolitan centers. Once other major variables are controlled, there is little regional variation between the Southeast and other areas.

The longitudinal model supports the consistent finding that core employment and larger family farming increase socioeconomic well-being over time. Counties with a greater extent of smaller family farming also had slightly less poverty. In contrast, industrialized farming is related to slightly higher poverty, paralleling the relationship found in the longitudinal model for median family income. Counties with larger business establishments, more unionized workers, and in regions outside the Southeast also had increased poverty. Education provided no significant shelter from poverty, although income transfers did. More urbanized counties and counties closer to metro areas also had no reduction in poverty. As noted previously, these relationships seem to reflect the pattern of industrial restructuring and diminished worker power over the 1970s decade.

Income Inequality

The relationships between economic structure and income inequality tend to follow those in the previous models (Table 6.4). Peripheral and state employment heighten income inequality relative to the core, and this relationship is stronger in the case of the periphery. Larger establishment size is related to lower income inequality. Smaller and larger family farming heighten and reduce income inequality, respectively. These models also provide the first cross-sectional evidence in support of Goldschmidt regarding the deterimental impacts of industrialized farming. However, the relationship between industrialized farming and higher income inequality is small.

The worker power variables have similar relationships with income inequality as found in the previous economic well-being models. The exception is unionization. Counties with a greater unionized workforce have slightly higher inequality in 1980. Although this is counter to expected relationships, it is consistent with some other studies (Jacobs, 1985). Jacobs (1985) argues that areas with a greater unionized work force may have higher income inequality over time because union wage demands can lead employers to substitute nonlabor production factors for workers. If this occurs extensively, it will significantly increase "the supply of workers in unorganized industry and the resulting downward pressure on these wages will outweigh wage increments in the organized sector,"

TABLE 6.3

Regressions of Family Poverty on Farm and Industry Structure and Other County Characteristics[a]

Independent Variables	1970 Cross Section	1980 Cross Section	1980 with 1970 Independent & Lagged
Industry Structure			
Percent in Peripheral Employment	.030 (.032)	.088 (.061)	.111 (.064)
Percent in State Employment	.133 (.248)	.146 (.179)	.086 (.102)
Establishment Size	−.094 (−.003)	−.094 (−.002)	.061 (.001)
Farm Structure			
Smaller Family Farming	.048 (.000)	.083 (.000)	−.029 (−.000)
Larger Family Farming	−.073 (−.000)	−.158 (−.001)	−.059 (−.000)
Industrialized Farming	.016 (.000)*	.014 (.000)*	.029 (.000)
Worker Power Characteristics			
Percent Unionized	−.021 (−.021)*	.001 (.000)*	.026 (.017)
Per Capita AFDC Payments	−.180 (−.001)	−.191 (−.000)	−.043 (−.000)
Percent Nonwhite	.231 (.150)	.372 (.157)	.077 (.032)
Median Education	−.560 (−.040)	−.383 (−.025)	−.031 (−.001)*
Percent Unemployed	.121 (.520)	.179 (.340)	.050 (.136)

TABLE 6.3 continued

Independent Variables	1970 Cross Section	1980 Cross Section	1980 with 1970 Independent & Lagged
Spatial Characteristics			
Percent Farm to Rural Population	.101 (.063)	.222 (.116)	.113 (.045)
Percent Urban	−.037 (−.013)	−.095 (−.021)	−.007 (−.001)*
Metro Proximity	−.094 (−.002)	−.103 (−.002)	−.012 (−.000)*
Northeast	−.004 (−.001)*	.000 (.000)*	.078 (.013)
Eastern Mountains	−.050 (−.012)	−.016 (−.002)*	.008 (.001)*
Central U.S.	−.000 (−.000)*	.051 (.007)	.081 (.011)
West	.004 (.001)*	.013 (.002)*	.058 (.011)
Family Poverty	NA	NA	.805 (.512)
Intercept	.000 (.596)	.000 (.370)	.000 (−.013)*
R^2	.803	.740	.811

[a]Unstandardized coefficients are in parentheses
*Not significant at $p \leq .05$.

TABLE 6.4

Regressions of Income Inequality on Farm and Industry Structure and Other County Characteristics[a]

Independent Variables	1970 Cross Section	1980 Cross Section	1980 with 1970 Independent & Lagged
Industry Structure			
Percent in Peripheral Employment	.245 (.094)	.190 (.070)	.145 (.045)
Percent in State Employment	.187 (.148)	.132 (.086)	.112 (.071)
Establishment Size	−.175 (−.002)	−.185 (−.002)	−.009 (−.000)*
Farm Structure			
Smaller Family Farming	.050 (.000)	.102 (.000)	.002 (.000)*
Larger Family Farming	−.060 (−.000)	−.184 (−.001)	−.093 (−.000)
Industrialized Farming	.044 (.000)	.062 (.000)	.057 (.000)
Worker Power Characteristics			
Percent Unionized	.009 (.004)*	.039 (.016)	.040 (.013)
Per Captia AFDC Payments	−.202 (−.000)	−.255 (−.000)	−.120 (−.000)
Percent Nonwhite	.199 (.055)	.307 (.069)	.095 (.021)
Median Education	−.346 (−.010)	−.244 (−.008)	−.195 (−.005)
Percent Unemployed	.068 (.123)	.043 (.043)	.020 (.029)*

TABLE 6.4 continued

Independent Variables	1970 Cross Section	1980 Cross Section	1980 with 1970 Independent & Lagged
Spatial Characteristics			
Percent Farm to Rural Population	.136 (.036)	.188 (.052)	.034 (.007)*
Percent Urban	.051 (.008)	.035 (.004)	.057 (.007)
Metro Proximity	−.064 (−.001)	−.146 (−.001)	−.074 (−.001)
Northeast	−.010 (−.001)*	−.057 (−.005)	−.011 (−.001)*
Eastern Mountains	−.088 (−.009)	−.074 (−.006)	−.068 (−.005)
Central U.S.	.028 (.003)*	.039 (.003)*	.071 (.005)
West	−.034 (−.004)*	−.009 (−.001)*	.036 (.004)
Income Inequality	NA	NA	.500 (.398)
Intercept	.000 (.432)	.000 (.432)	.000 (.233)
R^2	.577	.597	.675

[a]Unstandardized coefficients are in parentheses.
*Not significant at p ≤ .05.

thereby creating greater aggregate inequality (Jacobs, 1985:176). The findings suggest that while unions raise family income overall, they may stratify the work force and slightly heighten inequality among various segments of labor.

The spatial variables also tend to follow previous patterns. More centrally located counties, with lower farm populations, generally outside the Southeast, have lower income inequality. In contrast to previous models, however, the percent urban has a small but positive relationship with income inequality.

The longitudinal model reaffirms most of the relationships found in the comparable models for median income and poverty. Higher peripheral and state employment increase income inequality over time, and the relationship is stronger for the former. Counties with more industrialized farming had small increases in income inequality, while counties with more larger family farming had declines in inequality. Counties with more smaller family farming had no changes in income inequality. As expected, higher income transfers and education and a lower non-white population result in a more equitable income distribution. In contrast, as found in the cross-sectional models, a more unionized workforce slightly heightens inequality. Inequality increased in urban, less centrally located counties and somewhat more in the Central U.S. than in the Southeast.

Interpreting the Impacts of Farm Structure and Other Local Characteristics

The previous analyses show the effects of the independent variables within the entire conceptual model of inequality outlined by this study. For a more detailed understanding of the forces creating inequality, however, it is useful to examine the separate effects of each set of independent variables and how farm structure is mediated by industrial structure, spatial characteristics and worker power. The models in Table 6.5 first examine each set of independent variables and, beginning with county spatial characteristics, progressively incorporate other major sets of variables into the model. For a simpler and clearer examiniation of the relationships, I focus upon one time period (1980) and use a summary measure of economic well-being, which incorporates median family income, poverty, and income inequality. This measure was created through a principal axis factor analysis of the three previous indicators that revealed a one dimension solution. That is, the three items could satisfactorily be represented by one dimension, which I term local economic well-being. Factor scores were used to generate the index of economic well-being.[6] It should be noted that although median family income, poverty, and income inequality were related nationally such that a summary measure of the three items could be constructed, each indicator of economic well-being is important in its own right and merits separate consideration. The study of poverty and income distribution is undergirded by a large literature in sociology and economics and policy efforts at improving economic well-being often center specifically on poverty reduction.

The first model in Table 6.5 shows the effects of the spatial characteristics on economic well-being. All of the relationships are in expected directions with well-being highest in the Northeast and lowest in the Southeast followed by the Eastern Mountains. The percent farm to rural population has a small negative relationship with well-being. The spatial variables explain about 41 percent of the variance in well-being. The second model shows that farm structure alone explains only a very small amount of economic well-being. The relationships for smaller and larger family farming follow those suggested by the Goldschmidt hypothesis in that both are related to higher well-being. In contrast, industrialized farming has essentially no relationship to well-being. Model three supports segmented economy theory in that peripheral employment and smaller firm size are related to lower well-being. However, while state employment is related to somewhat better well-being than peripheral employment, the state is related to significantly lower well-being than the core. The industrial structure variables explain nearly 22 percent of the variance in well-being, nearly seven times that of the farm variables. Model four shows that the worker power indicators are all in the expected directions with the strongest relationship for education. These variables are the best set of predictors and explain nearly half the variance in well-being among counties.

The farm structure variables are incorporated with the spatial variables in model five. The positive direction of smaller family farming (unstandardized coefficient, .011, found in model two) reverses and is small but negative ($-.005$). This seems due to the association of smaller family farming with certain beneficial spatial characteristics, or those that raise economic well-being: smaller family farming is positively correlated with urbanization and metro adjacency (see Chapter 8 for further elaboration), so that a negative relationship emerges with well-being when these variables are controlled. Similar changes are observable for industrialized farming. The nonsignificant relationship in equation two now becomes negative. Again, this appears due to the more favorable location of industrialized farming, closer to more urbanized areas, particularly in the West. In contrast, the positive relationship between larger family farming and well-being in equation two becomes larger when spatial characteristics are controlled. This suggests that this type of farming is associated with more unfavorable locational characteristics, such as lower urbanization and distance from metropolitan areas.

The industrial structure variables are incorporated in model six. The coefficient for smaller family farming becomes slightly more negative, indicating that industrial structure mediates the relationship between smaller family farming and well-being. Smaller family farming tends to be associated with a more diversified industrial structure, including some types of core employment, which, if not controlled for, would suppress a stronger negative relationship between this type of farming and economic well-being. The coefficient for industrialized farming, in contrast, becomes smaller. This suggests that this farming may be associated

TABLE 6.5

Regressions of 1980 Economic Well-being on Farm and Industry Structure, Worker Power, and County Spatial Characteristics[a]

	1	2	3	4	5	6	7
Industry Structure							
Percent in Peripheral Employment			−.361 (−3.826)			−.249 (−2.637)	−.183 (−1.934)
Percent in State Employment			−.231 (−4.356)			−.231 (−4.348)	−.148 (−2.788)
Establishment Size			.211 (.066)			.095 (.029)	.143 (.045)
Farm Structure							
Smaller Family Farming		.111 (.011)			−.051 (−.005)	−.075 (−.007)	−.125 (−.012)
Larger Family Farming		.099 (.010)			.196 (.019)	.126 (.012)	.194 (.019)
Industrialized Farming		−.003 (−.000)*			−.086 (−.008)	−.032 (−.003)*	−.034 (−.003)
Worker Power Characteristics							
Percent Unionized				.193 (2.337)			.012 (.141)*
Per Capita AFDC Payments				.136 (.004)			.229 (.008)
Percent Nonwhite				−.198 (−1.285)			−.282 (−1.834)
Median Education				.389 (.391)			.303 (.304)
Percent Unemployed				−.169 (−4.928)			−.162 (−4.731)

TABLE 6.5 continued

	1	2	3	4	5	6	7
Spatial Characteristics							
Percent Farm to Rural Population	−.041 (−.329)				−.112 (−.900)	−.027 (−.200)*	−.202 (−1.621)
Percent Urban	.150 (.510)				.144 (.488)	.096 (.325)	.065 (.219)
Metro Proximity	.367 (.084)				.365 (.084)	.317 (.073)	.202 (.047)
Northeast	.461 (1.191)				.447 (1.155)	.394 (1.018)	.025 (.065)*
Eastern Mountains	.213 (.490)				.226 (.520)	.151 (.348)	.024 (.054)*
Central U.S.	.390 (.827)				.343 (.726)	.347 (.736)	−.035 (−.075)*
West	.249 (.717)				.268 (.772)	.296 (.853)	.022 (.064)*
R^2	.410	.033	.217	.489	.422	.494	.743

[a]Unstandardized coefficients are in parentheses.
*Not significant at $p \le .05$.

with somewhat poorer industrial quality. The positive coefficient for larger family farming is also reduced somewhat as compared to that in equation five, suggesting that larger family farming is related to better industrial structure.[7]

The final set of characteristics, worker power, is incorporated in model seven. The relationship between smaller family farming and economic well-being again becomes more negative, indicating that worker power characteristics, including a somewhat lower nonwhite population, mediate the effects of smaller family farming. The relationship between larger family industrialized farming and well-being becomes slightly more positive in this model. Although industrialized farming becomes significantly negatively related to well-being, the relationship is small and hardly differs from that found in the previous model. Worker power characteristics thus appear to play a much greater role in mediating the effects of smaller and larger family farming than they do industrialized farming. However, it should be recognized that the analysis covers only one time point. Counties with greater industrialized farming have somewhat high per capita AFDC payments and unionization rates (see Chapter 8) which could reduce potential deterimental impacts of such farming over time.

Table 6.5 also permits examination of ways in which industrial structure is modified by intervening and prior variables. The unstandardized coefficients in models three and six show relationships in the same expected direction. Previous analyses indicate that changes in model six are mainly from spatial rather than farm characteristics. The coefficient for state employment is of almost exact magnitude in both models, indicating it tends to have homogeneous effects little influenced by location. State employment is also fairly evenly spread through all regions, although there is slightly more in the West. In contrast, the more negative effects of peripheral (as opposed to core) employment and more positive effects of establishment size are both reduced in model six. Core employment and larger firm size are higher in the urban Northeast. The addition of the labor power variables in model seven indicates that these variables further mediate the effects of industrial structure. The coefficients for all three industrial indicators remain in the same direction but are reduced due to the differential association of industrial structure with worker power. For example, some of the effects of core employment are channelled through its association (evident in zero-order correlations) with greater unionization and a lower nonwhite population.

Finally, as was noted in the previous section and confirmed more strongly here, regional differences tend to decline once economic structure and worker power are controlled. The Southeast tends to rank lowest on the worker power indicators with the exception of unemployment, while the urban Northeast tends to rank highest. These differences are a result of the differential historical development of each region. When industrial structure and worker power are controlled, only a small residue of former historical differences remain.

In Summary: The Effects of the Independent Variables on Economic Inequality

As economic sectors, farming and industry structure can be expected to have the most direct impacts on economic outcomes, particulary those that are income related. The previous analyses show support for aspects of the Goldschmidt hypothesis and for segmentation theory at the general national level. In support of Goldschmidt, the analyses indicate that larger family farming or moderate sized, capital intensive units using little hired labor tend to improve county economic conditions. There is also some evidence that industrialized farming reduces well-being in that it raises income inequality slightly and limits future county economic potentials. In contrast to Goldschmidt, and in support of recent studies and some political economic perspectives, smaller family farming is related to poorer economic conditions at any one time point. But the longitudinal models for poverty and income inequality suggest that this farming does not have such adverse impacts on future well-being. The effects of the farm structures were shown to be mediated by local nonfarm industrial structure and somewhat less so by worker power. As segmentation theory indicates, core employment improves economic conditions. However, in contrast to earlier perspectives, state employment does not have impacts similar to the core but rather, to the periphery.

The worker power variables are related to economic inequality in expected directions: a lower nonwhite and higher educated population, higher levels of income transfers, and lower unemployment significantly improve local conditions. Greater unionization tends to be related to higher income but also leads to somewhat greater income inequality.

Spatial characteristics, urbanization, metro adjacency, and population with farm residence generally follow expected directions, even when economic structure and worker power are controlled. The previous analysis shows that while there are initial regional differences in inequality, these tend to diminish when economic structure and labor power are controlled.

Finally, the analyses reveal some temporal differences over the 1970 and 1980 periods. Higher education appeared less able to shelter workers from market exigencies in 1980 than in 1970. In contrast, the gap between the white and nonwhite population and between more and less unionized work forces appears to have widened. The longitudinal models tend to confirm common observations about the industrial restructuring process, as areas with larger firms, higher unionization, and outside the Sun Belt appeared to lose economic advantages over the decade.

INEQUALITIES OF UNEMPLOYMENT AND EDUCATION AMONG COUNTIES

In this section, the effects of the independent variables on nonincome indicators of well-being, unemployment and education are explored.

Unemployment

The models for unemployment (Table 6.6) explain considerably less variance than those for the income related indicators. As discussed previously, the census definition of unemployment is highly general and does not take into account the various complexities of this concept, such as the reason for and duration of unemployment. It also does not include individuals who have given up the job search or who are underemployed. Unemployment tends to be a more volatile indicator than income levels and distribution because it fluctuates more with the business cycle and other exogenous factors. Both the lack of preciseness with which unemployment is measured and causal complexities make explained variance lower than for the income indicators.

The cross-sectional models show a generally similar pattern of relation-ships for both 1970 and 1980. The periphery is not significantly different from the core in affecting local unemployment. While this contrasts with early segmented economy assumptions, it corroborates those of more recent studies (Beck et al., 1978; Schervish, 1983). Establishment size is negatively related to unemployment, as would be expected from segmented economy theory. In contrast, state employment is related to higher unemployment and more so in 1980 when the unemployment rate was highest. As discussed previously, an issue involved in analyzing the state sector is whether state employment actually worsens well-being through its earnings or employment structure, or whether state employ-ment represents service allocations that may be extended to poorer areas. Sheets et al. (1987) and Tomaskovic-Devey (1988c) argue for the first explanation in the case of local income levels. However, in the case of unemployment, state jobs have been shown to be the most stable, even tending to expand when unemployment is higher, suggesting a response to service demands (Schervish, 1983). Gurr and King (1987:107) for example, show that state employment is more heavily concentrated in declining cities and that state employment grew in such cities (while it remained stable or declined in growing cities) over the 1970s decade.

Smaller family farming is related to higher unemployment and larger family farming is related to lower unemployment, findings that parallel those for the income models. The relationship between smaller family farming and unemploy-ment is suggestive of the 'reserve army' hypothesis (Bonanno, 1987; Mottura and Pugliese, 1980) in which a large pool of small, part-time operators are main-tained to meet the fluctuating needs of rural employers. Industrialized farming is related to slightly higher unemployment in 1970, but in 1980 the relationship reverses entirely. This may reflect the need for workers during the peak produc-tion period prior to the farm crisis of the early 1980s.

The worker power variables have differential relationships with unemploy-ment. A higher nonwhite population and lower education appear to undercut the bargaining power of labor (as was also evident in the income models), thereby raising unemployment. For unionization and AFDC levels, the relationships are quite different and tend to be reversed from the income models. Counties with a more unionized work force and higher AFDC payments have higher unemployment. Higher income transfer payments increase workers' ability to withhold their labor power from low-wage employment and so may discourage less advantaged workers from taking the worst jobs. Unionization is also associated with certain types of core industries (steel, automobiles) that were subject to lay-offs and employment losses during the 1970s. As the relationship between unionization and unemployment is greater in 1980, unionized areas experienced increased employment setbacks, probably as a consequence of this restructuring.

The relationships for the spatial characteristics are also somewhat different from the income models. Unemployment is significantly lower in farm areas. As the presence of self-employment in farming will tend to mask unemployment (Briggs, 1981), however, these findings should be viewed tentatively. More urbanized areas had higher unemployment in 1970, but urban-rural differences became nonsignificant by 1980. Counties adjacent to metropolitan areas have lower unemployment. Unemployment was lower in the Southeast as compared to most other regions in 1970 but this relationship is less consistent in 1980.

The longitudinal model extends some of the previously noted relationships. Over time, the three industrial sectors differ little in the amount of unemployment they generate. In light of the cross-sectional models, this finding suggests that greater state employment may be a response to unemployment, since the state sector itself does not appear to produce greater unemployment over time. In order to further explore the relationship between the state sector and unemployment, I regressed the percentage of the work force in each of the economic sectors in 1980 on levels of the independent variables, including unemployment and the percent of the workforce in each sector for 1970. Counties with higher unemployment in 1970 had a significant growth in state employment over the 1970-1980 decade; counties with lower unemployment in 1970 had a significant growth in peripheral employment; and unemployment in 1970 had no significant relationship with the extent of core employment in 1980. This further supports the argument that state employment is a response to rather than cause of unemployment.

Counties with more larger family farming had reductions in unemployment; counties with more smaller family farming saw increases in unemployment. Over the same period, there was little change in unemployment in counties with greater industrialized farming. Counties with higher per capita AFDC payments did not have significantly higher unemployment, suggesting that any work disincentive would operate only as a short-term work/nonwork trade-off. More unionized counties and counties with higher nonwhite populations and lower education had higher unemployment, as was found in the cross-sectional models. Counties closer

TABLE 6.6

Regressions of Unemployment on Farm and Industry Structure and Other County Characteristics[a]

Independent Variables	1970 Cross Section	1980 Cross Section	1980 and 1970 Independent & Lagged
Industry Structure			
Percent in Peripheral Employment	-.029 (-.006)*	.020 (.007)*	-.029 (-.009)*
Percent in State Employment	.067 (.029)	.108 (.070)	.020 (.012)*
Establishment Size	-.142 (-.001)	-.044 (-.000)	.033 (.000)
Farm Structure			
Smaller Family Farming	.185 (.000)	.145 (.000)	.057 (.000)
Larger Family Farming	-.213 (-.000)	-.100 (-.000)	-.065 (-.000)
Industrialized Farming	.042 (.000)	-.040 (-.000)	-.005 (-.000)*
Worker Power Characteristics			
Percent Unionized	.341 (.080)	.526 (.219)	.295 (.099)
Per Capita AFDC Payments	.154 (.000)	.097 (.000)	.012 (.000)*
Percent Nonwhite	.169 (.025)	.159 (.036)	.084 (.018)
Median Education	-.301 (-.005)	-.234 (-.008)	-.134 (-.003)

TABLE 6.6 continued

Independent Variables	1970 Cross Section	1980 Cross Section	1980 with 1970 Independent & Lagged
Spatial Characteristics			
Percent Farm to Rural Population	−.216 (−.031)	−.235 (−.065)	−.017 (−.004)*
Percent Urban	.155 (.013)	.029 (.003)*	−.009 (−.001)*
Metro Proximity	−.234 (−.001)	−.214 (−.002)	−.105 (−.001)
Northeast	.050 (.003)*	−.019 (−.002)*	.070 (.006)
Eastern Mountains	.007 (.000)*	.061 (.005)	.050 (.004)
Central U.S.	.125 (.006)	−.090 (−.007)	−.107 (−.008)
West	.216 (.015)	.029 (.003)*	−.039 (−.004)
Percent Unemployed	NA	NA	.537 (.774)
Intercept	.000 (.075)	.000 (.107)	.000 (.049)
R^2	.320	.477	.636

[a]Unstandardized coefficients are in parentheses.
*Not significant at p ≤ .05.

to metro areas continued to have lower unemployment over the decade. The urban Northeast, as would be expected, had the greatest growth in unemployment. Finally, it should be noted that for every one percent rise in the 1970 unemployment rate, the 1980 rate rises by .77 percent, indicating that prior unemployment rates have a large impact on future employment potentials.

Education

The effects of economic structure on education are similar for both cross-sectional models (Table 6.7). Core and peripheral employment are not significantly different in their impact, while state employment raises education compared to both sectors. Again, the effects of the state sector may reflect job structure or service outlays or a combination of both, since the proportion of the labor force in educational industries is a component of the state sector. Greater establishment size is related to higher education in 1970 but is not significant in 1980. There are no significant differences among the farm indicators, although larger family farming has a slight negative relationship to education in both models. Greater unionization, higher AFDC payments, a lower nonwhite population, and lower unemployment increase levels of schooling. This suggests that traditional human capital attempts to upgrade local educational levels might be more successful if forms of worker power were increased. Education is higher in counties with a greater urban, more centrally located, nonfarm population. Regional differences are also evident, with the largest and most consistent differences seen in the Eastern Mountains region, whose populaton has significantly less education than the Southeast.

The longitudinal model shows that counties with greater peripheral employment and with larger business establishments in 1970 experienced declines in education, while 1970 levels of state employment had little effect on educational change. For the farm indicators, only counties with more smaller family farming had significant educational change, in this case, increases in educational levels. This suggests that smaller family farming has some benefits to localities. Education may increase in counties with a greater extent of smaller family farming because such farming is more integreated into urban networks and services, making schooling more accessible and necessary for employment. The relationships between education and levels of income transfers and unemployment are similar to those found in the cross-sectional models, while those for unionization and percent nonwhite are no longer significant. Counties in the Southeast (as compared to the rest of the nation) experienced educational gains over the decade.

In Summary: The effects of the Independent Variables
On Education and Unemployment

The analyses show that economic structure and other county characteristics have somewhat different effects on education and unemployment than on income related indicators of inequality. Core and peripheral employment differ little in their effects on unemployment. State sector employment is also related to higher county educational attainments compared to the other two sectors. Smaller family farming is related to higher unemployment; larger family farming is related to lower unemployment. There is no consistent relationship between unemployment and industrialized farming. The farm structure indicators had little impact on education. Greater unionization and higher transfer payments tended to raise unemployment while higher education and a lower nonwhite population lowered it. Educational attainments were higher in counties with greater unionization, higher transfer levels, lower unemployment, and a smaller nonwhite population. In sum, the models show that economic structure and worker power characteristics affect local educational attainments and levels of unemployment. This suggests that programs and policies to raise education or lower unemployment will not be successful unless the structural antecedents of these conditions are likewise addressed.

FARMING AND INDUSTRY STRUCTURE AND INFANT MORTALITY AMONG COUNTIES

This section extends the analysis of inequality by providing and testing a conceptual model of how current patterns of farming and industry shape health-related conditions. Social scientists rarely focus on the consequences of farming and industry structure for local health levels. Likewise, health area researchers consider farming and industry mainly as these relate to occupational health and epidemiological hazards. They have largely neglected an alternative way in which farming and industry structure can affect levels of health, that is, through the local socioeconomic order. This is a serious oversight, since the relationship between industrial and farm structure and local health conditions has become increasingly critical: current economic restructuring may affect the quality and quantity of health services available in an area as well as the resources individuals have for meeting health needs (Hosokawa, 1986; Miller, 1985). Infant mortality is an important health indicator and an actual measure of a population's ability to reproduce itself.[8] Infant mortality rates in the United States exceed those of nearly all developed nations, a reflection of inequities in structure of economic opportunity and a medical system that fully serves only those with the ability to pay.

A Conceptual Model of Infant Mortality

Several major ways in which economic structure may impact infant mortality are examined. First, because farming and industry have been shown to directly influence local socioeconomic conditions, they may likewise have direct effects on infant mortality. Second, farming and industry structure may affect infant mortality indirectly via their effects on stratification-related inequalities. Indicators

TABLE 6.7

Regressions of Median Education on Farm and Industry Structure and Other County Characteristics[a]

Independent Variables	1970 Cross Section	1980 Cross Section	1980 with 1970 Independent & Lagged
Industry Structure			
Percent in Peripheral Employment	.010 (.128)*	−.004 (−.047)*	−.041 (−.361)
Percent in State Employment	.112 (2.933)	.110 (2.061)	−.015 (−.265)*
Establishment Size	.103 (.040)	.008 (.003)*	−.074 (−.020)
Farm Structure			
Smaller Family Farming	−.020 (−.003)*	.020 (.002)*	.041 (.004)
Larger Family Farming	−.026 (−.004)*	−.040 (−.004)*	−.024 (−.002)*
Industrialized Farming	.027 (.004)*	−.014 (−.001)*	−.022 (−.002)*
Worker Power Characteristics			
Percent Unionized	.121 (1.697)	.177 (2.135)	−.001 (−.012)*
Per Captia AFDC Payments	.226 (.018)	.252 (.008)	.086 (.005)
Percent Nonwhite	−.261 (−2.371)	−.202 (−1.307)	.014 (.088)*
Percent Unemployed	−.184 (−11.055)	−.275 (−7.974)	−.036 (−1.510)

TABLE 6.7 continued

Independent Variables	1970 Cross Section	1980 Cross Section	1980 with 1970 Independent & Lagged
Spatial Characteristics			
Percent Farm to Rural Population	−.138 (−1.206)	−.102 (−.818)	−.042 (−.258)
Percent Urban	.181 (.885)	.131 (.444)	−.035 (−.118)
Metro Proximity	.054 (.018)	.084 (.019)	.032 (.007)
Northeast	−.008 (−.029)*	−.089 (−.229)	−.083 (−.215)
Eastern Mountains	−.281 (−.927)	−.257 (−.588)	−.056 (−.128)
Central U.S.	.185 (.560)	.029 (.060)*	−.038 (−.080)*
West	.084 (.346)	−.013 (−.037)*	−.070 (−.201)
Median Education	NA	NA	.767 (.533)
Intercept	.000 (9.623)	.000 (11.018)	.000 (6.159)
R^2	.586	.387	.602

[a]Unstandardized coefficients are in parentheses.
*Not significant at p ≤ .05.

commonly used to represent socioeconomic positions or levels, such as income, education, and poverty status (Gortmaker, 1979; Pampel and Pillai, 1986; Wicks and Stockwell, 1984; Farmer et al., 1984; Markides and McFarland, 1982), are related consistently to infant mortality. According to Gortmaker (1979), low income may affect the prenatal behavior of the mother, for example, by reducing the quality of her nutritional intake or by making it difficult for her to secure prenatal care. These factors are related to a greater risk of low birth weight, a major contributor to infant mortality. Low income also may increase environmental hazards for infants and constrain parental protection of offspring. Such hazards and constraints "can emerge in the form of inferior housing, poor sanitary facilities at home, lack of adequate food and clothing, inadequate hospital or postnatal care, [and] lack of transportation facilities..." (Gortmaker, 1979:285). Financial problems also are linked to increased family stress levels, which may adversely impact the quality of parental care. Educational levels reflect life-style and knowledge of health practices and health service utilization, which may decline with lower levels of schooling (Gortmaker, 1979; Hollingsworth, 1986).

Finally, farming and industry structure may influence infant mortality via their effect on other local characteristics that have been linked to infant mortality. Studies in the Goldschmidt (1978a) tradition have found lower numbers or quality of community services associated with larger farms (Fujimoto, 1977; Swanson, 1980), which suggests that farm structure may impact health care sevices. State employment is both an indicator of local income levels and service outlays, so that areas with greater state employment should have greater available health services. The relationship between health care services and health status, however, has been debated. Hollingsworth (1986:184) notes that one set of literature argues that greater access to health resources will result in better health status, while another argues that health outcomes are influenced less by access and more by social structural factors such as class and race. Although researchers generally hypothesize that greater access to health care lowers mortality (Pampel and Pillai, 1986), there have been divergent findings. Some studies have found that physician availability is not associated with improvements in infant mortality (Farmer et al., 1984) or general health (Fuchs, 1984), while rural health care programs have been associated with infant mortality reductions (Farmer et al., 1984).

Studies in the Goldschmidt tradition also argue that industrialized farms disrupt the social integration of the community (Goldschmidt, 1978a; Martinson et al., 1976; Poole, 1981). Teenage fertility reflects social disruption via family instability (Wilson and Neckerman, 1986). Since teenage pregnancy disrupts the stability of individual families, a high incidence of this in a community disrupts society as well. Mortality rates are higher for infants born to younger mothers as such infants are more likely to have low birth weight (Markides and McFarland, 1982). Also, socioeconomic conditions of teenage mothers make it difficult for them to care for infants. These mothers are often unmarried; their education has been interrupted; they have difficulties finding employment; and they seldom receive child support (Wilson and Neckerman, 1986). Extending the Goldschmidt hypothesis, then, large farms may disrupt community social integration as indicated by teenage fertility and thereby indirectly increase infant mortality. Poor economic conditions also have been related to family instability and in turn to infant mortality (Wilson and Neckerman, 1986), so that industry and farm structures that offer better economic opportunities should contribute to lower teenage fertility.

In addition to farm and industry structure, worker power and spatial characteristics are also assumed to affect infant mortality, socioeconomic levels, and mortality related factors. As shown in the previous analyses and confirmed in numerous other studies, worker power and spatial characteristics affect income and educational attainments. Indicators of worker power and spatial characteristics have also been associated with infant mortality and mortality related factors. Areas with lower unemployment (Gortmaker, 1979) and higher white populations (Rosenblatt and Moscovice, 1982; Smith, 1982) tend to have lower infant mortality, and both unemployment and nonwhite race/ethnicity have been associated with higher teenage fertility and other familial disruptions (Wilson and Neckerman, 1986). Widespread popular and academic debate surrounds the topic of the relationship between AFDC benefit levels and out-of-wedlock births. The traditional, politically conservative stance is articulated by Murray (1984) who argues that higher AFDC benefits are an incentive for lower class women to bear children and avoid marriage. In contrast, an extensive review of studies on this issue concludes "that welfare receipt or benefit levels have no effect on the incidence of out-of-wedlock births" (Wilson and Neckerman, 1986:251).

Finally, spatial characteristics, such as greater urbanization and metropolitan adjacency and location outside the South and Appalachian areas tend to be associated with better health status and lower infant mortality (Clifford and Brannon, 1985; Ross et al., 1979; Smith, 1982). Less centrally located areas, particularly farming locales, and areas with potentially poorer ancillary (e.g., educational) institutions are also less attractive to higher level health service workers, such as physicians (Langwell et al., 1985).

A causal model of the relationship between farm and industry structure and infant mortality is shown in Figure 6.1. Causal analysis demonstrates the linkages among a set of variables that are assumed to affect a dependent variable, in this case, infant mortality. I expect that four sets of exogenous (antecedent) independent variables, farm structure, industry structure, worker power and spatial characteristics, will have direct effects on infant mortality as well as indirect effects through the endogenous (intervening) variables, socioeconomic levels and mortality related factors. To simplify the analysis for the regional variables, I have included a comparison for Southeast Plains and Eastern Mountains with the rest of the nation. Median education and median income represent general socioeconomic levels. I follow the previous analyses by indicating that education influences income, although the obverse relationship is just as plausible (Schiller, 1980). The teenage fertility rate, an indicator of familial disruption, and physicians per capita, an indicator of service availability, represent mortality related factors. The measurement of teenage fertility, physicians per capita, and the three-year average infant mortality rate were described in the previous chapter.

FIGURE 6.1

Model of the Relationship Between Farm and Industry Structure and Infant Mortality

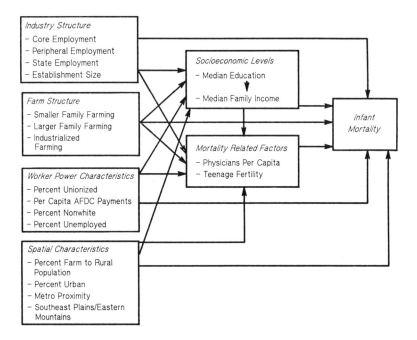

The Analysis

The analysis is based on data for the 1980 period. Because mortality rates may be unstable where incidence is less frequent (Farmer et al., 1984), counties that had fewer than fifteen infant deaths (total) over the three year period from 1978 through 1980 were excluded from the analysis. This resulted in the final selection of 1,440 counties.[9] Path analysis is used to evaluate the expected relationships. This technique involves using a series of regression equations in which independent variables are tested as to their significant, net effects on dependent variables. Path analysis allows examination of direct, indirect, and total effects of an independent variable on a dependent variable. It is particularly appropriate for this analysis, since I expect farm and industry structure to have both direct and indirect impacts on infant mortality. The path analysis employs a fully saturated model in which each exogenous variable impacts each endogenous variable and infant mortality. Only those variables exercising significant effects on the endogenous and dependent variables are included in the final model (Table 6.8).[10]

Statistical relationships and the amount of explained variance in the models for median income and education show marked similarities between these counties and the nation as a whole in 1980. Greater state employment, unionization, and AFDC levels, a smaller nonwhite and higher urban population, lower unemployment, and greater metropolitan proximity significantly raise educational levels. In contrast, no significant relationships with education are found for the farm variables or for the other worker power and spatial variables. The independent variables also have relationships with median income identical to those in the national model, and here the Southeast Plains and Eastern Mountains are shown to have significantly lower income than the rest of the nation.

The model for teenage fertility explains almost 70 percent of the variance in this variable. In contrast to expectations, both peripheral and state employment directly lower fertility to a small degree relative to the core. While the reason for this relationship is unclear, it indicates that familial disruptions are somewhat greater in the social milieu of heavily industrialized environments. It should also be noted that core employment lowers teenage fertility relative to the two other sectors, indirectly through its positive relationship with median family income. When indirect effects are taken into account, the total effects of the state and peripheral employment are small, only about half those of the direct effects.[11] Smaller family farming reduces teenage fertility while there is no direct relationship between teenage fertility and larger family farming. As the Goldschmidt literature would suggest, counties with a greater extent of industrialized farming have significantly higher teenage fertility, indicating the presence of a farming pattern disruptive to family stability.

Other significant relationships indicate that where the population has less access to resources for meeting consumption needs and to channels of power and influence, teenage fertility is higher: in counties with lower unionization and welfare benefits, a greater nonwhite population, lower income, higher unemployment, and in the Southeast Plains/Eastern Mountains, historically more rigidly stratified and poorer areas. Interestingly, although it is often argued that better education among the lower and working class is needed to reduce births to teenagers, there is no significant relationship at least between general education and teenage fertility once income levels and other variables are controlled. The largest coefficient in this model is for the relationship between higher AFDC rates and lower teenage fertility. This relationship seriously challenges the political right's arguments that a punitive welfare system is needed to reduce out-of-wedlock

TABLE 6.8

Path Coefficients (betas) for Variables Included in the Final Model of Farm and Industry Structure and Infant Mortality

Independent Variables	Dependent Variables				
	Median Education	Median Family Income	Teenage Fertility	Physicians Per Capita	Infant Mortality
Industry Structure					
Percent in Peripheral Employment	---[a]	-.212	-.088	.164	---
Percent in State Employment	.184[b]	-.100	-.058	.160	-.085
Establishment Size	---	.108	---	.112	---
Farm Structure					
Smaller Family Farming	---	-.149	-.089	---	-.066
Larger Family Farming	---	.116	---	---	-.113
Industrialized Farming	---	---	.128	---	---
Worker Power Characteristics					
Percent Unionized	.182	.092	-.159	---	---
Per Capita AFDC Payments	.176	.212	-.323	.162	-.075
Percent Nonwhite	-.208	-.075	.226	---	.418
Percent Unemployed	-.241	-.283	.116	-.139	---

TABLE 6.8 continued

			Dependent Variables		
Independent Variables	Median Education	Median Family Income	Teenage Fertility	Physicians Per Capita	Infant Mortality
Spatial Characteristics					
Percent Farm to Rural Population	----	-.074	----	-.160	.185
Percent Urban	.212	.071	----	.263	-.127
Metro Proximity	.077	.315	----	----	----
Southeast Plains/ Eastern Mountains	----	-.079	.104	----	----
Socioeconomic Levels					
Median Education	----	.173	----	.112	-.112
Median Family Income	NA	NA	-.259	----	-.121
Mortality Related Factors					
Teenage Fertility	NA	NA	NA	NA	.075[c]
Physicians Per Capita	NA	NA	NA	NA	----
R^2	.397	.773	.674	.259	.502

[a] Denotes a variable that has no significant effect and hence is not included in the final model.
[b] Unless other wise indicated, all variables are significant at $p \le .01$.
[c] Significant at $p \le .02$.

births. The analysis supports the contentions of Wilson and Neckerman (1986) that teenage fertility is less related to factors that encourage births than to factors actively discouraging women from having unwanted births; that is, opportunities for higher income and employment are incentives for avoiding pregnancy and the disruption it causes in teenagers' lives.

Counties with greater peripheral and state employment have a higher rate of physicians per capita. The presence of state employment indicates educational and public administrative institutions that bear an ancillary relationship to health service practitioners. The relationship between peripheral employment and physicians per capita is likely due to the association of the latter with health services, considered part of the peripheral sector. None of the indicators of farm structure are associated significantly with this variable. Counties with higher education and welfare benefits, lower unemployment, and lower farm and rural populations have greater physicians per captia. Such findings correspond to those of Langwell et al. (1985): the location of physicians does not depend on the health needs of certain areas. Rather, in a for-profit medical system, physicians and health services are generally situated where patient profits can be more easily turned over, such as in urban rather than rural areas and in more economically viable areas. Physicians also tend to locate in faster growing, less agricultural areas offering educational institutions and attractive living conditions (Langwell et al., 1985), which may lead them to bypass highly industrialized, core employment areas as well.

The economic structure, worker power, spatial, and mortality related variables explain about half of the variation in county infant mortality rates. Infant mortality is affected by a combination of structural factors related to child and maternal care. Counties with greater state employment and both smaller and larger family farming have lower infant mortality. Counties with better worker power resources in the form of higher levels of income transfers and a lower nonwhite population, and counties whose residents are in better socioeconomic positions (indicated by both education and median income) have significantly lower infant mortality. These findings support studies (Farmer et al., 1984; Pampel and Pillai, 1986; Wicks and Stockwell, 1984) reporting an inverse relationship between socioeconomic levels and infant mortality. Local socioeconomic conditions circumscribe mothers' ability to secure prenatal care and adequate nutrition and the context of early infant care. Racial differences reflect persistent inequities in health, particulary prenatal, care, family stability, and numerous other resources that have led historically to higher infant mortality among nonwhites. Where the state is less supportive of the reproduction of the work force as indicated by lower income transfers, infant mortality is also greater.

Counties with a higher farm population and more rural population have higher infant mortality. This is consistent with much of the literature on spatial inequities in health care and status. The demographic and socioeconomic characteristics of the rural population, coupled with the limited availability of health services, places rural localities' health status at greater risk (Rosenblatt and Moscovice, 1982; Wright and Lick, 1986). Rural residents tend to be older, poorer, and less educated than those in urban areas. Other studies have found that rural areas have poorer health status compared to urban areas on a number of frequently employed indicators: rural areas have higher infant and maternal mortality (Rosenblatt and Moscovice, 1982:587), higher crude death rates in some states, and equal or higher rates of serious chronic health conditions (Wright and Lick, 1986:462). Although rural areas have experienced no shortage of hospital beds as a consequence of postwar Hill—Burton legislation (Hollingsworth, 1986), they experience large inequities in health care, including the distribution of physicians, registered nurses, federal health payment outlays, and long-term care for the elderly (Farmer et al., 1984; Wright and Lick, 1986). Health services were more evenly distributed over rural areas in the past but have become increasingly concentrated in urban areas, particularly since the 1980s.

Of the two mortality related factors only teenage fertility significantly affects infant mortality. The findings thus seem to support empirical and conceptual literature indicating that physician availability and access to health resources are relatively less important than social structural factors (e.g., stratification position or race) in predicting health status (Hollingsworth, 1986; Farmer et al., 1984). Lower teenage fertility indicates a more stable child rearing context and lower family stress from early parenthood and limited family resources, which reduces infant mortality.

Path analysis shows how intervening variables modify the effects of the farm and industry structure. Peripheral employment has only an indirect effect on infant mortality through its negative relationsip with median income and teenage fertility (the physicians per capita variable is not included in the infant mortality model). When the various paths through these intervening variables are calculated, the total effect of peripheral employment is to raise infant mortality slightly (.023) relative to the core. This total effect results largely from peripheral employment's negative relationship to family income. State employment has a direct effect of (−.085) in reducing infant mortality and many smaller effects through education, median family income, and teenage fertility. When these indirect paths are included, the total effect of state employment is to reduce infant mortality (−.101) relative to the core. Smaller family farming lowers infant mortality directly and indirectly through teenage fertility but raises infant mortality indirectly through its negative relationship with income. The total effect of smaller family farming is to reduce infant mortality slightly (−.052). Larger family farming reduces infant mortality directly and indirectly via median family income and via median family income's relationship to fertility. When these paths are calculated, the total effect of larger family farming is to reduce infant mortality (−.129).

Finally, the total effect of industrialized farming, all of which is indirect through teenage fertility, is positive but virtually negligible (.010).

In Summary: The Effects of Farm and Industry Structure on Infant Mortality

This analysis develops a conceptual model in which patterns of farming and industry structure are expected to affect infant mortality directly, as well as indirectly, through their impact on county socioeconomic status and mortality related factors. Although the model explains a good deal of the variance, one limitation is the inability to include all of the relevant mechanisms by which farm and industry structure could affect infant mortality.[12] The analysis finds support for many of the expected relationships.

Counties with a greater extent of smaller family farming have lower teenage fertility and lower infant mortality. This supports the traditional Goldschmidt hypothesis that smaller units are related to greater community well-being. However, the beneficial effect of smaller units does not extend directly to economic well-being as smaller family farming is related to significantly lower income. It appears, then, that counties with a greater extent of smaller family farming have achieved the social conditions, low teenage fertility, conducive to lower infant mortality without concomitant high income levels.

Counties with a greater extent of larger family farming have higher median income and lower infant mortality. In contrast to expectations, however, larger family farming displays no significant direct relationship with education, teenage fertility, and physicians per capita, indicating that such counties do not possess other characteristics related to lower infant mortality. Counties with greater larger family farming appear less well linked to the institutions and services that could reduce infant deaths. Langwell et al. (1985), for example, found that physicians tend not to locate in areas where most of the population is engaged in farming. Educational expenditures per pupil and levels of schooling are also lower in such areas, the latter in part a consequence of out-migration of the better educated rural population (Seninger and Smeeding, 1981).

Industrialized farming is related significantly to only one variable, teenage fertility. Because higher teenage fertility is, in turn, related to higher infant mortality, industrialized farming contributes indirectly (and in a very small way) to the infant mortality process.

The three industrial sectors differentially affect infant mortality and mortality related factors. Counties with greater state employment have significantly higher education, lower teenage fertility, a greater number of physicians per capita, and lower infant mortality. Although state employment directly contributes to lower median family income, total effects on infant mortality remain negative. These results indicate that state employment reduces infant mortality largely through its effect on nonincome mortality related factors. Service outlays and ancillary health and educational institutions are resources provided by the state that may lower the infant mortality rate. Counties with greater peripheral employment have significantly lower income, lower teenage fertility, and higher per capita physicians as compared to the core. As noted previously, the social and economic milieu of highly industrialized core counties appears to raise fertility slightly as well as to lower physicians per capita. However, when the total effects of peripheral employment are calculated, peripheral employment is found to slightly increase infant mortality relative to the core, mainly as a result of its negative reltionship with income.

Among the more interesting findings of this analysis is that counties with higher level of AFDC benefits, lower unemployment, and higher income are related to lower teenage fertility. Births to teenagers are thus reduced when access to employment and income opportunities becomes more equitable. This challenges conservative perspectives by showing that a punitive welfare system does not decrease births to teenagers. And it challenges conventional notions that general education is the main solution to teenage pregnancy.

Finally, the findings have implications for research in community health and in the industrial and agricultural social sciences. This study supports much previous research that has found that persistent inequities due to socioeconomic position, race, regional, and rural location contribute to higher infant mortality (Clifford and Brannon, 1985; Rosenblatt and Moscovice, 1982; Pampel and Pillai, 1986; Farmer et al., 1984; Gortmaker, 1979). Unlike previous studies, however, I attempt to link the types of economic structures present in a locality with mortality rates. Industrial and farm structure affect the structure of local social relations, thereby shaping income, educational, and related conditions. A dramatic and tragic consequence of the social order is the higher infant mortality rate of those groups on the lowest rungs of the stratification hierarchy.

CONCLUSIONS

The relationships described in the previous analyses represent national patterns among counties during the 1970-1980 period. Although the data permit broad generalization, they present limitations as well. First, the use of secondary data necessarily constrains the study to specific time points and to indicators that may not fully capture the complexity of concepts. Second, while the county has been used as a unit of analysis in numerous tests of the Goldschmidt hypothesis and in labor market research, as any unit of higher aggregation, it may obscure variations between less aggregated units such as communities. Finally, the findings must be regarded as historically specific, national averages rather than as constant across time periods and within each section of the county. The next chapter addresses the latter limitation by examining differences between various agricultural regions.

One of the most consistent findings of this study is that larger family farming contributes to better economic conditions, including higher and more equitably distributed incomes and lower unemployment. In addition, this farming pattern is associated both directly and indirectly with lower infant mortality. Comparison of these results with those of other studies requires consideration of the salient indicators of this farming pattern. Larger family farming represents capital-intensive, part-owner and tenant operated farming employing little hired labor and conducted in counties with much of their land in farming. This farming pattern is not simple commodity production in the sense that operators own all production factors. Rather, it relects the differentiation of simple commodity producers by the market economy. Though the dimensions of farm structure used in this study have not been examined in other tests of the Goldschmidt hypothesis, the findings suggest support for studies reporting positive contributions of nonindustrialized farms using little hired labor.

However, the positive benefits of larger family farming do not extend directly to educational levels or to physicians per capita, which are unrelated to larger family farming. Despite the economic viability of larger family farming counties, higher education and other services appear limited in 1980. It might also be added that such limitations arise precisely out of historically uneven development processes in which a more educated population and better services come to be centered in urban rather land extensive, farming areas.[13]

The hypothesis that smaller family farming improves socioeconomic conditions is generally not supported. Indeed, most findings indicate the reverse relationship: counties with a greater extent of this farming pattern have considerably poorer income levels and distribution at any cross-sectional time point and higher unemployment. The smaller family farming dimension reflects a pattern of concentration of small-scale farms that are owner-operated, used as a home residence, and part-time. Few studies have examined farming patterns at this end of the farm size continuum: Goldschmidt's work has tended to direct discourse and research to the deterimental impacts of large-scale farms. Previous studies examining linear relationships, particularly those whose findings have been mixed, may have overlooked the curvilinear relationships and negative impacts of the smallest farms. This study thus supports Skees and Swanson's (1986) observation that the linear assumption of the Goldschmidt hypothesis requires modification.

Another reason that negative relationships between economic conditions and smaller family farming emerge here but have appeared less frequently in earlier research is because this study has controlled for important intervening (industrial structure and worker power) and antecedent (spatial structure) variables. The relationship between smaller family farming and economic well-being changes from positive to progressively negative when these variables are added to the regression models (Table 6.5). Smaller family farming counties are associated with some beneficial characteristics of industrial employment and worker power and have favorable locational characteristics such as greater urbanization and metropolitan proximity. All of these variables would obscure a negative relationship between smaller family farming and economic well-being if not controlled.

Despite their poorer economic conditions, counties with a greater extent of smaller family farming have slightly lower teenage fertility, lower infant mortality, and greater educational gains over time. Also, counties with greater smaller family farming do not have higher poverty or income inequality over time, although median family income remains low. Smaller family farming counties appear better linked to state institutions and urban consumption and labor markets. Off-farm employment opportunities also give small farm operators access to health insurance coverage and other work benefits that reduce infant mortality.

Small farmers are not a homogeneous group. For some, farming is vital for family subsistence, either in its own right or as supplement to off-farm employment. For others, farming may be more of a hobby, retirement strategy, and/or convenient shelter for nonfarm income. The latter group is often viewed critically by production economists and traditional family operators: such small farmers are seen as opportunistically tapping into the farm programs and tax advantages of 'real farmers' and as gentrifying rural areas. In general, however, the proportion of small operators who actually bask in rural affluence, as indicated by high family income, appears very small during the period of this study. Using data from a national probability sample of 5,700 famers, Carlin and Crecink (1979) show that more than three-quarters of the operators of small farms (those with sales less than $20,000) had total family incomes below the nonmetropolitan median. Total family incomes of small producers are low despite opportunities for off-farm employment. Further, Carlin and Crecink (1979) argue that policy approaches to assisting farmers with low family incomes and farmers with low farm sales need not differ because of the extensive overlap between farmers in each group.

Although this study cannot disentangle variations within smaller family farming, the picture that emerges is consistent with Carlin and Crecink's (1979) observations as well as with theoretical perspectives that decribe the impoverishment of areas dominated by small-holder agriculture. The precise routes by which smaller family farming disadvantages counties cannot be discerned from the analysis but several can be suggested. First, sales from smaller units appear insufficient to support families at adequate consumption levels. Second, higher poverty despite opportunities for off-farm employment (even in core industries) indicates that part-time farmers may help underwrite the social costs of maintaining industry's labor force. That is, as noted previously, employer costs of reproducing the labor force and hence, wages, may be lower because employees can produce food for home or market consumption. Third, higher unemployment in counties with more smaller family farming suggests that this farming retains redundant labor. Smaller family farming may therefore serve an industrial reserve function, allowing employers access to local labor when needed, and enabling industry to offer lower wages because it can draw from a surplus labor pool.

In sum, the findings for unemployment and economic well-being seem to support Kautsky's (1988, Volume 1:190) observations regarding the proletarianization of small producers:

> large-scale industry brings about a deterioration in the labour-power available for the small farm, at the same time as it accelerates the reduction in its size, and as a result, worsens the actual technique of cultivation. And...large-scale capital in rural areas...pushes their [farmer-workers'] exploitation and degradation to the extreme.

The analysis indicates some support for the traditional Goldschmidt hypothesis that industrialized farming leads to poorer socioeconomic conditions. The most consistent support comes from the analysis of income inequality. The longitudinal models of poverty, median family income, and income inequality also show that industrialized farming limits future county economic gains. Industrialized farming is related to lower economic well-being as measured by the pooled index of the three income measures, and the relationships follow the expected direction (but are not significant) in the cross-sectional analyses of poverty and median income. In addition, industrialized farming is disruptive to social integration as indicated by its relationship to teenage fertility. However, most of the previous relationships between industrialized farming and scioeconomic conditions are small; moreover, no significant and/or consistent relationships are found with industrialized farming and unemployment or education.

Considering the long-standing and at least implicit acceptance of the Goldschmidt hypothesis by many researchers, one might question why industrialized farming does not show a stonger negative relationship to well-being as found in Goldschmidt's (1978a) and other (particularly less recent) studies. There are several possible reasons for this. First, postwar changes such as the accelerated decline of farming, growth of manufacturing and service sectors (particularly in rural areas), and alternative forms of state intervention have resulted in a dramatically different political economy than that observed by Goldschmidt in the early 1940s. These changes have undoubtedly mediated some of the negative effects of industrialized farming. For example, opportunities for nonfarm employment provide additional off-farm income and can drive up the wages paid by industrialized farms (Skees and Swanson, 1986). Higher AFDC benefits are a nonmarket source of income and can supplement earnings of seasonal workers. The association of industrialized farming with industrial employment and aspects of worker power such as higher AFDC payments and slightly higher unionization rates (see Chapter 8) also suggest that localities make structural adjustments to such farming. Social welfare policies and support for labor organizations in particular reflect conscious, political efforts among state and local populations to counter the destabilizing effects of industrialized farming and other low income employment.

A second issue is that the nature of industrialized farming itself has undergone change since the time of Goldschmidt. Large farms have become more capital intensive, and there is evidence, from California citrus farms for example, that some seasonal jobs are converting into longer-term employment (Fritsch, 1984). Successful organizing attempts, such as those of the United Farm Workers Union, and coalitions between farm worker and consumer/environmental groups over pesticides and other agricultural issues, strengthen the power of farm workers to demand better job conditions. Should industrialized farming become more rationalized and labor more organized, wages and job conditions may begin to approach those in nonfarm, large-scale industry.

Finally, methodological issues may affect the findings. It can be difficult to discern the negative effects of industrialized farming in a national analysis that uses county-level data. Although industrialized farming is present throughout the country, it is more concentrated in the West and parts of the South; regionally specific analyses, such as those presented in the next chapter, might better illuminate the effects of such farming. But even here the use of county level data can still obscure relationships between less aggregated units such as towns. This is particularly true for West and Southwestern counties, which are much larger in land area than counties in other parts of the nation. Relatedly, because farm labor may be migrant or may not reside in the county where industrialized farming is present, the full negative effects of industrialized farming may be obscured. This issue probably has little effect on the national relationships as the number of migrants is small (an estimated 200,000 during the 1970s), constituting at most about 8 percent of the farm labor force (Holt, 1984:23). Goldschmidt (1978a) also confronted this issue in the analysis of Arvin and Dinuba as both communities used migrant laborers. He argued that the effects of industrialized farming were not to be evidenced just in the low quality of life of the farm labor force but spilled over to the resident workforce as well as to community institutions and services.

Capital's power and labor's resistance become embodied in industrial structures that influence the level of local inequality. In counties with more core employment, employers have greater need and ability to support a labor force at higher levels of consumption. Such counties have higher median family income, a lower poverty level, and lower income inequality. In contrast, counties with greater peripheral and state employment have poorer income levels and distribution. As noted previously, peripheral employment is more labor intensive and lower profit, making it more difficult for employers to respond to wage demands. Workers are also less organized in this sector. The magnitude of the differences between the state and periphery indicates that the two sectors have relatively similar impacts. The relationships for state employment and income levels and distribution vary from earlier conceptual and empirical research on the segmented economy but tend to support recent studies, particularly those using aggregate rather than individual data. Core and peripheral employment also display similar impacts on county unemployment rates, supporting recent revisions of segmented economy theory regarding unemployment (Schervish, 1983).

This study extends segmented economy perspectives by examining extra-economic indicators of inequality or those related but less reducible to economic structure. The analyses show that segmented economy assumptions are not directly transferable to these other aggregate indicators. For example, core employment is not related to higher educational attainments. Nor does it directly diminish familial disruptions as indicated by teenage fertility or lower infant mortality. However, the higher and more equitably distributed income levels that the core does bring to localities are essential preconditions for each one of these.

The relationships between employment in the state sector and local inequality are particularly intriguing and generally have not been explored in previous studies. State employment is related to significantly poorer income and greater income inequality as compared to the core. Counties with a greater proportion of state employment have higher unemployment, in contrast to expectations, but also higher education and physicians per capita. State employment also directly lowers teenage fertility and infant mortality. These relationships show that while state employment does not contribute to overall higher, more evenly distributed incomes as productive employment in the core would, it results in significant improvements in health, education, and social integration and thus ameliorates some noneconomic inequities.

In order to understand these relationships, the following issues merit consideration. First, state employment impacts county inequality in two major ways, through the positions and associated wages it generates and through the provision of state services. In studies that examine the effects of the state sector on the earnings of its employees, the first impact can be delineated. But in studies that examine aggregate effects, the two impacts are interrelated. Simply put, the state must fund employment positions in order to implement its various programs and services. In general (and with certain exceptions such as government capitals, military bases, and ordnance centers) a locality's dependence on local, state, and federal government funding will be reflected in the size of its administrative bureaucracy (Gurr and King, 1987). Recent studies dispute the benefits of state employment by showing that the state sector is characterized by a high proportion of secondary, low-wage jobs and high minority and female employment (Sheets et al., 1987; Fligstein, 1983). The relationships between state employment and poorer income conditions both cross-sectionally and over time appear more reflective of the state's impact via its employment structure rather than service outlays.[14]

In contrast, the few studies examining unemployment have rather consistently shown that unemployment is lowest in the state sector. I therefore attribute the positive relationship between state employment and unemployment found only in the cross-sectional model (indicating that the state did not produce unemployment over time) more to a service response of the state. This is further supported by an analysis which shows that counties with higher unemployment in 1970 have higher state employment in 1980, indicating that unemployment is followed by an expansion of jobs in the state sector.

Gurr and King (1987) provide additional insight as to how state employment and local economic well-being are related. They argue that there is a tendency for national, regional, and local governments to allocate fiscal resources (for employment, transfer payments, private sector contracts and other programs and services) to declining localities. These allocations tend to stabilize decline (e.g., unemployment, poverty, deteriorating services), but in the process, local political autonomy may be jeopardized; moreover, state investment often fails to stimulate the high wage, private sector. In the attempt to attract private business, localities are compelled to provide ever growing incentives, which may contribute to further decline and another round of state investment. To the extent that the state begins to assume responsiblity for local well-being, the economic base of a locality shifts from dependence on the private sector to the public. Greater dependence on the state for employment or services, with the few exceptions noted above, would thus seem to be related to poorer economic conditions.

I also find that the power of workers influences the levels at which they are able to reproduce themselves. The indicators of worker power are related to income levels and distribution generally as expected. There is some indication that unions, income transfers and education had diminished capacity to shelter workers from market exigencies over the 1970s and that more unionized areas had slightly higher income disparities. Worker power variables also have significant relationships with education, indicating that in order to increase educational levels, localities should bolster income transfers and policies to sustain lower unemployment. Higher AFDC payments particularly benefit localities by raising educational levels and lowering teenage fertility and infant mortality. The worker power variables have a somewhat different relationship with unemployment (as a dependent variable) than they do with other indicators of socioeconomic conditions. Areas with greater unionization have higher unemployment cross-sectionally and over time. This may reflect the fact that unionized workers are more subject to lay-offs. However, viewed over time it suggests that capital reduces employment opportunities when worker organizations become too strong. Higher AFDC payments also appear to slightly withhold redundant labor from the market. Finally, counties with a higher nonwhite population consistently have lower socioeconomic conditions on virtually all indicators, indicating the persistence of racial and ethnic inequities.

In examining county spatial and locational characteristics, I find that rural areas (notably those most distant from metropolitan centers) are poorer. This illustrates the persistence of uneven economic development over time. However, it is worth noting that when the quality of the county industrial base and aspects of worker power are controlled, other U.S. regional differences diminish. This suggests that differences in economic inequality historically regarded to be a consequence of 'regional culture' or ecology were actually more a consequence of regional political economy or of the balance of power between capital and labor embodied in a particular area.

A final point is the adequacy of the proposed conceptual model for the explanation of inequality. I have argued that local levels of inequality are a function of the conflicting relationship between capital and labor over the conditions and terms of employment and, in the case of farming, over relationships of exchange in land, capital, and employment markets. In addition to economic structure, human action as evidenced in the power of workers plays a part in mediating inequality. Finally, spatial characteristics confine economic structures and worker power to certain localities and regions and reflect historical characteristics that reach into the present. In a statistical sense, the conceptual models presented 'explain' most of the variation in levels of income and distribution and a substantial amount in the indicators of unemployment, education, social disruption, and health. Ultimately, however, the adequacy of any model of inequality depends not on explained variance but on the insights it sheds in interpreting present conditions and in the strategies it offers for achieving social justice.

Local Inequality: Regional Comparisons

The preceding chapter examined the effects of economic structure, worker power, and spatial characteristics on socioeconomic inequality at the national level, providing general support for the conceptual framework articulated in this book. The long-standing argument that industrialized farms contribute to poorer socioeconomic conditions was given some support, while the converse relationship that family farming benefits localities was qualified and extended. Differences within family farming were shown to affect localities, with larger rather than smaller family farming improving socioeconomic conditions.

This chapter continues the discussion of the previous issues by addressing inequality at the regional level. I focus on two questions. First, do the national average relationships for farm structure described in the preceding chapter differ from region to region? Second and more broadly, how relevant is the conceptual model of inequality across different regional settings? To explore these questions, theoretical issues involved in interregional studies are first discussed. I review the general perspectives that have emerged to account for regional disparities in economic structure and socioeconomic conditions and outline specific reasons as to why the impacts of farm structure may vary spatially. I then analyze empirically the effects of farm structure and other county characteristics in the five major national regions, those areas sharing similarities in agriculture and other economic activities, climate, history, and physiography. Finally, detailed regional analyses focusing on more homogeneous agricultural commodity areas are presented.

Regional comparisons of social structural relationships are important for several reasons. First, they illuminate general processes of social change. National social structural changes, such as the restructuring of agriculture and industry do not have uniform effects over all areas of the country because of the prior unevenness of development. Regions represent an amalgamation of characteristics that mediate wider, societal processes. Relatedly, understanding regional differences is important for policy formulation. As regions are characterized by different proportions of rich and poor, farm and nonfarm people, economic structures, and so forth, covering all areas under the same tax, agricultural, or other federal policy inherently benefits certain regions over others. Differences in location are also a potential reason for divergent findings about the Goldschmidt hypothesis. Regional analyses demonstrate whether or not the effects of farm structure are spatially invariant, thereby contributing to a resolution of the Goldschmidt debate. Finally, with the exception of the Office of Technology Assessment studies (Swanson, 1988) and studies limited to a few select areas (Gilles and Dalecki, 1988), there are no regionally comparative tests of the Goldschmidt hypothesis. The present study offers the first view of relationships that are directly comparable across major U.S. regions.

THEORETICAL PERSPECTIVES ON REGIONAL ECONOMIC DISPARITIES

Regional variations in economic structures, whether in the farm or nonfarm sector, and in socioeconomic conditions are complex and still poorly understood by social scientists. Classical economic perspectives as well as early Marxian perspectives focused on the uniformity of the development process and the reduction of regional differentials over time. Contemporary social scientists recognize the unevenness of the development process but debate its fundamental causes, temporal persistence, and benefits to society. The current literature on interregional differentials can be characterized by two contrasting approaches each with an extensive and diverse literature: the neoclassical and structural/political economy.

The Neoclassical Perspective

The neoclassical economic perspective "is based upon assumptions of economic rationality amongst entrepreneurs who seek an optimal location defined in terms of a single criterion, or on the basis of trade-offs between several criteria" (Lever, 1985:11). This perspective argues that enterprises are located where they can best maximize profits: where they are best able to utilize available productive resources, such as land, labor, and capital and where they can capture appropriate markets.[1] Regional differentials in the location of firms and industries are seen as functional for society as well as for business because they reflect the optimal allocation of market forces. At least implicit in the neoclassical argument is a symbiotic relationship between capital and labor, that a growth in profits for capital means an increase in wages and living standards for workers. To the extent that resources, such as characteristics of labor supply (levels of education or skill) and location to markets, fail to match up with the exigencies of capital, regional imbalances, such as impoverishment in some areas and affluence in others, may exist. However, such imbalances are thought to be relatively impermanent and do not reflect the normal operation of the economic system. Rather, factors of production are seen to adjust geographically in a somewhat automatic fashion. For example, labor migration from areas of labor surplus to labor deficit is viewed as a relatively routine, unproblematic process. In short, the neoclassical model implies a general tendency toward interregional convergence of income and socioeconomic conditions.

The Structural/Political Economy Perspective

The contrasting structural/political economy perspectives emphasize that entrepreneurial decisions must be viewed in a broader social context "in which the interplay of capital and labor is based upon power coalitions whose interests are usually in conflict" (Lever, 1985:29). Like neoclassical perspectives, structural perspectives recognize that businesses are profit maximizers. However, the particular regional characteristics that allow profit maximization are given different emphasis, and regional imbalances are viewed as pervasive, persistent, and as benefiting mainly segments of capital.

Under the structural/political economy umbrella, there are a variety of perspectives that deal with regional disparities within first world societies. These include: attempts to develop general, abstract laws about the spatial development of the capitalist mode of production; specifying how regionally different modes of production articulate with one another; applications of underdevelopment theory to first world settings; and analyzing spatial differentiation as a historically evolved process emergent from accumulation. For reviews and critiques of these perspectives, see Massey (1978), Markusen (1987), and Brenner (1977).

Viewing regional differences as a consequence of the accumulation process offers a particularly fruitful and dynamic approach that has come to characterize much of the recent literature. A study on regional economic development in the South by Wood (1986) builds squarely upon this approach, derivative from Marxian principles. Wood (1986) argues that the rate of exploitation in the textile industry (the industry most responsible for shaping post-Civil War Southern economic development) was higher in the South than in the North because textile owners took advantage of the preexisting powerlessness of Southern workers in order to extract greater surplus value. Once established, the industry continued to build upon the powerlessness of labor through its control over political and social institutions as well as the wage. As other Southern industries followed the lead of textiles, socioeconomic well-being continued to lag behind the North.

An outpouring of new scholarship by geographers, regional scientists, and economists now focuses on how changes in the accumulation process, nationally and globally, affect the response of capital and labor in particular regions and locales, linking changes in the wider economy to change within component spatial units (Markusen, 1987; Storper and Scott, 1986; Lipietz, 1986; Sayer, 1986; Clark, 1986; Massey, 1984; Storper and Walker, 1984; Bluestone and Harrison, 1982).[2] The movement of capital is seen as a continual search for profit which leaves some areas impoverished and others flourishing, a process which generates:

> spontaneous, unregulated patterns of growth and contraction, which are by their very nature unbalanced...Periodically, of course, crises will occur as barriers to further expansion of accumulation are reached...Hence, it will

become ncessary to restructure production to allow accumulation to pro-
ceed. Crucially for present purposes, this restructuring may involve the
geographical reshaping of productive activity to take advantage of openings
for greater profits (Rees, 1984:31).

Regional disequilibrium is thus viewed as the normal outcome of the operation of the economic system. In contrast to neoclassical perspectives, capital does
not share profits automatically with workers—rather this depends on a variety
of factors that empower labor vis-à-vis capital, such as labor's ability to organize.
In interpreting the locational decisions of capital, political economy stresses labor
force characteristics (e.g. docility, skill levels) over nonlabor characteristics such
as proximity to consumer markets and environmental attributes, which can be
compensated for by technology. The decline of nondurable manufacturing in
Northern cities, for example, is seen to result from the ability of capital to gain
greater mobility over time while labor has remained relatively constrained. The
changing global economy had intensified the movement of firms and industries
since the 1970s. Economic development has become an ephemeral process, with
regions experiencing burst of growth alternated with stagnation. The rapidity and
unpredictability of post-fordist economic change pose a continual challenge to
documenting the factors that make capital mobile and more likely to locate in
certain areas.

FARM STRUCTURE AND SOCIOECONOMIC CONDITIONS: THE REGIONAL QUESTION

Conceptual Issues and Perspectives

The previous perspectives focus on regional differentials in the location
of nonfarm industries and in socioeconomic conditions. Several conceptual issues
make the analysis of regional variations in farming impacts problematic. First,
virtually all research on uneven development in first world societies centers on
nonfarm industries employing wage labor. The regional dynamics of simple commodity units such as family labor farms are not given attention, so there is little
theoretical precedent for describing how their effects might vary interregionally.
Agricultural social scientists also have not focused explicitly on developing
explanations for regional variations in the effects of farm structure: while a few
tests of the Goldschmidt hypothesis document whether or not regional differences
exist, they are less clear in delineating the reasons for such differences.

Another problem is that the biological and ecological requirements of
farming make regional analyses particularly complex. The dynamics of farming
are not only affected by available labor, technology, and input and market location, but also by agroclimatic factors such as soil, rainfall, temperature, and
topography. These factors affect the types of commodities that can be grown in

a particular area and the commodity in turn affects the internal structure of farming units. For example, the longer growing season, sufficient rainfall and fertile soil found in Iowa, Illinois, and Indiana make these states favorable for corn production, which has been produced typically on moderate-size family operated farms. Citrus fruits requiring a milder climate are typically produced by large, industrialized farms of the South and Southwest. Farm structure is thus partly determined by the exigencies of the commodity, and the selection of the commodity is intertwined with ecological and other regional factors.

A third problem noted previously as common to all regional analyses is how to define a region. This is an important issue because the findings of any interregional analysis will be in part a function of the way in which regions are delimited (Fuguitt and Beale, 1978). The literature, particularly on farming, has not evolved to the point where there is consensus about the criteria that should be used to define a region. As a result, researchers delineate regions in different ways, such as by agroclimatic factors (Gilles and Dalecki, 1988), common agrarian and social history (Buttel et al., 1986; Skees and Swanson, 1986), predominate farming type (MacCannell and Dolber-Smith, 1986), combination of farming type/commodity (Flora and Flora, 1986), or, as in this study, by similarities in agricultural and industrial structure, history, and ecology. A related and seldom discussed issue is the appropriate scale at which a region should be delineated. Most analysts consider a region as incorporating areas in more than one state, but beyond this the selection of a particular scale appears arbitrary. The various ways of considering regional location in the Goldschmidt studies (see Table 3.1) affect results differentially and make it difficult to compare relationships across settings.

Although there are no clear explanations for interregional variations in the effects of farm structure, two approaches that parallel the previous perspectives on general regional development can be reconstructed from the literature. I term these approaches ecological and structural. The ecological approach shares assumptions about society with neoclassical perspectives. The structural approach shares those of structural/political economy perspectives. The ecological approach stresses adaptation and symbiotic relationships attained through maximizing proper use of environmental resources. The structural approach focues on conflicting social relations, particularly the balance of power between labor and capital, and stresses the importance of labor over other resources.

The Ecological Approach

This approach (Coughenour, 1984; Gilles, 1980; Dunlap and Martin, 1983) argues that particular farm structures develop in specific regions because farmers adapt to the configuration of local resources, such as land, climate, topography, technology and labor. The existence of specific farm structures in a region tends to reflect a functional and symbiotic relationship between people and their environment. The commodity is of interest because regional ecological conditions circumscribe the types of production that may take place. The effects of farm structure on socioeconomic conditions may differ by region because: regions vary by the types of farm production present; and agroclimatic and other ecological features of certain regions influence how adaptive some types of farm structures are. For example, small farms in a dry area requiring much irrigation would be expected to generate lower income than small farms in more fertile areas. Consequently, larger farms using irrigation networks and the latest technology may be the more adaptive form in dry areas. An assumption implicit in the ecological approach is that socioeconomic conditions should be higher in regions where farming units have more appropriately adapted to existing resources.

The Structural Approach

Structural approaches (e.g., Buttel et al., 1986; Flora and Flora, 1986; Goldschmidt, 1978a, 1978b; Harris and Gilbert, 1982; MacCannell and Dolber-Smith, 1986; Reif, 1987) emphasize social relations as the basis of farm impacts while incorporating many of the insights of the ecological perspective. Like the latter, they recognize that ecological conditions circumscribe the types of farm units and the commodities specific to a region. However, with the exception of labor resources, ecological constraints are seen to be of more limited importance and to be diminishing over time as capital circumvents them through technology.

Studies from the structural approach show that ecological and crop-related characteristics help explain why various types of farming might arise initially in certain regions but that wider social relations are generally more determinant of their ultimate form. For example, Wells (1984) argues that the nature of California strawberry production required a fluctuating demand for labor and a quality, skilled labor force. Prior to the mid-1960s, these exigencies were met largely through industrialized, wage-labor production. As the balance of power shifted more to the side of labor during the subsequent period (due to the mobilization of farm workers, lessening of control of employers over farm labor policy, and the role of the state in regulating land and labor) it was more advantageous for larger growers to replace wage labor with sharecropping. Pfeffer (1983) points out that despite widely varied ecological settings and commodity exigencies, wheat production on the Great Plains, cotton production in the South and industrialized farming in California were characterized initially by concentrated landholdings and nonfamily labor. Differential problems of labor recruitment in the first two areas gave rise to the later predominance of family operated units in the Plains and sharecropping in the South. Gilbert and Akor (1988) argue that climatic and topographic factors, population growth, the quality and quantity of local labor, state subsidies, and ethnicity account for divergences in the development of dairying. Larger, industrialized dairy farms have come to predominate in California while smaller, family operated units are found in Wisconsin.

The shape and structure of agriculture in a given region are thus seen to result from the pattern of social relations in an area as well as initial environmental conditions. Extending the argument to examine why the socioeconomic impact of different types of farming might vary interregionally, structural perspectives emphasize the nature of social relations in the wider, nonfarm economy. As noted earlier, factors such as unionization, labor laws favorable to hired workers, nonlabor market guarantees (such as welfare and food stamps) and nonfarm employment empower labor and supplement income thereby mediating the effects of farm structure (Skees and Swanson, 1986). This position is generally supported by the empirical analysis in the previous chapter. To the extent that all these factors vary regionally, the same type of farming might have different impacts in different places. Finally, like the ecological approach, structural perspectives also give importance to the commodity. However, the commodity is not of interest in and of itself but rather because it presupposes a particular labor process (and thus internal relations of production) and external relations of exchange (Friedland et al., 1981). Variations in commodities at the regional level are important not so much because they flow from particular ecological circumstances but because they suggest that particular regions will be characterized by particular social relations.[3]

To recapitulate, the ecological and structural perspectives differ in their emphasis of the factors creating interregional variations and in a sense, their underlying view of society. Although I have focused on distinguishing the two approaches, it should also be noted that they overlap on certain issues. For example, social or class relations are easily incorporable in the ecological approach, although they would not be given the primacy accorded in most structural research.

Bases of Regional Variations in Farm Impacts

Why might we anticipate regional variations in the effects of farm structure? The structural and ecological literature provide alternative but general perspectives on this question from which a more coherent set of responses can be drawn. First, as both perspectives recognize, different types of farming units are located in different regions, such as the greater presence of family labor farming in the Midwest and industrialized farming in California and other areas of irrigated agriculture. In addition, there may be differences within farm units themselves that vary regionally. Industrialized farms in California, for example, utilize a more highly skilled, longer-term, organized labor force than industrialized farms in other parts of the county.

Second, a combination of social structural forces and relations at the regional level may affect the ways in which farming influences well-being. These include nonfarm economic structure, labor force characteristics, and the balance of power between labor and capital, given lengthy discussion in previous chapters. In addition, related aspects of social relations, such as political sentiments, traditions of popular activism, and agrarian and social histories vary in different sections of the country. These factors can affect the ability and willingness of a populace to offset potentially destabilizing effects of industrialized farms or alternatively to protect family farming. For example, public sentiment against corporate farming led to the enactment of statutes restricting the activities of this type of farming in ten states, mainly in the Midwest, by 1982 (Krause, 1987). Some states tax farmland owned by nonfamily corporate farms at higher rates than family enterprises. Alternatively, in areas where large farm owners have more political clout or local acquiesence, other restrictions such as acreage limitations on irrigation use may be bypassed, as in the Imperial Valley of California. Laws regulating the organizing ability and conditions of labor likewise vary by state. United Farm Worker pressure in California during the 1970s facilitated passage of legislation supporting farm workers' right to strike, to receive some unemployment insurance, and to outlaw short-handled hoes, which had crippled lettuce workers (Dyson, 1986:334).

Third, factors external to a region in the national and global political economy may affect farm impacts at the regional level. National policy and conditions of the world economy have uneven effects. For example, commodity-specific farm programs tend to benefit some parts of the country over others. Midwestern farms were particularly hard hit during the farm crisis as the rising dollar and other factors dampened global demand for cash grains.

Finally, physical environmental factors also shape the regional dynamics of farming. These include spatial location relative to urban agglomerations and other regions and places—factors discussed in previous chapters—as well as natural resources or elements such as water, minerals, climate and physical landscape. While these factors unquestionably create regional differentials, communication, transportation, and information age computer technology have superceded or reduced many former barriers to marketing, pricing, and input needs of farm production. Likewise, various mechanical and chemical technologies have reduced dependency on agroclimatic factors. Biotechnologies will lessen environmental dependencies even further. Some of these changes have been reflected in the movement of commodities to different areas, such as cotton growing from the deep South to Texas and California and corn production, which now extends to irrigated areas of the high Plains. In sum, like nonfarm industry, the dynamics of farming are becoming less determined by nonhuman environmental factors and more by the balance of social relations at the regional, national and global levels.

The previous factors help clarify the meaning and significance of a region. A region or any other populated areal unit is not merely a surrogate for the type of agricultural commodity grown in an area or agroclimatic measure. Regions reflect spatial forms of human activity, embodying numerous characteristics such as patterns of social relations, location in the national political economy, historical factors as well as nonhuman environment—all of which affect the dynamics of farming and levels of socioeconomic well-being. A drawback to the multiplicity of these conditions is that it is often difficult to discern precisely which ones are responsible for regional variations.[4] On the other hand, comparative regional analyses enable empirical generalizations to be examined under different social contexts. This helps establish the credibility of generalizations or clarifies the contexts under which they are supported. More broadly, by comparing relationships under various settings, regional analyses illuminate the real complexities of social life.

Empirical Evidence for Regional Differentials in Farm Impacts

One of the few sets of studies focusing on regional variations in farming impacts are those commissioned by the Office of Technology Assessment.[5] The studies examine five U.S. agricultural regions for the 1970-1980 period. The relationship between measures of agricultural concentration and rural community conditions in 98 agricultural counties in California, Texas, Arizona, and Florida was investigated by MacCannell and Dolber-Smith (1986). They conclude (1986:59) "with some qualification" that their study "supports Goldschmidt's original large industrial farm/small farm thesis." Flora and Flora (1986) examined 234 agriculturally dependent counties in seventeen states in the Great Plains and West, which were classified by farming system type: wheat, livestock, wheat/livestock, and mixed crops/livestock. For each system, they analyzed the impacts of medium and large size farms on community well-being indicators such as median family income, poverty, housing conditions, and retail trade. Despite the different farming system type, the relationship between farm size and well-being was generally similar: the "economic vitality of the rural community is enhanced by the growth of medium-size farms" (Flora and Flora, 1986:194).

The remaining OTA studies report more divergences from the Goldschmidt hypothesis. Skees and Swanson (1986) studied 706 nonmetropolitan counties in thirteen Southern states, excluding Florida and Texas. Counties with the greatest increases in farm sales over the 1970-1980 period had greater poverty. Other farm structure and community relationships did not consistently support the Goldschmidt hypothesis. An illuminating finding of this study, noted previously, is that a greater number of both large- and small-scale operations contributed to higher unemployment, while a greater number of medium-size farms was associated with lower unemployment.

Van Es et al. analyzed 331 counties in the Corn Belt states grouped by grain, dairy, and mixed grain and livestock farms. In contrast to Goldschmidt, they found that "those counties with relatively stronger presence of larger farms tend to be somewhat better off than those counties where the process of concentration in agriculture has not progressed so far (van Es et al., 1986:551). Moreover, they point out that the impact of farm structure on population and quality of life in the Corn Belt is relatively small when compared to nonfarm employment even in agriculturally dependent counties.

Buttel et al. (1986) examined 105 counties in 17 Northeastern states. Counties where the farm population, proportion of fully owned farms, and total farm sales declined had greater poverty. But changes in farm scale and in the number of incorporated farms had negligible impact on community well-being. As a whole, the farm indicators also explained little of the variation in socioeconomic well-being, leading Buttel et al. (1986) to conclude that socioeconomic well-being is more a function of nonfarm and urban influences than farming.

Another recent study (Gilles and Dalecki, 1988) tested the Goldschmidt hypothesis for the Corn Belt and Great Plains. For both regions, an increase in farm scale was related to better socioeconomic conditions; an increase in the number of hired farm workers was related to significantly poorer conditions in the Corn Belt but not in the Plains; and an increase in tenancy had no significant effects in either region.

Several conclusions can be drawn from the empirical research on regional variations. First, compared to nonfarm industry, farming is not a strong determinant of socioeconomic conditions in most regions, even agriculturally dependent Corn Belt counties (van Es et al., 1986). Second, the effects of medium size farms tend to be constant over the regions examined: the studies verify or imply that such farms are related to better socioeconomic conditions. The impacts of small and large farms by region are less clear. Swanson and Skees's (1986) study, the only one of the previous studies to directly test for curvilinear relationships, suggests that small farms may lower well-being. The effects of large-scale farms do not hold a consistent pattern across regions.

EXPECTED RELATIONSHIPS

Regions represent innumerable human and nonhuman characteristics, allowing social relationships to be tested under different conditions. I expect to find that the conceptual model of local inequality is supported across various regional settings; as argued earlier, much of the difference in economic inequality between regions can be attributed to the different configurations of economic structure, worker power, and spatial characteristics. The conceptual and empirical literature indicates that the effects of farm structure may be mediated by regional factors such as: internal social structural forces, including nonfarm industrial structure and the nature of social relations between capital and labor; spatial location and related ecological features specific to a region; and external factors arising from a region's position in the national and global political economy. Because no one study can completely disentangle the variety of ways in which regional location affects farm structure impacts, I limit the quantitative analysis primarily to the first two sets of factors, which include industrial structure, worker power and spatial characteristics.[6] Controlling for these characteristics will tend to regularize relationships between farm structure and socioeconomic conditions so that they follow more similar patterns across regions.

To test the relationships, I shall employ the variables and types of analyses employed in the previous chapter. County farm structure is measured by a set of three indexes termed smaller family farming, larger family farming, and industrialized farming, which were developed from a factor analysis of items from the Census of Agriculture. Industry structure is measured by the percentage of the county labor force employed in three industrial sectors, the periphery, state, and core with the last serving as the excluded reference category in the regression analysis. The average establishment size of county businesses is also used as an indicator of industrial structure. The power of workers vis-à-vis employers is operationalized by five indicators: the percent unionized, AFDC payments per capita, the percent nonwhite and unemployed, and median education. County spatial characteristics are the percent rural farm and urban population and an index of metropolitan proximity. The measurement of the independent variables is described in detail in Chapter 5. The dependent variable, economic well-being, is measured by factor scores generated from a principal axis factor analysis of three indicators: median family income, percent of county families in poverty, and family income inequality. This variable was described in the preceding chapter. As previously shown, income related economic measures are useful and conceptually relevant dependent variables because they vary more systematically with economic structure than, for example, indicators of education, unemployment, or health. They are also preconditions for better socioeconomic well-being, including lower infant mortality and teenage fertility.

Cross-sectional and longitudinal multiple regression analyses similar to those in the previous national analyses are employed. The cross-sectional analyses are for two time points, 1980 and 1970, with focus on the former. The longitudinal analyses test the effects of the independent variables at the 1970 time point on 1980 economic well-being, and an additional control, the 1970 value of the dependent variable, is included. These later analyses permit examination of the effects of the independent variables on changes in economic well-being. The analyses are performed for the nation and for each of the five major agricultural regions: Urban Northeast, Eastern Mountains, Central U.S. Agriculture, Southeast Coastal Plains, and West. In addition, a brief analysis based upon finer disaggregation within each region is presented.

THE ANALYSIS

Regional differences in economic well-being in 1980 tend to follow anticipated patterns (Table 7.1). Economic well-being is considerably higher in the Northeast than the rest of the nation, at about the national average for the Central U.S. agricultural region, and lowest in the Southeast and Eastern Mountains. Better

TABLE 7.1

Means for Major Variables by Region, 1980 Period

	U.S.	Northeast	Eastern Mountains	Southeast Plains	Central U.S.	West
Economic Well-being	0.000	.823	-.179	-.604	-.002	.087
Industry Structure						
Percent in Peripheral Employment	.576	.535	.556	.584	.613	.572
Percent in Core Employment	.265	.308	.294	.254	.234	.241
Percent in State Employment	.159	.157	.150	.162	.153	.187
Establishment Size	7.067	8.850	8.263	7.340	5.518	5.794
Farm Structure						
Smaller Family Farming	50.000	52.326	52.046	48.744	48.450	48.635
Larger Family Farming	50.000	49.942	44.840	46.121	57.791	46.742
Industrialized Farming	50.000	49.854	46.688	49.024	51.033	55.061
Worker Power Characteristics						
Percent Unionized	.212	.302	.215	.140	.202	.213
Per Capita AFDC Payments	$74.73	$102.55	$61.14	$45.65	$82.02	$86.27
Percent Nonwhite	.114	.049	.088	.293	.067	.101
Median Education	11.540	12.000	10.954	11.182	11.827	11.829
Percent Unemployed	.068	.083	.081	.064	.048	.076
Spatial Characteristics						
Percent Farm to Rural Population	.142	.092	.093	.076	.264	.104
Percent Urban	.354	.435	.269	.368	.333	.428
Metro Proximity	5.251	7.800	5.342	5.444	3.731	4.880
	(N=3037)	(N=510)	(N=695)	(N=543)	(N=898)	(N=391)

quality employment, as indicated by core industries and larger establishment size, is found in the Northeast. Farm structure also follows previously noted regional patterns. Predominate regional farming patterns are: smaller family farming in the Northeast and Eastern Mountains; larger family farming in the Central U.S.; and industrialized farming in the West and somewhat in the Central U.S. The Southeast appears characterized by a more dualistic structure, with values highest for both smaller family and industrialized farming than for larger family farming. Workers have considerably less shelter from the demands of low-wage employment in the Southeast as indicated by low unionization rates, welfare payments, educational levels, and high nonwhite population. In contrast, the values on the previous variables for the Northeast indicate substantially greater bargaining power for workers. Unemployment, however, is also particularly high in the Northeast and in the Eastern Mountains as well. Spatial characteristics likewise vary across region. Central U.S. counties are characterized by the highest farm populations and greatest distance from metropolitan areas while the most urbanized population is found in the Northeast.

Comparative Analyses for Five Agricultural Regions

The first analysis explores the relationship between farm structure and economic well-being for 1980 (Table 7.2). It shows the initial relationships by region and for the entire nation without controlling for antecedent spatial characteristics and mediating influences of worker power and industrial structure. It is expected that these relationships will vary interregionally but become more consistent as the control variables are introduced. Farm structure explains relatively little variation in well-being and only about 14 percent of the variance even in the most highly agricultural part of the country, the Central U.S. Smaller family farming is significantly negatively related to economic well-being in the Northeast and Eastern Mountains but positively related in the other regions. Significant relationships for larger family farming are found only in the Northeast and West, although these run in opposite directions. In contrast to the Goldschmidt hypothesis, industrialized farming is related to better economic conditions in the Northeast, Eastern Mountains, and West.

In the complete cross-sectional models for 1980, the amount of explained variance in economic well-being is high (from about 70 to 78 percent) and relatively similar across the five regions and the nation indicating that the conceptual model holds quite well under different regional conditions (Table 7.3). It should be noted that because region of the country is not controlled in the national analysis, the relationships are dominated by those regions that have the largest number of counties. As expected, the initial relationships for farm structure and local inequality presented in the previous table change considerably when industrial structure, worker power, and spatial variables are controlled. The preceding chapters described how all these variables may come to mediate the effects of

TABLE 7.2

Regressions of Economic Well-being on Farm Structure by Region, 1980[a]

	U.S.	Northeast	Eastern Mountains	Southeast Plains	Central U.S.	West
Intercept	.000 (−1.003)**	.000 (−.618)*	.000 (−3.978)**	.000 (−1.285)**	.000 (−2.634)**	.000 (.859)**
Smaller Family Farming	.111 (.011)**	−.251 (−.016)**	−.176 (−.015)**	.215 (.021)**	.323 (.046)**	.274 (.017)**
Larger Family Farming	.099 (.010)**	.317 (.019)**	−.021 (−.003)	−.121 (−.014)	.083 (.009)	−.474 (−.045)**
Industrialized Farming	−.003 (−.000)	.192 (.026)**	.282 (.101)**	.069 (.006)	−.011 (−.002)	.226 (.009)*
R^2	.033	.078	.038	.028	.138	.069

[a]Unstandardized coefficients are in parentheses.
*Significant at $p \leq .05$.
**Significant at $p \leq .01$.

TABLE 7.3

Regressions of Economic Well-being on Farm and Industry Structure and Other County Characteristics by Region, 1980[a]

	U.S.	Northeast	Eastern Mountains	Southeast Plains	Central U.S.	West
Industry Structure						
Percent in Peripheral Employment	-.182 (-1.934)**	-.289 (-2.540)**	-.116 (-.989)**	-.245 (-2.742)**	-.329 (-3.654)**	-.321 (-3.188)**
Percent in State Employment	-.146 (-2.747)**	-.097 (-1.235)**	-.152 (-2.675)**	-.135 (-2.515)**	-.074 (-1.452)**	-.260 (-4.043)**
Establishment Size	.153 (.048)**	-.001 (-.000)	.203 (.050)**	.163 (.051)**	.062 (.026)**	.102 (.052)**
Farm Structure						
Smaller Family Farming	-.107 (-.010)**	-.175 (-.011)**	-.216 (-.018)**	-.116 (-.011)**	-.152 (-.022)**	-.135 (-.008)**
Larger Family Farming	.165 (.016)**	.367 (.022)**	.251 (.034)**	.130 (.015)**	.153 (.017)**	.049 (.005)
Industrialized Farming	-.157 (-.003)**	-.051 (-.007)	-.039 (-.014)	-.067 (-.006)*	.058 (.011)**	.024 (.001)
Worker Power Characteristics						
Percent Unionized	.018 (.223)	-.008 (-.082)	.060 (.639)*	-.079 (-1.921)**	.038 (.596)	.116 (1.577)**
Per Capita AFDC Payments	.234 (.008)**	.048 (.001)	.102 (.006)**	.110 (.007)**	.136 (.005)**	.241 (.007)**

TABLE 7.3 continued

	U.S.	Northeast	Eastern Mountains	Southeast Plains	Central U.S.	West
Worker Power Characteristics cont.						
Percent Nonwhite	-.289	-.170	-.108	-.353	-.503	-.311
	(-1.881)**	(-1.671)**	(-.743)**	(-1.866)**	(-3.849)**	(-2.800)**
Median Education	.297	.134	.392	.138	.184	.391
	(.298)**	(.366)**	(.261)**	(.135)**	(.277)**	(.374)**
Percent Unemployed	-.157	-.334	-.285	-.135	-.041	-.034
	(-4.573)**	(-6.463)**	(-8.196)**	(-4.917)**	(-1.448)	(-.816)
Spatial Characteristics						
Percent Farm to Rural Population	-.220	-.178	-.192	-.127	-.140	-.071
	(-1.767)**	(-1.398)**	(-2.112)**	(-1.985)**	(-1.121)**	(-.796)*
Percent Urban	.062	.149	-.016	.020	.187	.109
	(.209)**	(.337)**	(-.057)	(.064)	(.614)**	(.329)**
Metro Proximity	.202	.307	.206	.284	.155	.100
	(.047)**	(.040)**	(.043)**	(.062)**	(.046)**	(.023)*
Intercept	.000	.000	.000	.000	.000	.000
	(-2.537)**	(-2.049)**	(-2.193)**	(.280)	(-1.758)**	(-2.673)**
R^2	.741	.705	.740	.734	.776	.740

[a]Unstandardized coefficients are in parentheses.
*Significant at p ≤ .05.
**Significant at p ≤ .01.

farm structure. In the case of larger and smaller family farming, the relationships tend to become similar across regions. Smaller family farming is significantly and negatively related to economic well-being in all five regions. Larger family farming is related to better economic conditions in all five regions and the relationships are significant for all regions except the West. The relationships for industrialized farming, however, differ across region. Industrialized farming is related to poorer economic conditions in the Southeast and to better conditions in the Central U.S. (although both of these relationships are small), while no significant relationships are found in the other regions.

The relationships for industrial structure, worker power, and spatial characteristics remain relatively stable across regions and follow the national averages. Counties with greater peripheral and state employment have significantly poorer economic well-being than those with greater core employment. Peripheral employment also tends to reduce economic well-being relative to state employment. Larger establishment size is related to better economic conditions in all regions but the Northeast. The greater bargaining power of labor, as indicated by higher AFDC payments and education and a lower nonwhite population and unemployment, is related to better economic conditions in all five regions. Unionization rates, however, do not vary as systematically, and the relationship for the Southeast Plains is in the opposite direction as hypothesized. Although the Southeast has much lower unionization rates than the nation as a whole, some states such as Alabama, Arkansas, and Louisiana have unionization rates higher than the Southern average (as a consequence of industries such as oil and steel) yet comparatively poorer economic conditions. The presence of unions may heighten inequality between segments of the organized and unorganized workforce within the South. Finally, the relationships for spatial characteristics are generally consistent across regions, with lower farm and higher urban populations and closer metropolitan proximity related to greater well-being.

The models for 1970 (Table 7.4) explain similar amounts of variance, from 77 to 83 percent, somewhat more than models for 1980. The relationships for smaller family farming follow the same direction as in the 1980 models but no longer are significant in the Northeast and West. Larger family farming continues to be positively and significantly related to better economic conditions except in the West, where the relationship is of insignificant magnitude. Industrialized farming has little relationship to economic well-being in any of the five regions or the nation as a whole. The small but significant positive relationship found in the Central U.S. in the previous 1980 model may have been due to regionally and temporally specific conditions: large, industrialized farms may have been particularly profitable during the Midwest agricultural boom prior to the farm crisis, which could be reflected in greater rural affluence. Finally, the relationships for the industrial structure, worker power, and spatial variables also generally follow the same direction as in the 1980 models, indicating their stability over time as well as place.

TABLE 7.4

Regressions of Economic Well-being on Farm and Industry Structure and Other County Characteristics by Region, 1970[a]

	U.S.	Northeast	Eastern Mountains	Southeast Plains	Central U.S.	West
Industry Structure						
Percent in Peripheral Employment	-.124 (-1.104)**	-.190 (-1.289)**	-.110 (-.882)**	-.214 (-2.033)**	-.264 (-2.149)**	-.228 (-2.048)**
Percent in State Employment	-.140 (-2.551)**	-.077 (-1.034)**	-.236 (-4.140)**	-.102 (-1.582)**	-.093 (-1.661)**	-.214 (-3.026)**
Establishment Size	.163 (.044)**	.052 (.007)	.188 (.045)**	.199 (.062)**	.098 (.033)**	.162 (.069)**
Farm Structure						
Smaller Family Farming	-.062 (-.006)**	-.058 (-.003)	-.163 (-.014)**	-.140 (-.012)**	-.180 (-.022)**	-.089 (-.006)
Larger Family Farming	.060 (.006)**	.136 (.008)**	.214 (.030)**	.101 (.101)**	.115 (.011)**	-.010 (-.001)
Industrialized Farming	-.014 (-.001)	.004 (-.000)	-.005 (-.002)	-.010 (-.001)	.011 (.002)	.011 (.000)
Worker Power Characteristics						
Percent Unionized	.042 (.409)**	.019 (.170)	.007 (.054)	-.050 (-1.211)*	.090 (.926)**	.131 (1.308)**
Per Capita AFDC Payments	.212 (.012)**	.049 (.002)*	.060 (.006)**	.200 (.021)**	.172 (.010)**	.147 (.009)**

TABLE 7.4 continued

	U.S.	Northeast	Eastern Mountains	Southeast Plains	Central U.S.	West
Worker Power Characteristics cont.						
Percent Nonwhite	−.180	−.116	−.131	−.340	−.365	.015
	(−1.147)**	(−1.217)**	(−.912)**	(−1.645)**	(−2.494)**	(.172)
Median Education	.457	.281	.410	.221	.316	.587
	(.320)**	(.239)**	(.297)**	(.155)**	(.227)**	(.406)**
Percent Unemployed	−.111	−.188	−.235	−.117	−.060	−.014
	(−4.698)**	(−5.144)**	(−9.600)**	(−5.444)**	(−2.305)**	(−.479)
Spatial Characteristics						
Percent Farm to	−.128	−.115	−.175	−.170	−.045	−.049
Rural Population	(−.783)**	(−.606)**	(−1.194)**	(−1.440)**	(−.254)*	(−.384)
Percent Urban	.037	.181	.051	.047	.105	.062
	(.125)**	(.405)**	(.184)	(.144)	(.292)**	(.185)
Metro Proximity	.150	.290	.127	.175	.154	.025
	(.035)**	(.035)**	(.028)**	(.037)**	(.039)**	(.006)
Intercept	.000	.000	.000	.000	.000	.000
	(−3.026)**	(−1.602)**	(−2.738)**	(−.693)	(−1.366)**	(−3.577)**
R^2	.804	.828	.755	.811	.795	.766

[a]Unstandardized coefficients are in parentheses.
*Significant at p ≤ .05.
**Significant at p ≤ .01.

TABLE 7.5

Longitudinal Regressions of 1980 Economic Well-being on 1970 Farm and Industry Structure and Other County Characteristics by Region[a]

	U.S.	Northeast	Eastern Mountains	Southeast Plains	Central U.S.	West
Industrial Structure						
Percent in Peripheral Employment	-.140 (-1.248)**	-.052 (-.362)	-.112 (-.858)**	-.167 (-.731)**	-.241 (-2.352)**	-.142 (-1.278)**
Percent in State Employment	-.085 (-1.545)**	.041 (.563)	-.098 (-1.633)**	-.115 (-1.879)**	-.102 (-2.180)**	-.146 (-2.070)**
Establishment Size	-.053 (-.014)**	-.050 (-.007)	-.017 (-.004)	-.010 (-.003)	-.058 (-.024)**	-.099 (-.042)**
Farm Structure						
Smaller Family Farming	.030 (.003)**	-.054 (-.003)	-.034 (-.003)	-.031 (-.003)	.013 (.002)	.009 (.001)
Larger Family Farming	.058 (.006)**	.136 (.008)**	.067 (.009)	.104 (.010)**	.086 (.010)**	.050 (.005)
Industrialized Farming	-.043 (-.004)**	-.055 (-.008)	-.020 (-.008)	-.036 (-.004)	-.024 (-.005)	-.088 (-.004)*
Worker Power Characteristics						
Percent Unionized	-.045 (-.443)**	-.096 (-.882)**	-.038 (-.295)	-.041 (-1.051)	.023 (.288)	.023 (.231)
Per Capita AFDC Payments	.020 (.001)	.008 (.000)	.017 (.002)	.023 (.003)	.037 (.003)	.080 (.005)
Percent Nonwhite	-.047 (-.295)**	.002 (.020)	.013 (.085)	-.105 (-.536)**	-.158 (-1.294)**	-.061 (-.727)*

TABLE 7.5 continued

	U.S.	Northeast	Eastern Mountains	Southeast Plains	Central U.S.	West
Worker Power Characteristics cont.						
Median Education	.027	−.051	.093	.050	.090	.163
	(.019)**	(−.045)	(.064)**	(.037)	(.077)**	(.113)**
Percent Unemployed	−.038	−.054	−.043	.004	−.026	−.056
	(−1.616)**	(−1.528)	(−1.681)	(.176)	(−1.185)	(−1.880)
Spatial Characteristics						
Percent Farm to	−.059	.058	−.078	.002	−.031	−.029
Rural Population	(−.362)**	(.314)	(−.513)**	(.017)	(−.209)	(−.223)
Percent Urban	−.026	−.143	−.116	−.151	.086	.020
	(−.090)*	(−.328)**	(−.404)**	(−.489)**	(.284)**	(.060)
Metro Proximity	.061	.109	.064	.142	.048	.078
	(.014)**	(.014)**	(.014)**	(.032)**	(.015)*	(.019)*
Economic Well-being, 1970	.790	.924	.781	.691	.526	.655
	(.788)**	(.949)**	(.744)**	(.731)**	(.628)**	(.658)**
Intercept	.000	.000	.000	.000	.000	.000
	(.856)**	(1.145)**	(.472)	(.967)*	(.516)	(−.325)
R^2	.824	.816	.837	.796	.807	.763

[a]Unstandardized coefficients are in parentheses.
*Significant at p ≤ .05.
**Significant at p ≤ .01.

When the effects of prior levels of economic well-being are included in the longitudinal models, little variance remains to be explained by the other independent variables, resulting in a smaller number of significant findings (Table 7.5). The level of smaller family farming in 1970 has no significant relationship to changes in economic well-being over the 1980 period for any of the five regions. Counties with a greater extent of larger family farming in 1970 had significantly better economic well-being in 1980 in the Northeast, Southeast, and Central U.S. The relationships for the two other regions are also in the positive direction. Industrialized farming tends to reduce economic well-being over time in all five regions but the relationship is significant only in the West.

The relationships for the other variables also exhibit more regional variation than in the cross-sectional models. This is not surprising in light of the economic shifts of the 1970s, which differentially altered regional patterns of social relations and fortunes. Counties with greater peripheral and state employment in 1970 continued to have worse conditions in 1980 in most regions. Economic well-being tended to deteriorate in counties with larger business establishments but less so in the Eastern Mountains and Southeast. The balance of power between workers and employers had somewhat differential effects on changes in economic well-being. As in the cross-sectional models, the impacts of unionization varied regionally, although significant relationships are found only in the Northeast, where economic conditions worsened in counties with higher unionization rates. The relationships for the other worker power characteristics tend to follow anticipated directions although many are not significant. Interestingly, while higher education led to small economic gains over the decade in most regions, it did not protect Northeast counties against the changes of the 1970s and even contributed to slight decreases in economic well-being. Finally, spatial characteristics had differential impacts on well-being. Counties with higher farm populations had significantly poorer conditions in the Eastern Mountains. More urbanized counties in the Northeast, Eastern Mountains, and Southeast experienced significant declines in well-being, while the reverse occurred in the Central U.S. Economic conditions significantly deteriorated in counties furthest from metropolitan areas, and this was consistent across all regions.

In summary, the initial relationships between larger and smaller family farming assumed more consistent patterns across regions once other county characteristics were controlled. However, the relationships for industrialized farming were less consistent across time and place. In 1970, industrialized farming was not significantly related to economic well-being in any region or the nation as a whole. In 1980, industrialized farming was negatively related to well-being in the Southeast but positively related in the Central U.S., while the relationships in other regions were not significant. To further disentangle these relationships for 1980, subregional variations are examined. This set of analyses explores whether or not the effects of industrialized farming depend upon more specific environmental and commodity related conditions found within each region, allowing the relationships to be tested under a set of even more homogenous criteria.

Comparative Analyses for Agricultural Subregions

The subregions were developed by Fuguitt and Beale (1978) and adapted for county level data by Carlin and Green (1988). The subregions reflect more uniform mixtures of locational and economic characteristics than the five major national regions. Four subregions commonly examined in other studies and associated with specific agricultural commodities, climate, and landholding patterns were selected: the Great Plains, Corn Belt, Cotton Belt, and Southwest. The Great Plains and Corn Belt are part of the larger Central U.S. region. The Great Plains is a major wheat and livestock area extending east from central Montana to Minnesota and south to central Texas. The Corn Belt extends from southern Minnesota to central Missouri and eastward to central Indiana. Compared to the Corn Belt, the Great Plains is characterized by larger-size family operated farms, lower rainfall, and harsher climatic conditions (Flora and Flora, 1986; Gilles and Dalecki, 1988). The old coastal plain Cotton Belt, which extends in a horseshoe pattern from the western half of South Carolina through Georgia, Alabama, and Mississippi, is part of the Southeast region. Cotton and sugar cane are still grown in the Cotton Belt and the plantation system was concentrated in this area (Skees and Swanson, 1986). The Southwest, part of the West, incorporates most of California, Nevada, Arizona, New Mexico, and southern Texas. Much of this area contains heavily irrigated, industrialized agriculture.

The models for the Great Plains and the Corn Belt explain nearly similar amounts of variance (Table 7.6). The relationships in these models are also similar in direction and magnitude. In both subregions, smaller family farming has a significant negative relationship to well-being, while larger family and industrialized farming are positively related to well-being. Thus, despite somewhat different commodity/agroclimatic settings, the subregional relationships are similar and follow those of the wider Central U.S. region in 1980. The relationships for the Coastal Plain Cotton Belt also tend to follow those found in the Southeast region. Smaller family farming is significantly negatively related to economic well-being; larger family farming is significantly positively related. Industrialized farming has a small negative relationship to well-being and the unstandardized beta is larger than that found in the relationship for the wider Southeast region. The coefficient, however, is not significant, in part due to the smaller size of the subregional sample. For the Southwest, the relationships for larger family and industrialized farming are nonsignificant, as was found in the model for the entire West. While smaller family farming was significantly negatively related to economic well-being in the model for entire West, this analysis shows a smaller but still negative relationship.

Regional differences in the effects of farm structure generally appear to hold at subregional levels under even more homogeneous agroclimatic and

TABLE 7.6

Regressions of Economic Well-being on Farm and Industry Structure and Other County Characteristics for Four Subregions, 1980[a]

	Great Plains	Corn Belt	Southwest	Old Cotton Belt
Industry Structure				
Percent in Peripheral Employment	-.420 (-3.995)**	-.411 (-3.358)**	-.207 (-2.523)**	-.206 (-2.502)**
Percent in State Employment	-.105 (-1.760)**	-.094 (-1.410)**	-.260 (-4.353)**	-.128 (-2.037)**
Establishment Size	.075 (.042)*	.097 (.023)*	.027 (.016)	.110 (.037)**
Farm Structure				
Smaller Family Farming	-.319 (-.051)**	-.092 (-.010)**	-.072 (-.004)	-.145 (-.021)**
Larger Family Farming	.253 (.030)**	.172 (.012)**	-.001 (-.000)	.129 (.022)*
Industrialized Farming	.090 (.014)**	.124 (.020)*	.002 (.000)	-.080 (-.032)
Worker Power Characteristics				
Percent Unionized	.019 (.367)	-.022 (-.290)	.174 (2.865)	-.113 (-2.417)**
Per Capita AFDC Payments	.131 (.004)**	.138 (.005)**	.226 (.006)*	-.038 (-.003)
Percent Nonwhite	-.497 (-3.919)**	-.248 (-4.286)**	-.181 (-1.643)**	-.641 (-3.183)**

TABLE 7.6 continued

	Great Plains	Corn Belt	Southwest	Old Cotton Belt
Worker Power Characteristics cont.				
Median Education	.092	.020	.410	.179
	(.144)**	(.044)	(.341)**	(.162)**
Percent Unemployed	.029	−.091	−.140	−.003
	(.993)	(−2.927)*	(−4.144)**	(−.093)
Spatial Characteristics				
Percent Farm to Rural Population	−.219	−.268	−.087	−.153
	(−1.562)**	(−1.617)**	(−1.099)	(−2.285)**
Percent Urban	.255	.215	.127	.077
	(.698)**	(.541)**	(.407)**	(.256)
Metro Proximity	.119	.274	.117	.246
	(.036)**	(.050)**	(.028)**	(.069)**
Intercept	.000	.000	.000	.000
	(.608)	(.657)	(−2.587)**	(1.745)
R^2	.701	.709	.767	.782
	(N = 475)	(N = 197)	(N = 364)	(N = 203)

[a]Unstandardized coefficients are in parentheses.
*Significant at p ≤ .05.
**Significant at p ≤ .01.

commodity-related conditions. This suggests that sources of regional variations in farm structure impacts may be less a consequence of specific nonhuman environmental attributes and more a consequence of wider regional social structural arrangements.

CONCLUSION

Regional economic inequality can be attributed to the same forces affecting inequality at the national level—economic structure, worker power and spatial characteristics. The model of inequality developed here is generally consistent across regions, as indicated by the direction of most relationships and explained variance of the cross-sectional models. The longitudinal regression models also explain similar amounts of variance, but the relationships tend to vary more interregionally, particularly for the worker power characteristics. Changes in the national economy of the 1970s appear to have differentially altered the balance of power between capital and labor, giving previous sources of empowerment diminished capacity to shelter workers or advance their interests in some regions. This is most pronounced in the case of the Northeast, where counties with higher unionization and to some extent, higher education experienced deterioration in economic conditions and where higher AFDC payments and white ethnicity provided no significant future economic advantages.

Another major purpose of this chapter is to address whether or not the national average relationships outlined in the previous chapter remain consistent across regions. The initial relationships between larger and smaller family farming and economic well-being assume a more consistent direction across regions once the other county characeristics are controlled. As in the national analyses, counties with a greater extent of smaller family farming tend to have poorer conditions, while counties with a greater extent of larger family farming have better conditions. Interregional variations in the impacts of larger and smaller family farming thus seem in large part to depend upon the industrial structure, worker power, and spatial characteristics found in a particular area.

The effects of industrialized farming on economic well-being are less consistent across time and place even when major county characteristics are controlled. There are no significant relationships between industrialized farming and well-being in any region in 1970. In 1980, industrialized farming is related to slightly lower well-being in the Southeast and higher well-being in the Central U.S. The most consistent findings are those for the longitudinal models. Although the relationships are statistically significant only for the West (in part due to the large amount of variance explained by the independent lagged variable), counties with a greater extent of industrialized farming in 1970 tend to show poorer conditions in 1980 across all regions. As noted previously, there are many reasons why the impacts of farming could vary regionally. By holding constant industrial structure, worker power, spatial characteristics, and particularly in the last analysis, aspects of agroclimatic and commodity related factors, the influence of these potential intervening and antecedent factors are reduced or eliminated.

There are several possible explanations as to why regional variations remain in the case of industrialized farming. Because of the limitations of the data, especially the level of aggregation in the county unit of analysis, the following discussion should be viewed as tentative.

· First, the more variable findings for industrialized farming suggest that it is integrated into regional political economies in different ways than are smaller family labor operations. Particularly because of its dependency on wage labor, industrialized farming is affected by a number of different social forces than those affecting family labor operations. Although previous studies have not used the same farm structure measures as this one, the findings for the Central U.S., Great Plains and Corn Belt are similar to those of other studies of the same general areas (van Es et al., 1986; Gilles and Dalecki, 1988), which report a positive relationship between scale and well-being. The Midwest context of protection of family farming, state regulation of corporate farming, and history of agrarian populism may offset any deleterious impacts of industrialized farming. The strong Midwestern farm economy of the 1980 period may also have acted to raise economic well-being in counties with significant number of industrialized farms. In contrast, the Southeast is characerized by a quite different agrarian history of plantation agriculture and later sharecropping. The old Cotton Belt, the bastion of plantation agriculture, still contains many large farming operations. Skees and Swanson (1988) indicate that this area is particularly vulnerable to the adverse effects of industrialized farming. This labor coercive agrarian history, as well as the tendency of the state in the South more so than in other areas to support the interests of capital (Wood, 1986), is less likely to buffer the effects of industrialized farming. Based on the social and historical contexts of industrialized farming in different regions, we can expect to find that this type of agriculture has a less damaging impact in the Midwest and more damaging impact in the South.

A second reason for regional differences is that the nature of industrialized farming may vary in different areas. While the measures of farm structure allow us to make broad generalizations about major structural patterns, they cannot account for internal variations in all farming characteristics. In the case of industrialized farming, such characteristics include wage and skill levels of farm workers, the extent of labor organization, and the seasonality of employment. For example, as noted previously, California industrialized farming offers more highly skilled, longer-term, state regulated employment and has a greater proportion of organized farm workers than other areas. California farm laborers also made great strides in wage increases, particularly during the 1964-1974 period, with farm worker wages increasing 120% compared to a 59% rise in wages for industrial workers (Majka and Majka, 1982:241). Compared to the national average in 1981, median daily earnings for farm workers were 26 percent higher in the West, at the national average in the North Central states, and below the national average in both the Northeast and South (U.S. Bureau of the Census, 1983b, Table 1182:671). The number of workers per farm also varies by region and commodity. Western states (particularly California, Washington and Oregon) have the highest proportion of farms employing twenty or more seasonal workers (Fritsch, 1984:72). Most of these large units are involved in vegetable and fruit production and tend to be associated with more rationalized farm production (job stratification based upon skill), higher wages, and a labor force with greater potential for union organizing (Hayes, 1984; Mamer, 1984). Thus, industrialized farming may have less adverse impacts in the West than in the South because internal characteristics of farming units vary from region to region.

Finally, the methodology I use in this study may influence the regional variations observed. County level data may bear upon the findings in at least a couple of ways. As noted in the previous chapter, while the full impacts of industrialized farming may not be discernable in areas such as the West that use greater migrant labor, this issue is probably of limited importance: migrant laborers numbered at most about 200,000 or 8 percent of the hired farm work force throughout the 1970s. Even in California during the mid-1970s, the vast majority (74 percent) of seasonal farm workers were local people; only 15 percent migrated from other areas within the state and about 11 percent were interstate migrants (Majka and Majka, 1982:4). The number of foreign workers during the 1970s was also relatively small (approximately 37,000-41,000 from 1971 through 1975) and regionally dispersed, employed in commodities such as Florida sugarcane, East Coast apples and Maine lumber, and in Western sheepherding (Martin and North, 1984:174-175). The county as a unit of analysis may also obscure relationships at less aggregate levels, such as the community. This becomes more important in the West, as counties tend to be much larger than in the rest of the country. Another issue is that as family labor farms predominate in the U.S., very high levels of industrialized farming may be required before the impacts of such farming can be discerned. Even in California in the 1970s, 84 percent of operators farmed fewer than 500 acres (Small Farm Viability Project, 1977:7). Finally, as this study has found few significant relationships between industrialized farming and well-being in the West, in contrast to the MacCannell and Dolber-Smith (1986) study, it may be that the specific methodology of controlling for industrial employment, worker power, and spatial characteristics diminishes the effects of industrialized farming.[7]

In sum, there are a number of possible reasons for the interregional differences found in the cross-sectional models. However, these differences should not be overemphasized. The long term implications of industrialized farming are clear: counties with a greater extent of this farming in 1970 did not have better conditions in any region in 1980. Industrialized farming tends to limit future economic potentials wherever it is found.

Farming and the Nonfarm Sector: Industry and Other Local Linkages

The previous chapters explore how inequality results from the configuration of farm and industry structure, worker power and spatial characteristics of the locality. This chapter addresses a related issue, the link between these local attributes, particularly industrial structure, to farm structure and change. Two major questions are investigated. First, what local characteristics help to sustain smaller and larger family farming and industrialized farming over time? Second, what factors differentiate counties having a predominate type of farming pattern from one another? Does, for example, the industrial base of a county characterized by industrialized farming differ from that of a county characterized by smaller family farming?

The relationship between local characteristics and farm structure is a little studied but significant academic and policy-related issue. The shape and structure of agriculture at any historical moment are influenced by a multiplicity of local, national, and global conditions. As discussed in Chapter 2, explanations of agricultural change have tended to center on factors such as the internal dynamics and capital accumulation strategies of production units and, more recently, on external forces such as state agricultural policy and the international division of labor. Without minimizing the importance of these agriculturally related and nonlocal factors, a neglected issue is that agricultural structure can also be a function of prevailing nonfarm conditions in a locality. These conditions include the factors identified previously (industrial structure, worker power, and spatial characteristics) as well as general socioeconomic levels. Focusing on the effects of local characteristics thus explores an alternative way of interpreting agricultural change. It also addresses a frequently noted criticism of the Goldschmidt literature. Most studies are premised on a one-way causality, in which farm structure is assumed to affect the community while community impact on agriculture is overlooked (Beaulieu et al., 1988; Korsching and Stofferahn, 1986; Moxley, 1986).

Relationships between farms and their nearby communities also have important policy implications, an issue more fully developed in the last chapter. If local characteristics have a bearing on farm structure, then efforts to control agricultural change (such as stabilizing declines of moderate size operations) should not be limited to the farm sector (Carlin and Green, 1988). Rather, this implies that agricultural policy should be broadened into a general rural development policy that addresses other economic sectors and local characteristics influencing farming.

INDUSTRY STRUCTURE, OTHER LOCAL CHARACTERISTICS AND FARMING

The existing literature examining community impacts on farming has been characterized as fragmented and not tied to any systematic investigation of the topic (Beaulieu, et al., 1988). This analysis explores how aspects of local social systems, industrial structure, worker power, spatial characteristics, and levels of economic well-being affect farming.[1] Researchers generally consider industrial structure and spatial characteristics such as urban proximity and regional location to be the major nonfarm factors influencing farming (Beaulieu et al., 1988; Moxley, 1986; Salant and Munoz, 1981). That local socioeconomic conditions have a 'continuative effect' on the structure of farming over time is considered a corollary of the Goldschmidt hypothesis (Green, 1985). The issue of human agency in the form of worker power characteristics, particularly labor organizations and income transfer levels, has not been examined in any previous study.

Industry

Industry influences farming through the labor, land, and product markets. It can be expected to have differential impacts on family labor and industrialized, hired labor dependent farms. Probably the most commonly noted impact on family farms is that industry becomes a source of additional employment, contributing to farmers' household income. Added nonfarm income can increase the viability of family farms, particularly during downturns in the agricultural economy. This is one reason why smaller operations dependent on off-farm income were not as hard hit as moderate size, full-time family farms during the 1980s farm crisis (Leistritz and Murdock, 1988). A study of Iowa labor markets also found that off-farm employment is critical in sustaining communities with many small family farms (Korsching and Stofferahn, 1985b). In addition to farm viability, the internal structure of the farm operation may change if operators and family members secure off-farm employment. Farmers may compensate for the family labor that is now allocated to industrial employment through investing in machinery or other inputs that reduce labor requirements, switching to less labor intensive commodities, hiring farm labor, or reducing the scale of operations, with the latter the most common strategy (Beaulieu et al., 1988).

The causal interpretation usually given to the part-time farming/industry relationship is that off-farm employment subsidizes ongoing farming operations and assists new operators in entering farming on a part-time basis (Beaulieu et al., 1988). While motivations for part-time farming vary tremendously, an in-depth study of Georgia farmers found that the desire for additional household income through 'a sideline business' was the primary reason for part-time farming outweighing even lifestyle considerations (Barlett, 1986). This suggests that the converse relationship is also plausible: part-time farming may supplement wages in the industrial sector.

The labor market impacts of nonfarm industry would seem less beneficial to operators of large-scale industrialized farms. Competition for hired labor between industry and industrialized farming may result in higher wages for farm laborers. As noted in previous chapters, it is precisely the growth of nonfarm employment in rural areas that appears to have mediated some of the negative consequences of industrialized farming reported by early scholars. The presence of nonfarm employment may also alter the internal structure of industrialized farming as employers substitute capital for labor inputs in the face of escalating labor costs. It may even drive out industrialized farming altogether.

Industry also affects farming through the land market (Salant and Munoz, 1981). The location of new industry is generally accompanied by land speculation and a rise in prices (Salant and Munoz, 1981). Increasing land prices are barriers to entry for beginning farmers while land equity is a major asset of most established farmers. Thus, when land prices rise, larger well-established farms may continue to grow because of their superior investment positions. This can lead to greater concentration of landholding and wealth (Boxley and Walker, 1979). Alternatively, an influx of nonfarm industry and rising land prices presents new opportunities for the sale of farmland and thus for the general reduction of the number of farms in a locality. Greater demand for land for nonfarm use also may result in higher taxes. Nearly all states have recognized this issue and instituted forms of preferential property taxation that allow farmland to be taxed on agricultural use value rather than on market price (Boxley and Walker, 1979).

Finally, nonfarm industry influences farming through the product market. The presence of businesses supplying farm inputs or engaging in the marketing and processing of farm outputs can particularly help sustain family operations since these are less likely than industrialized farms to be connected into nonlocal supplier-processor networks. Privatized industries supplying consumer goods and services (such as retail stores, banks, and medical care) and state services (such as schools and public transportation) facilitate household reproduction and therefore may support family operations.

An issue that has not been considered by any previous study is how industrial segmentation affects farming. Obviously, higher wage core employment would have greater labor market benefits for part-time farmers and would be more likely to lead to positive wage rollouts for workers on industrialized farms. However, peripheral industries tend to be most attracted to rural areas where less skilled, cheaper, and marginally employed or unemployed labor is available. An Alabama study (Wheelock, 1979) found that growth in low-wage, labor intensive manufacturing was more likely to occur in counties with a large proportion of small farms.

Employment in the state sector, particularly in schools, tends to be important in rural areas. The state sector also reflects service outlays. Education, social welfare, agricultural extension, and other government services should facilitate the survival of family operations. Thus, although core industries may have greater capacity to financially sustain family operations, the relative lower frequency of these in rural areas may mean that family farming is more interrelated with the peripheral and state sectors.

Spatial Characteristics

Population density, distance from metropolitan centers, and location in the national and regional political economy shape the structure of farming. The cost and availability of land in more densely populated and metropolitan areas promotes the transfer of farmland into nonfarm use. Because metropolitan areas have higher land prices and greater employment opportunities, they also tend to have smaller farms. In a study of Southern counties, Beaulieu et al. (1988) found that urbanized areas were more likely to support the growth of small farms while rural areas were more likely to support the growth of medium and large farms. Large-scale industrialized farms also are sometimes located close to cities because of urban consumer markets. Finally, as shown in previous chapters, the uneven development of farming historically has meant that farm structure coincides with regional location with concentrations of larger family farming in the Midwest, industrialized farming in the West and parts of the South, and smaller family farming in the Eastern Mountains, Northeast, and South.

Local Socioeconomic Conditions

Another potential influence on farm structure is a locality's socioeconomic well-being. Goldschmidt (1978a) surmised while farming affected socioeconomic conditions, the reverse also occurred: socioeconomic conditions could in turn influence farm structure. Better conditions can facilitate the reproduction of farm households and thereby sustain family farming. Green (1985) tested this hypothesis for Missouri counties over the 1934–1978 period using quality of life indicators including literacy and level of farm debt. Although few significant relationships were found, counties with better conditions did tend to have the smallest increases in scale, thus indicating some support for the reverse of the Goldschmidt hypothesis.

Worker Power Characteristics

Although previous research has generally not examined the impact of ethnicity, education, unemployment, level of income transfers, and unionization upon farm structure, it seems reasonable to expect that such impact exists. These characteristics reflect a population's influence upon how economic production is organized around it. While people have little capacity to modify conditions such as geographic location or the presence of extractive resources, they exert some control over educational attainment, the establishment of labor organizations, and political decisions such as acceptable levels of social welfare. Although farmers are generally unable to receive AFDC because of their assets, higher AFDC payments suggest a climate of liberal state support for household reproduction and therefore, family farming. Similarly, family farming would seem more likely to be sustained within a more favorable socioeconomic context of higher education and unionization and lower unemployment.

A larger nonwhite population may be related to the presence of hired farm labor and industrialized farming. In contrast, localities with higher minority populations may have less family farming. Limited access to capital and other resources and discrimination in land purchases continue to force black-operated units out of farming (Beauford and Nelson, 1988). Mechanization of cotton, New Deal agricultural policy, and opportunities in Northern and urban industry, contributed to massive black out-migration from farming areas in the South during the early half of this century. On balance, the viability of the farm sector, particularly of family farming, should be strengthened by the same worker power characteristics that contribute to local well-being.

THE ANALYSIS

The examination of the impact of local nonfarm forces on farming has two stages. The first focuses on factors contributing to the survival of smaller and larger family farming and industrialized farming over time. This involves using longitudinal multiple regression analyses similar to those employed in previous chapters. The longitudinal analyses test the effects of the independent variables at the 1970 time point on the indexes of farm structure (measured in 1978) while controlling for a county's initial (1969) scores on these same indexes. These analyses allow the effects of the independent variables on changes in farm structure to be examined. The second stage examines the characteristics that differentiate counties having a predominate pattern of farming—smaller family, larger family, or industrialized farming, from one another. This is addressed through discriminant analysis for two time points, 1980 and 1970. The purpose is to understand what local characteristics, particularly in the nonfarm industrial base, define each farming pattern in the 1970 period, and if the same characteristics are useful in defining the patterns in the later decade.

The major variables have been described in previous chapters. Smaller and larger family farming and industrialized farming are indexes developed from a factor analysis of items from the Census of Agriculture. Industry structure is measured by the average establishment size of county businesses and the percent of the county labor force employed in the periphery, state, and core with the latter serving as the excluded reference category in the regression analysis.

Characteristics that empower a locality's workers are measured by: the percent unionized, AFDC payments per capita, the percent nonwhite, percent unemployed, and median education. County spatial characteristics are regional location, the percent rural farm and urban population and an index of metropolitan proximity. Economic well-being is a factor-score index composed of median family income, percent of families in poverty, and family income inequality.

Local Nonfarm Support for Patterns of Farming Over Time

This analysis examines the effects of industrial structure, worker power, spatial characteristics, economic well-being, and farm structure at the 1970 period on county farm structure in 1980 (Table 8.1). The explained variance in all three models is very high (and the betas are correspondingly low for nonfarm variables), as would be expected with the large lagged effects of the prior levels of farm structure.

TABLE 8.1

Longitudinal Regressions of Farm Structure on Industry Structure and Other County Characteristics[a]

	Smaller Family Farming	Larger Family Farming	Industrialized Farming
Industry Structure			
Percent in Peripheral Employment	.010	−.002	.024
	(.896)*	(−.167)*	(2.179)
Percent in State Employment	.026	.007	.015
	(4.886)	(1.393)*	(2.733)
Establishment Size	−.037	−.003	−.001
	(−.104)	(−.008)*	(−.004)*
Farm Structure			
Smaller Family Farming	.968	.011	.011
	(.968)	(.011)	(.011)*
Larger Family Farming	−.091	.921	−.010
	(−.091)	(.921)	(−.010)*
Industrialized Farming	.111	.038	.968
	(.111)	(.038)	(.968)
Worker Power Characteristics			
Percent Unionized	.013	.017	.019
	(1.359)	(1.764)	(1.946)
Per Capita AFDC Payments	.065	.038	−.004
	(.038)	(.023)	(−.003)*

TABLE 8.1 *continued*

	Smaller Family Farming	Larger Family Farming	Industrialized Farming
Worker Power Characteristics cont.			
Percent Nonwhite	−.048	−.010	−.004
	(−3.154)	(−.654)	(−.247)*
Median Education	−.000	−.008	.021
	(−.004)*	(−.058)*	(.153)
Percent Unemployed	−.014	−.017	−.010
	(−6.190)	(−7.409)	(−4.492)
Spatial Characteristics			
Percent Farm to Rural Population	.010	.042	.005
	(.665)*	(2.660)	(.300)*
Percent Urban	.018	−.016	−.007
	(.622)	(−.553)	(−.239)*
Metro Proximity	.024	−.020	−.005
	(.059)	(−.047)	(−.011)*
Northeast	−.046	.007	.011
	(−1.218)	(.188)*	(.295)*
Eastern Mountains	−.021	.008	.012
	(−.509)	(.185)*	(.297)*
Central U.S.	−.011	.003	.018
	(−.248)*	(.071)*	(.397)
West	.008	−.010	.015
	(.240)*	(−.286)*	(.446)
Economic Well-being	−.002	.034	.013
	(−.016)*	(.354)	(.132)*
Intercept	.000	.000	.000
	(−1.737)	(.768)*	(−2.256)
R^2	.947	.969	.953

[a]Unstandardized coefficients are in parentheses.
*Not significant at $p \leq .05$.

Turning first to smaller family farming, it is apparent that local characteristics affect this pattern over time. Counties with relatively higher levels of smaller family farming in 1980 were characterized by an industrial structure of small firms and somewhat greater state than core employment. State employment might sustain smaller family farming through its employment or service functions. There is also some support for previous arguments that smaller family farming is more reproducible in an industrial context of small, peripheral firms, possibly because it supplements low wages. As would be expected, smaller family farming tends to be sustained in a more urbanized, metropolitan proximate spatial context. Higher AFDC payments and a lower nonwhite population also contribute to the maintenance of this pattern. Smaller family farming tends to be higher in counties that had more industrialized and less larger family farming, suggesting that the fragmentation of local landholdings accompanies industrialized farming over time.

The model for larger family farming also demonstrates that a number of local factors influence this farming pattern. However, in contrast to smaller family farming, larger family is not differentially sustained by any particular segment of industrial structure. Many of the nonfarm factors supporting larger family farming are locational: low levels of urbanization, distance from metropolitan areas, and a higher farm population. Higher AFDC and a lower unemployed population also help to sustain this farming. The positive and significant relationship between economic well-being and larger family farming supports the converse of the Goldschmidt hypothesis that better socioeconomic conditions strengthen family farming over time. Finally, larger family farming tends to be higher in counties that have a greater extent of farming in general, irrespective of the particular farm pattern.

The greater frequency of nonsignificant findings indicate that local characteristics have less influence on industrialized farming than they do on smaller and larger family farming. Counties with poorer quality jobs, as indicated by peripheral and state employment, have slightly higher levels of industrialized farming over time. This suggests that industrialized farming is less able to compete with the higher wage employment generated by the core sector. Industrialized farming also has minor relationships with higher unionization and education. Earlier patterns of farm structure have little effect on the development of industrialized farming. There is no evidence that industrialized farming has expanded into areas occupied formerly by family farms during the 1970s. Finally, industrialized farming was more likely to grow in the Central U.S. and West than in other areas of the country.

Nonfarm Characteristics and Predominate Farming Patterns

The section extends the analysis of farm and nonfarm interrelationships by examining the local characteristics that distinguish each farming pattern. Discriminant analysis is used to identify which characteristics differentiate between counties having a predominate farming pattern. Discriminant analysis is a statistical procedure that identifies the linear sets of independent variables (discriminant functions) that are most important in distinguishing between two or more groups (Klecka, 1984). It also allows the importance of an individual variable as a discriminator net of other variables to be assessed. The analysis is performed for 1970 and 1980 so that it is possible to make comparisons among the variables defining the farming patterns for each time point.

In order to identify the nonfarm factors characterizing each pattern, counties first had to be classified by predominate type of farming. Because the indexes for industrialized and larger and smaller family farming are standardized at the same value (a mean of 50, standard deviation of 10) direct comparisons among them are possible. I examined each county's scores on the three patterns for both 1969 and 1978 and chose to pattern on which they scored the highest (for both years) to define that county's predominate pattern. Counties that did not have the same pattern for both years were considered to be borderline cases and were eliminated. Only 332 counties did not have consistent scores, so that the discriminant analysis is based on 2,705 counties.[2] Counties were almost evenly distributed among three patterns. The same variables used in the previous analysis, industrial structure, worker power, spatial characteristics, and economic well-being are used to identify counties by predominate farming pattern. However, in order to examine the industrial structure of counties in more detail, I disaggregated the core, peripheral, and state sectors into 40 component industries which are comparable for both 1970 and 1980.

I use stepwise discriminant analysis to find variables that are good discriminators among the major U.S. farming patterns. This procedure selects variables for inclusion in a function if they make a significant (set at the $p \leq .05$ level), individual, net contribution to discriminating among the groups.[3] Variables that fail to enter a function may have been good discriminators alone but make insufficient contributions when combined with other variables. The stepwise procedure helps to cull variables that contribute little individually or in combination to the explanation of farming differences and is particulary useful given the large number of industrial categories now in the analysis. The stepwise procedure also is appropriate because the effects of nonfarm impacts on farming is an exploratory issue not centered in any theoretically developed literature and addressed by few empirical studies.

The canonical correlation defines the degree of relatedness between the three groups of county farming patterns and the discriminant function. Two discriminant functions are mathematically possible in distinguishing among the three groups, and conventional criteria such as the eigenvalues of the functions and the canonical correlations indicate both are necessary for each year. In the analysis for 1970, the canonical correlation of .768 for the first function and .563 for the second indicate substantial relatedness (Table 8.2). Each discriminant function represents a dimension of local characteristics, and the group centroids indicate how far apart along the dimension the three groups are located. For 1970, two distinct nonfarm dimensions are evident from the group centroids. The first dimension distinguishes larger family farming counties (1.779) from

TABLE 8.2

Results of Discriminant Analysis for Predominate Farming Patterns, 1970

Item	Standardized Coefficients		County Means		
	Function 1	Function 2	Smaller Family Farming	Larger Family Farming	Industrialized Farming
Industry Structure (Percent Employment)					
Agriculture, Forestry and Fisheries	.236	-.178	.092	.261	.120
Mining	.077	-.057	.015	.014	.029
Textiles and Apparel	.101	.293	.062	.013	.038
Miscellaneous Nondurable Manufacturing	.054	.086	.036	.016	.030
Furniture, Lumber and Wood	-.047	.133	.037	.007	.039
Primary Metals	.120	.156	.015	.007	.009
Fabricated Metals	.068	.150	.016	.011	.009
Machinery, except Electrical	.261	.174	.019	.019	.010
Electrical Machinery	.157	.072	.019	.014	.010
Transportation Vehicles	.049	.126	.020	.011	.014
Miscellaneous Durable Manufacturing	.065	.138	.026	.014	.017
Trucking and Warehousing	-.010	.106	.014	.013	.011
General Merchandise Stores	.023	.135	.019	.016	.018
Food, Bakery, and Dairy Stores	.094	.006	.025	.023	.025
Motor Vehicle and Automotive Trade	.074	.138	.027	.028	.027
Other Retail Trade	.160	.016	.050	.059	.050
Banking and Credit Agencies	.078	.052	.012	.013	.012
Repair Services	.024	.120	.014	.014	.013
Private Household Services	.089	-.108	.020	.018	.023
Hospitals	.018	.109	.028	.028	.028

TABLE 8.2 continued

Item	Standardized Coefficients		County Means		
	Function 1	Function 2	Smaller Family Farming	Larger Family Farming	Industrialized Farming
Other Health Services	.084	.183	.018	.022	.016
Schools and Colleges	.081	.265	.077	.075	.078
Worker Power Characteristics					
Percent Unionized	−.116	.150	.275	.252	.255
Per Capita AFDC Payments	−.052	−.229	$41.91	$50.31	$46.36
Percent Nonwhite	−.040	−.251	.097	.050	.137
Percent Unemployed	−.080	.027	.048	.036	.051
Spatial Characteristics					
Percent Farm to Rural Population	.551	.885	.191	.359	.120
Percent Urban	−.147	−.207	.344	.325	.354
Metro Proximity	.002	.292	5.759	3.767	4.969
Northeast	.026	−.197	.194	.096	.199
Eastern Mountains	−.117	.211	.491	.021	.177
Central U.S.	.964	−.498	.069	.785	.090
West	.038	−.422	.046	.041	.279
Economic Well-being	.092	−.238	−.096	.089	.076
Canonical Correlation	.768	.563			
Group Centroids					
Function 1			−.669	1.779	−.961
Function 2			.897	−.102	−.770
Percent of Cases Correctly Classified			79.19	83.69	66.77
Total Number of Counties			908	852	945
Wilks' Lambda	.273				

TABLE 8.3

Results of Discriminant Analysis for Predominate Farming Patterns, 1980

Item	Standardized Coefficients		County Means		
	Function 1	Function 2	Smaller Family Farming	Larger Family Farming	Industrialized Farming
Industry Structure (Percent Employment)					
Agriculture, Forestry and Fisheries	-.159	.682	.059	.174	.081
Mining	.063	.186	.021	.022	.033
Food and Kindred Products	-.054	.086	.019	.022	.017
Chemical and Allied Products	.001	.148	.012	.006	.011
Furniture, Lumber and Wood	-.139	-.018	.035	.008	.033
Fabricated Metals	.056	-.134	.015	.011	.008
Machinery, except Electrical	.185	-.043	.025	.028	.015
Electrical Machinery	.084	-.004	.021	.015	.011
Railroad Service	-.044	.086	.007	.008	.008
Other Transportation Services	-.043	.152	.007	.005	.009
Wholesale Trade	.076	-.061	.034	.043	.032
General Merchandise Stores	.077	-.183	.016	.013	.014
Food, Bakery, and Dairy Stores	-.029	.095	.028	.025	.029
Motor Vehicle and Automotive Trade	.122	-.066	.023	.027	.023
Banking and Credit Agencies	.117	.031	.017	.019	.017
Insurance, Real Estate, and Other Finance	-.084	.097	.020	.018	.023
Private Household Services	.098	.127	.008	.008	.009
Entertainment and Recreation Services	-.011	.202	.006	.005	.009
Other Health Services	.164	-.078	.029	.036	.025
Schools and Colleges	.046	-.080	.085	.084	.088
Welfare, Religious, and Nonprofit Organizations	.099	-.136	.018	.019	.088

TABLE 8.3 continued

Item	Standardized Coefficients		County Means		
	Function 1	Function 2	Smaller Family Farming	Larger Family Farming	Industrialized Farming
Legal, Engineering and Other Professional Services	-.120	.114	.011	.010	.014
Public Administration	-.086	.186	.051	.046	.068
Establishment Size	.128	.030	7.951	6.083	7.098
Worker Power Characteristics					
Percent Unionized	-.108	-.184	.226	.206	.207
Per Capita AFDC Payments	-.168	.356	$68.27	$81.55	$76.74
Percent Nonwhite	.014	.310	.101	.066	.152
Median Education	.012	-.170	11.356	11.788	11.537
Spatial Characteristics					
Percent Farm to Rural Population	.746	-.698	.107	.258	.073
Percent Urban	-.251	.255	.356	.334	.367
Metro Proximity	.020	-.423	6.200	4.005	5.459
Northeast	.113	.172	.194	.096	.199
Eastern Mountains	-.127	-.292	.491	.021	.177
Central U.S.	.934	.461	.069	.785	.090
West	.112	.292	.046	.041	.279
Economic Well-being	.150	.319	-.017	.076	.012
Canonical Correlation	.788	.567			
Group Centroids					
Function 1			-.665	1.867	-1.044
Function 2			-.897	.125	.749
Percent of Cases Correctly Classified			80.73	83.57	63.81
Total Number of Counties			908	852	945
Wilks' Lambda	.259				

industrialized (−.961) and smaller family (−.669) farming counties; the second distinguishes smaller family (.897) from industrialized (−.770) farming counties. On the basis of the information provided by the two functions, about 79 percent of the smaller family farming counties, 84 percent of the larger family farming counties, and 67 percent of the industrialized farming counties could be correctly classified. The lower accuracy with which industrialized farming is predicted suggests that it is less likely a function of local characteristics, a point I shall return to at the end of this chapter.

The standardized discriminant function coefficient represents the relative contribution of its associated variable to the function net of the other variables. The sign of the coefficient indicates whether the variable is making a positive or negative contribution to the function. Only variables that make a significant contribution to discriminating among the three groups have been included in Tables 8.2 and 8.3. Their standardized coefficients are reported in the first two columns while the remaining columns contain the means for each variable by predominant county farm structure.

For 1970, variables with positive coefficients are more descriptive of larger family farming counties and variables with negative coefficients are more descriptive of industrialized and smaller family farming counties, as indicated by the direction of the centroids on the first function (Table 8.2). The variables loading highly in the direction of larger family farming counties reflect locational characteristics, the predominance of this farming pattern in the Midwest, and in areas with a higher farm population. Once other variables, particularly location, are controlled, larger family farming counties have a fairly diverse industrial structure. Although employment is greater in agriculture and other extractive industries, these counties are also characterized by some high wage industries, notably machinery, metals, and other durable manufacturing. A relatively large retail sector is supported and employment in schools and health services is present. Perhaps owing to a greater agrarian tradition, unionization rates are somewhat lower. Finally, the positive coefficient for well-being and negative coefficient for unemployment indicate that larger family farming counties are characterized by better economic conditions than are industrial or smaller family farming counties.

The second function indicates that a more diverse economy is found in smaller family farming counties than in industrialized farming counties. The proportion of the population employed in agriculture and related industries is lower in smaller family counties. There is greater employment in peripheral industries (such as textiles and apparel) and even in a few core industries (such as metals, machinery, and other durable manufacturing). Smaller family farming counties are also characterized by a more diverse (albeit generally low wage) service sector as indicated by greater employment in general merchandise stores, repair services, hospital and health services, and schools. As would be expected from the greater industrial base, unionization rates are also higher. Smaller family farming counties are located more in the Southeast and Eastern Mountains, closer to metropolitan areas and also in counties with a higher farm population. In addition to the comparisons with smaller family farming noted above, industrialized farming counties have higher AFDC payments, a greater nonwhite and urban population, and tend to be located more in the Central U.S. and West. Once all major local influences are controlled, economic well-being is also higher in industrialized farming than in smaller family farming counties.

The results for the discriminant analysis for 1980 show a two function pattern and discriminating variables that are similar to those found in 1970 (Table 8.3). The first function separates larger family farming from industrialized and smaller family farming counties. Larger family farming counties are still characterized by their spatial distinctiveness—high rural and farm populations, and Midwest location. The economy of larger family farming counties, however, has changed somewhat. These counties have become less agriculturally specialized, as shown by the negative loading of agricultural employment. Employment in core industries, particularly, machinery and larger business establishments (observable when other local characteristics are controlled) indicates the persistence of better quality industrial employment. Other forms of employment have now come to more strongly differentiate larger family farming counties, particularly the motor vehicle trade, wholesale trade (which includes farm products) and banking and credit agencies. The expansion of banks, lending institutions and the wholesale trade coincides with the agricultural boom of the late 1970s. The greater frequency of negative loadings on the nonfarm, industrial variables (relative to 1970) also suggests that larger family farming counties have lost some of their previous economic diversity. For example, these counties are no longer characterized by greater employment in food and other retail stores. Larger family farming counties continue to have higher economic well-being, but not lower unemployment as found in the previous decade.

In 1980, industrialized farming counties still have a less diverse industrial structure than smaller family farming areas. This is indicated by the higher level of agricultural employment in industrialized farming counties and by the negative loadings on some types of nonfarm employment. However, industrialized farming counties also appear to have been affected by changes in the growth and spatial distribution of services and other industries and by the strong farm economy of the 1970s. These counties seem to have become more specialized around agribusiness and related financial and transportation activities and other traditionally rural activities such as mining and recreation. As compared with smaller family farming counties, industrialized farming counties now have greater employment in: mining; food and kindred products and chemicals; and services including transportation, railroads, food retail, finance, private households, recreation, and public administration. In smaller family farm counties, textile employment is no longer a distinguishing feature, but industries such as fabricated metals and services such as retail chains, health and schooling continue to employ a higher proportion of the labor force. Characteristics of worker power follow similar patterns to those in 1970; however, educational levels now appear higher in smaller family farming counties. Spatial variations also follow the 1970 patterns. Finally, industrialized farming counties continue to have higher economic well-being than smaller family farming counties once other local factors are controlled.

CONCLUSIONS

In much research, the structure of farming tends to be viewed exclusively as a consequence of macrosocietal economic, political, and historical factors. This chapter explores an alternative set of influences, how the socioeconomic and spatial structure of a locality affect farming. I have investigated and outlined factors that maintain farming patterns over time; also, I have examined the distinct local characteristics associated with the various farming patterns.

Counties where larger family farming predominates are highly rural and, situated more in the Midwest. The nonfarm employment that is present involves segments of core industry, schools, and retail trade. Economic well-being is highest in areas of larger family farming. Over time, larger family farming tends to be supported in local contexts where the land market is more suitable, in terms of low population density, distance from metropolitan areas, and potential for farm residence and where some aspects of worker power are greater.

Smaller family farming counties tend to be dependent on peripheral manufacturing (such as textiles and apparel and other nondurable manufacturing), some types of core employment, and state services such as schools. These counties are located closer to metropolitan centers and are found more in the Eastern Mountains and South than in other areas of the country. The coincidence of low-volume, part-time farms in areas of low-wage employment and slightly higher unemployment suggests that analysts ought to be skeptical about inferring a symbiotic and mutually beneficial relationship between part-time farming and industry.

The distinguishing features of industrialized farming and its reproduction over place and time are less easily determined from local characteristics. Unlike family farming in which producers are tied to the community through residence, employment, use of community services and trade, and so forth, the presence of industrialized farming seems to be shaped to a greater extent by nonlocal, political economic forces. These would include the same forces shaping the temporal and spatial organization of hired labor or capitalist enterprises in the nonfarm sector that have been reviewed in previous chapters. For example, studies on industrialized farming have noted the importance of forces such as consumer demand, rate of return on investments from farming as compared to nonfarm industry, technology, methods of labor recruitment and retention, and state policy (Friedland et al., 1981; Krause, 1987).

Despite the differential impact of local characteristics, the general context of industrialized farming counties can be described. The nonfarm, industrial base of these counties seems to be comprised of lower wage industries that are less competitive with industrialized farming and that may perform agribusiness functions such as processing and transportation. Employment in agriculture as a distinguishing feature appears to have become more important in 1980, indicating that these counties have become more agriculturally specialized relative to the other counties. Industrialized farming counties are also characterized by typically rural, land dependent industries, such as mining and recreation. The lower employment in educational, health, and retail services (relative to other counties when all variables are controlled) also suggests that some consumption services are not well supported in these counties. Industrialized farming counties tend to have a higher nonwhite population, but other indicators such as levels of AFDC suggest that the power of workers is relatively high. In terms of spatial location, these counties fall between smaller family and larger family farming in degree of rurality and are found more in the West.

The local context of the farming patterns has several implications for the future development of the agricultural sector. Many of the peripheral industries such as textiles and nondurable manufacturing that have supported smaller family farming in the past began to decine in the 1970s, making this type of farming more vulnerable as well. The persistance of part-time farming has been argued to obscure long term trends toward concentration and centralization in agriculture, which may thus become more pronounced if small, part-time units decline. Another issue is that while rural land markets and distance from urban centers and industry seem to have supported larger family farming in the 1970s, these factors became liabilities in the 1980s. Declining land values eroded the tax base of family farming communities and led to increased consolidation of schools, hospitals, and other rural services. Distance from urban areas is also a double-edged sword: while it helps preserve land for farm use, it reduces sources of nonfarm income that have become more critical in sustaining farms.

The overwhelming costs of farm subsidies in the face of national fiscal decline and the deepening impoverishment of rural areas have led many to argue that agricultural programs are insufficient to deal with the crisis in rural areas. What is needed is a broad based development program that encompasses the nonfarm sector and the social and economic needs of all rural people. This chapter reinforces and extends these arguments by showing that even the farm sector is dependent upon local economic and social structure: a general rural development program is needed not only to strengthen rural America but for the future of family farming as well. The following, final chapter of this book considers this issue more fully. In addition to summarizing the conclusions and implications of this study, I focus on how state policy and programs and the empowerment of rural people can be used to transform current trajectories of agricultural and industrial development.

Conclusions

This chapter draws together the themes and findings of previous chapters and points to new directions for research and policy. This study has explored how postwar economic restructuring, particularly of the farm sector, contributes to socioeconomic inequality at the local level. It addresses a long standing debate with a rich and diverse literature that questions whether the development of large-scale, industrialized farms, as compared to family operations, jeopardizes local well-being.

This study has taken a different tack from previous research in several ways. First, I have argued that a more general set of assumptions about the origins of inequality underlies the Goldschmidt question: that is, it presupposes that socioeconomic disparities among localities must be viewed in large part as a consequence of the way economic production is organized within them. Framing the question in this way has allowed me to examine it in the context of recent, multidisciplinary political economic and other structural perspectives and more importantly into a general conceptual framework about inequality across space.

If the structure of the local economy is to be taken as central to the creation of inequality, the capacity of producers and their households to modify the conditions of production must be considered a corollary issue. People are not passive victims of farming or industry structure and continually attempt to alter the ways in which surplus is extracted whether through the wage relationship or through market exchange in the sphere of circulation. Many of these attempts reflect the heroic efforts of previous and contemporary generations of the working class as embodied in protective legislation, social welfare programs, workplace organizations, and other factors that increase the bargaining power of labor.

A final consideration still neglected by much social science research is how spatial location determines inequality and individuals' life chances. The uneven distribution of economic sectors and history of social relations embedded in different areal settings contribute to disparities in opportunities and living standards. Spatial location is particularly relevant to an understanding of the Goldschmidt question, since it is concerned fundamentally with differences among localities.

To recapitulate, I have argued that in order to properly address the Goldschmidt debate, it must be situated in the context of a broader conceptual framework on inequality in which three elements are key: the structure of production in farming and in industry, the bargaining power of workers and their households, and locational characteristics.

Second, in addition to the conceptual framework, this study differs from others by its focus on the structure of the contemporary farm system which many have argued is becoming dualistic—with a large number of small, part-time farms and a concentrated sector of large-scale industrialized farms that account for expanding proportions of farm sales. In contrast, much of the literature is still premised at least implicitly on populist assumptions about the economy, that is, that simple commodity production should typify the farm sector while industrialized farming is a historical aberration. This is evident in that researchers typically contrast dichotomous farm types (industrialized and family farms), and overlook variations within family labor farming such as small, part-time units. In short, there is a lack of recognition that farming, particularly family labor based production has responded to the changing nature of capitalism. The problem of adequately characterizing contemporary farm structure is not exclusive to the Goldschmidt studies but rather stems from our limited theory about the development of farming in modern societies as well as a lack of appropriate data.

This study has identified three national patterns of farm production distinguishable by their scale of operations and the circuits by which capital has penetrated agriculture. Industrialized farming generates high volume sales and is dependent on hired labor. Larger family farming is capital-intensive, depends on family labor, and is integrated into land and capital markets through part-ownership, tenancy, and heavy technological expenditures. It can be considered a modern equivalent of simple commodity production, characterizing operations by family farmers who have become increasingly market oriented in the attempt to stay in farming. Smaller family farming reflects the differentiation of family labor producers into marginalized, part-time farmers operating small holdings with low volume sales. These three production systems correspond to empirical observations about the contemporary structure of U.S. farming and to conceptualizations such as Kautsky's (1988). For the purposes of testing the Goldschmidt hypothesis, they allow not only for contrasts between industrialized and family farming but for exploring differences within family farming as well.

Third, this study describes how the nonfarm economy and other local characteristics articulate with farming. Industrial structure, worker power, spatial characteristics, and prior socioeconomic levels are critical to sustaining family operations and influence the development of industrialized farming. Most previous research has centered on the effects of farm structure on communities, neglecting communities' impact on farm structure.

Finally, this study focuses on national patterns of relationships across U.S. counties, providing an overall summary answer to the Goldschmidt question. Like other studies of U.S. industrial structure (Jacobs, 1982, 1985; Tomaskovic-Devey, 1988a; Bloomquist and Summers, 1982) and farming (Buttel and Larson, 1979; Harris and Gilbert, 1982; Heaton and Brown, 1982; Goldschmidt, 1978b), I have assumed that national level findings can yield valid and useful insights about the effects of economic structure. Alternatively, national level studies are always vulnerable to the charge that there are exceptions to every generalization. While I have attempted to deal with this issue in part by examining regional variations, there are obviously innumerable, more detailed sections of the country that the analyses have not explored. Any regional analysis is susceptible to a similar critique, that there are always subregional units where findings may not hold, and further, that the way a region is defined will determine results.

ECONOMIC STRUCTURE, WORKER POWER, SPATIAL CHARACTERISITCS AND INEQUALITY

Given the previous summary points, I turn now to a discussion of the major findings. I outline how the elements of the conceptual framework affect observable patterns of inequality, with particular focus on the relationship between farm structure and local socioeconomic conditions.

Farm Structure

This study provides limited support for the Goldschmidt hypothesis that industrialized farming reduces socioeconomic conditions across U.S. counties. But the detrimental impacts of this production system are neither automatic nor strong; further, they are not apparent at any particular historical point (cross-sectionally) in every region of the county. Most impacts appear to take time to work through and ultimately become evident in levels of local economic well-being. That is, where industrialized farming takes holds, the potential for future economic well-being tends to decline. The context of industrialized farming, extensive use of relatively low wage, seasonal, unskilled hired labor, and its association with specialized industries, such as agribusiness and forms of extractive employment, appears to be incapable of generating high and equitable levels of economic well-being over time. Some of the impacts of industrialized farming are also observable cross-sectionally at the same time point: counties with greater industrialized farming have inequitable income distributions and they are prone to greater disruption of the social fabric, as indicated by births to teenagers. In sum, the economic context of industrialized farming is characterized by internal disparities between rich and poor, and cumulative underdevelopment in the long run.

This study also has shown that the effects of industrialized local farming are not predetermined but can be modified by nonfarm factors. The political economic environment surrounding industrialized farming today is strikingly different from that at the time of Goldschmidt, a consequence of postwar changes, including the growth of industrial employment in rural areas, increased state intervention on behalf of workers and their households, and the expansion, although limited, of unions and labor legislation. The association of industrialized farming with some types of industry indicate the presence of alternative employment sources which can increase demand for workers and wages on industrialized farms. As shown in the preceding chapter, the state appears to heavily underwrite the costs of reproducing the labor force in counties characterized by industrialized farming, as evidenced by their higher per capita AFDC rates (observable when other factors are controlled). Industrialized farming counties are also relatively favorably endowed with other worker power and spatial characteristics, falling between larger family and smaller family farming counties in level of unionization, unemployment, and degree of rurality. Large nonwhite populations, however, make industrialized farming counties more vulnerable to low-wage employment and greater impoverishment. Although these local nonfarm attributes influence the course of development and impacts of industrialized farming, they have an even greater bearing on family labor production. Industrialized farming appears less responsive to local attributes and more strongly influenced by social relations in the larger economy.

That the sociopolitical context mediates the effects of industrialized farming is particularly evident in the regional analyses in the set of cross-sectional models for 1980. Industrialized farming is related to poorer economic conditions in the Southeast but to better conditions in the Central U.S. In the Midwest, agrarian social relations such as greater state regulation of corporate farming and tradition of protection of family farming, coupled with the strong Midwestern farm economy of the late 1970s may make industrialized farming more redistributive of benefits while the more coercive agrarian and labor history of the South offers greater leeway for exploitation.

The findings with regard to smaller family farming indicate that the Goldschmidt hypothesis needs serious revision. Over the regions of the country and time periods examined, this pattern of production is related to poorer income conditions particularly in the cross-sectional analyses; there is less evidence for long-term impacts. Nationally, counties with a greater extent of this farming also have considerably higher unemployment. While studies in the Goldschmidt tradition have been preoccupied with the effects of full-blown capitalist agriculture, capital entered farming through the back door so to speak, generating small units that impoverish localities to at least the same degree as industrialized farming. The routes by which smaller family farming disadvantages counties were considered in Chapter 6 and include insufficient farm sales to cover household reproduction, retention of redundant labor, and subsidizing low-wage nonfarm employment. These findings must be qualified by recognizing that there are various motivations for and conditions under which small, particularly part-time units may not jeopardize local well-being. There may be subregional and commodity specific exceptions; also, where farming is pursued only for lifestyle or tax purposes, impacts may not be detrimental. But by and large the findings here as well as other research (Carlin and Crecink, 1979; Tweeten, 1984) suggest that while units operated on these bases may be spatially interspersed throughout the rural economy, the general pattern of smallholder agriculture is not of this type: counties whose landscape is dotted with small farms are characterized by a landholding and production system that provides inadequate combinations of income and employment opportunities.

This study also shows that smaller family farming articulates with the nonfarm sector in closer and more complex ways than do the other two farming patterns. Counties where smaller family farming predominates have a larger industrial base and are particularly dependent on peripheral manufacturing, some types of core employment, and schooling. They appear better linked to urban consumption and labor markets. Their higher health status and educational attainments may be a consequence of these structural linkages. Thus, once industrial structure, worker power, and spatial characteristics are controlled, a negative relationship between smaller family farming and economic well-being emerges but one that does not necessarily extend to extraeconomic arena.

The findings indicate that a closer look at the political economic implications of small, part-time farms is warranted. That is, rather than focusing on the benefits of these farms for stabilizing the decline of family production or enhancing lifestyle, their function and significance for capital ought to be questioned. While the legitimation function of part-time units has been explored (Bonanno, 1987), much more study is needed on the articulation of this farming with the nonfarm economy and the types of activities smallholder households must engage in order to reproduce themselves. Focusing on these issues helps explain why smallholder, part-time farming can have detrimental consequences to farm households and their communities. As noted by a number of analysts (Goss et al., 1980; Gasson, 1988; Kautsky, 1988) farmers' work time is considerably lengthened by both on- and off-farm work leading to self-exploitation and deterioration in labor power. This study shows that in smaller family farming counties unemployment is higher and many of the existing jobs are in lower wage industries. Employers maintain and benfit from a cheaper, accessible labor force that subsidizes part of its consumption costs.

A final issue is the extent to which part-time farming will continue to provide meaningful economic and legitimation functions. Part-time farming is said to be an inherently unstable form of production as units tend to turnover more rapidly and are less likely to remain in the hands of the family (Gasson, 1988:158). The decline of rural industries such as types of nondurable manufacturing may diminish the potential for part-time farming in some areas, making the erosion of family farming more pronounced. A counter to this, however, is the recent trend toward the growth of the informal economy (Kolko, 1988). As employers have cut wages and full-time jobs and the state has decreased its support of the social wage, households have been forced to bear increasing costs of their reproduction. Farming may come to be more of a necessity for employed rural workers than a lifestyle choice.

A consistent finding of this study is that a production system of family operated commercially-oriented farms—larger family farming—results in better socioeconomic conditions for localities, including higher and more evenly distributed incomes, lower unemployment, and lower infant mortality. Producers of larger family farms have class positions that more closely approximate the petite bourgeoisie. They operate units that are large enough to support their households without much operator off-farm work but not so large as to require a great deal of hired labor. They are neither exploited like wage laborers nor extensively profiting from the work of others. Though the indicators of inequality used in this study are limited, the findings are in line with Goldschmidt's (1978a): moderate-size units that sustain the household without extensive hired labor result in a more homogeneously middle class community where living conditions are better and distribution of income and other resources is more democratic.

In contrast to Goldschmidt's (1978a) observations on Dinuba, however, it is less clear whether consumption needs are well met by services in larger family farming areas. Compared to other counties, larger family farming counties are situated in more isolated rural environments. Despite their location and farming dependency, such counties have a relatively diversified nonfarm sector, with employment in schools, core industries and some types of trade predominating. However, these counties appear to have lost some of the diversity of the nonfarm sector from 1970 to 1980, as indicated by the discriminant analyses for both years. Also, as shown in Chapter 6, once nonfarm variables are controlled, larger farmily farming counties do not have significantly higher education or physicians per capita. These findings suggest that larger farmily farming counties have not been favorably affected by postwar changes in the service economy. During the prewar period of Goldschmidt's study, rural communities were crisscrossed by small businesses that provided for the consumption needs of a spatially dispersed population. The postwar period witnessed large scale out-migration from rural areas, leaving behind a less educated and increasingly elderly population. These changes slowed in the 1960s and even reversed slightly in the 1970s. But by the 1980s, rural areas once again reverted back to lower growth rates. Added to these changes has been the trend toward specialization and centralization of services occurring throughout both urban and rural areas but which is obviously exacerbated more in less densely populated places. The sectoral shift to service employment has also been slower in rural areas (Henry et al., 1988). In the 1980s, deregulation of transportation and banking raised credit and transporation costs more highly in rural than urban areas, thereby limiting access more in the former.

A final point is that the benefits of larger family farming ought to be seen in light of its temporal persistence and in the costs it entails for producers and their households. Larger family farming reflects the compromises over control over factors of production that producers have had to make in order to remain competitive: partial or complete withdrawal from landownership; dependence on borrowed capital to sustain highly capital intensive operations; and increased segmentation of management of operations. These compromises reduce producers' autonomy and make them vulnerable to interest rates, prices and rents. Moreover, the ability to self-exploit or to reduce consumption levels, which in the past gave such farmers a competitive edge over hired labor dependent producers, is now an unrealistic strategy. Household consumption levels can simply not be reduced enough to sustain today's highly leveraged operations. Larger family farming lacks the advantages of smaller family farming in terms of off-farm income and the economies of scale and power in exchange relationships of industrialized farming. As shown in Chapter 2, it is precisely those farms with the characteristics of larger family farming that have been most devastated by the farm crisis.

In sum, family farmers are faced with a system of production that is neither genuinely of their making nor responsive to their needs but one that has evolved out of the exigencies of the wider economic system. The findings of this study do not augur well for the deepening dualism of the farm sector and increased marginalization of larger family farming. Rather, they suggest that a trend toward large scale industrialized and small farms will heighten socioeconomic inequality. However, it also should be recognized that levels of inequality in rural localities are only in limited part a function of the farm sector. Of more importance to the future well-being of rural areas will be the trajectories of development of non-farm industry and the balance of power between workers and employers.

Industrial Structure

The findings for industrial structure support and extend current research on economic segmentation. It was argued that in localities with greater core employment, socioeconomic conditions would be higher since employers have greater need and ability to buy off the labor force through higher consumption levels; historically, labor has won more concessions in the core. The reverse is true in the peripheral sector: employers have little need to buy off labor, and labor has won fewer concessions. It is not surprising that a county having a higher level of core employment also shows a higher income level, lower poverty level and less income inequality. State employment has negative impacts on economic well-being much like those of the peripheral sector. These findings support recent studies about the similarity between the peripheral and state sectors in terms of the quality of positions generated and suggest that former segmented economy assumptions about more favorable conditions in the state sector (Hodson, 1978) need to be revised, particularly when dealing with areal units. Dependence on the public sector (with exceptions such as administrative and ordnance centers) also appears to characterize communities in economic decline, those the private sector no longer considers worth exploiting (Gurr and King, 1987). The size of county business establishments, a firm level indicator of the segmented economy, has an influence on economic well-being comparable to that of core employment. In general, these relationships remain constant, regardless of time period or location examined, although there is some indication that counties with large firms lost previous economic advantages as a consequence of restructuring over the 1970s.

This study extends segmented economy research by examining indicators of inequality less reducible to economic structure and by focusing on the consequences of segmentation at the local rather than individual level. It supports recent research that finds little difference in the amount of unemployment generated by the core and peripheral sectors. Although core employment is not significantly related to higher educational levels, lower teenage fertility, or lower infant mortality, it creates the preconditions for each one of these through raising income levels. There is further evidence that state employment, potentially through its expenditures for services, can ameliorate noneconomic inequities and help reproduce the labor force through improved health and education facilities.

Worker Power

The resources and characteristics that strengthen the power of workers and their households relative to the interests of capital strongly influence the levels at which a local workforce can reproduce themselves. From an empirical standpoint, the worker power attributes explain greater variation in local economic well-being than economic or spatial structure. Localities whose populations are in better positions to press for material demands as a consequence of greater market security or higher state support of social welfare, group attributes such as higher educational attainments and ethnic status, and low unemployment, tend to have better economic conditions. Somewhat of an exception to this is the extent of labor organization, which over time and particularly in the closed-shop Northeast tends to diminish economic returns and raise unemployment. This suggests that in areas where class struggle has become too strong, employers react by closing income and employment opportunities. There is also some indication of a fractionalization and weakening of worker power in 1980 as compared to the previous decade. Higher levels of welfare transfers and education seem less able to shelter local labor forces from poorer economic conditions. Differences between union and nonunion workers and between white and nonwhite populations appear to have increased.

This study broadens previous work by examining how worker power affects extraeconomic conditions of localities. One interesting finding is the relationship between aspects of worker power and education attainments and births to

teenagers—where family welfare is strongly supported and adequate job opportunities exist, educational attainments are higher and teenage fertility is lower.
These results suggest that fundamental social structural changes empowering
workers and their households are necessary to raise educational levels and reduce
births to adolescents.

Spatial Location

A community's geographic region and distance from a metropolitan center
are important determinants of its level of well-being. Even after taking into account
economic structure and work force characteristics, more geographically isolated
areas rural areas have poorer economic well-being, higher unemployment, poorer
education, and higher infant mortality. The tendency for historical differences
between rural and urban areas is thus to persist and perhaps to become compounded in the development process. The study also confirms a continuation
of longstanding and well-known regional disparities such as greater inequality
in the South and Appalachia. However, regional differences tend to diminish once
economic structure and worker power characteristics are taken into account,
indicating that apparent regional disparities in socioeconomic well-being are much
a function of contemporary configurations of industrial structure and worker power
found in different areas.

Locality and Inequality: In Summary

In attempting to answer the questions posed by the Goldschmidt studies,
I have proposed a general model of how socioeconomic inequities are generated
across localities. This model is derived from political economic assumptions about
the social order. Capital has different bases for supporting workers' consumption
levels, production units are differentially advantaged in the sphere of exchange,
workers and households possess different resources, and the state varies in its
degree of support of the interests of capital over labor. All of these social forces
are unevenly spread across and historically embodied in different areal settings—
which translates to variations in the socioeconomic levels at which workers and
households in a particular locality can reproduce themselves. In its empirical form,
the model advocated here explains a great deal of inequality among localities,
both at the national and regional levels.

STARTING POINTS FOR NEW RESEARCH

While the findings of this study broaden and challenge previous research,
they raise new questions of their own. The nature of census data and the time
period are inherent constraints that call for the use of other methodologies and
historical points to address the issues presented. From an empirical standpoint,
there is a need to replicate this study using finer grained units of analysis and

more detailed methodology. The varied routes by which farming and industry affect local well-being should be explored through case studies of localities. Although I have addressed this issue through considering previous research and extrapolating from my findings, the use of county-level census data precludes comprehensive treatment of the topic. Comparative studies of similar production units in different areal settings (for example, industrialized farming in California as compared to Florida) also can provide information about a potential source of regional differences in the effects of industrialized farming, internal variations in production units. The conceptual approach taken in this study should be also subject to continual refinement and refraction with ongoing social reality. Future research should examine new forms of production arising in agriculture and industry, extend analysis of the effects of economic structure to extraeconomic and nonlocal impacts, broaden the notion of worker power, and continue to build social science theory that takes seriously the day-to-day experiences of people across places. The need for these new conceptual directions is detailed in this section.

With regard to farming, theory needs to be directed to the shape and structure of the farm sector in late fordism and beyond, as we move into a new regime of accumulation. This is a large mandate, since much of our current theory is inadequate for explaining the lines along which agriculture has developed under fordism itself. Areas of inquiry still needed include: the variety of forms production units take and the methods by which surplus is extracted from them; the functions of agriculture for the wider economy; and the paths by which crises in farming have originated and worked themselves out.

This study has pointed to the need to reformulate the Goldschmidt hypothesis and for new research thrusts assessing the impacts of farm structure. First, most generally, studies should focus on charting the effects of actual rather than idealized versions of the contemporary farm system. Most of our assumptions about family labor producers are based on surveys assessing motivations for farming in which lifestyle considerations (agrarian values, traditional rural upbringing for children, closeness to nature) play an important role. Certainly subjective experiences provide useful insights about why producers engage in farming, but we must look beyond these to gauge their political economic implications: to what extent are reported motives for farming rationalizations for self-exploitation or attempts to hold on to a last bastion of workplace autonomy? For despite family operators' often reported satisfaction with their communities and lifestyle, their rates of mental distress and disorder (whether they are part- or full-time operators and even if their financial situation is good) are generally higher than for urban, nonfarm residents, belying the notion that farming today is anything close to peaceful, bucolic existence (Coye, 1986; Keating, 1987; Belyea and Lobao, 1990). Reseachers should more fully question the social costs farmers have paid and the trade-offs they have made in terms of control over production factors, leisure time, and consumption levels in order to remain in farming.

Detailed documentation of how families balance household and farm resources and local labor market opportunities in order to survive in farming (e.g., Gasson, 1988) is needed. Researchers should also extend their focus from the positive functions of part-time farming for households to the functions provided to capital (e.g., Bonanno, 1987)—with this latter focus a starting point for greater understanding about why small, part-time units might have detrimental community impacts.

Second, the Goldschmidt hypothesis should be reframed by questioning not only if industrialized farms have adverse impacts but where and under what conditions. The reflexive nature of the relationship between farming and industry, the power of people to offset the demands of capital and to change the course of local economic development, changes in the internal organization of industrialized farms, and the uneven effects of state policy and macroeconomic conditions are all reasons why the impacts of industrialized farming might differ over time and place.

Third, future research should extend the Goldschmidt hypothesis to extra-economic impacts of farm structure in the locality. Heffernan and Heffernan (1986) set new research directions by showing how the recent farm crisis affected the social-psychological well-being of farmers and this study has shown that the structure of farming is related to family stability and levels of health. The political effects of industrialized farming have been examined at the local level by only a few studies (Goldschmidt, 1978a; Fujimoto, 1977). Local environmental effects of specific farm structures particularly merit investigation. There is evidence that large industrialized farms are associated with certain environmental damages because they have more resources that enable them to engage in excessive, detrimental practices. Such damages include: soil compaction due to use of large, heavy machines; drops in the water table due to groundwater mining; and groundwater contamination and pollution of lakes and rivers from greater chemical use (MacCannell, 1988:27-28). Finally, it should be recognized that indicators of well-being do not necessarily serve as proxies for one another and that farm structure may have alternatively beneficial or detrimental effects depending upon the aspect of well-being examined.

Fourth, research should consider the effects of farm structure beyond the locality. The nonlocal effects of farm structure have generally been the domain of a few economists questioning the relationship between food costs for consumers produced by farms of various sizes (Heady and Sonka, 1974). The most devastating effect of the current trend toward a dualistic farm structure, however, may not be evident in the local community or in food costs per se but in the closing of what little democracy currently exists in food production—that is, in control of our nation's food supply and in access to farming as a viable, lifetime vocation for those who want to farm. As farming is the last important industry not entirely contained by a few international corporations (MacCannell, 1988:24), its preservation is a critical national issue.

Finally, a major issue is that the entire agricultural system has wrought serious environmental and health related concerns. Fordist agriculture has been premised on the production of low-cost, uniform food commodities using extensive natural resources and agrochemicals such as pesticides which skyrocketed in usage in the postwar period (Kenney et al., 1989; Coye, 1986). This system began to be challenged by the 1960s when a new surge of farmworker organizing, coalescing with the emergence of the environmental movement, focused public attention about pesticide residues in the environment and in humans (Coye, 1986). The Environmental Protection Agency (EPA) was established in 1970 to regulate and approve the use of agricultural chemicals, including pesticides. But the poor quality or even falsified data submitted to EPA, staffing shortages, and lack of activism still make regulation problematic. An independent study reported that 38 percent of 3,350 pesticides have no toxicity data available (Coye, 1986:171). Coye (1986:180) estimates that about 313,300 farm workers out of 4 million may have suffered a pesticide related illness in 1982 alone. Of the 300 pesticides registered for use on food, only about half can even be detected by current tests, and violations run about 3 percent for all commodities tested (Coye, 1986:185-186). Other environmental issues concern the use of antibiotics for livestock, which may sicken individuals and have long-term effects on the immune system: an estimated one-half of the antibiotics used in the United States are fed to livestock (Coye, 1986:186). Pesticide and nitrate contamination of groundwater supplies now affects almost half (1,437) of the counties in the United States (Nielsen and Lee, 1987:19). As with other epidemiological indicators, socioeconomic differentials in large part determine who is subject to greater exposure to residues of agricultural chemicals: rural residents in agricultural areas, minorities and the poor.

Turning to industry structure, this study has raised several general questions about the segmented economy that require deeper investigation. First, research should continue to probe the differential effects of industrial structure over different places and times. While the effects of core industry on economic well-being did not change much over the decade examined, its benefit for localities may have diminished over broader and in more recent time periods (see Tigges, 1988). The need to revise segmented economy theory regarding the impact of the state sector, differences in the quantity of unemployment generated by each sector, and extensions to extraeconomic quality of life indicators was also noted earlier.

Most importantly, we should begin questioning the extent to which segmented economy theory remains a relevant perspective as the economy moves out of the fordist era. The new system emerging "rests on a startling flexibility with respect to labor processes, labor markets, products, and patterns of consumption" (Harvey, 1988:107). In the manufacturing sector, there is a tendency toward less job stratification and more flat hierarchies. The division of labor has become more flexible with workers performing multiple tasks, often in teams. There is greater movement and ability of firms to seek out specific types of labor pools with requisite skill, work ethics, and traditions of labor organization. Manufacturers have increasing capacity to produce a variety of products in small batches to keep up with rapidly changing consumer markets and fads. All of these attributes diverge from the highly stratified divisions of labor, union controlled job tasks, and mass production of bulk commodities that characterized traditional core sector manufacturing firms under fordism. To what extent manufacturing and services as a whole will move toward this new accumulation model is a topic of considerable current debate (Lipietz, 1986; Harvey, 1988; Clark, 1986; Davis, 1978) but one that calls the utility of the segmented economy approach increasingly into question.

This study has argued for and demonstrated the importance of examining how the actions and resources of workers and their households affect local inequality and the organization of economic production. Future studies should incorporate and broaden the notion of worker power. In addition to market security, workforce characteristics, and the employment situation, other bases of resistance that might vary locally or statewide include regulatory actions that limit the operations of big capital in the farm and industrial sectors, such as zoning and plant closing laws, workers' health and safety legislation, and legislation regarding non-family farm corporations and environmental resource management. Other evidence of historical and contemporary resistance of workers and their households is embodied in routine politics, particularly in local platforms and voting behavior, and in the nonroutine political action, including strikes and protests.

A final issue stressed throughout this volume is the importance of incorporating the concept of space into social science theory and research. While the analyses considered some aspects of this concept, the meaning and signifcance of space particularly for studies of social relations requires deeper systematic investigation. That social scientists are moving in this direction is evident in new theoretical developments in class analysis (e.g. Giddens, 1981), the incorporation of spatial dimensions to often aspatial research, such as that on political behavior (see Agnew, 1987), and in the growing use of contextual analyses to show the effects of local social structure on individual behavior.

Beyond the arena of social science research, there is a pressing political need for further focus on the central topic of this volume, the impacts of economic structure on local well-being and consumption levels. As a consequence of the current restructuring of farming and industry, producers can be expected to have shorter tenure on each job (or farm) and more varied work experiences that crosscut occupations and industries. Particular labor market experiences and issues will be potentially less salient than in the past as a basis for mobilizing farmers or workers. On the other hand, the recent, marked falls in many Americans' consumption levels as described in Chapter 2, coupled with the social effects of economic dislocation, including suicide and depression among farmers, depression among the unemployed, and homelessness, and are increasingly becoming cause for concern and outrage. At the same time, serious objections are being raised to the environmental impacts of industry, such as oil spills, hazardous waste disposal, and nuclear plant contamination, and of farming particularly soil erosion, pesticide tainted food, use of antibiotics for livestock, and goundwater contamination.

These events have several implications. First, there seems to be at least a tacit recognition by the public that many aspects of the quality of American life are deteriorating. Second, issues of consumption levels and quality (rather than traditional labor market issues) have become a new catalyst for political mobilization, as was somewhat evident during the 1988 Jackson presidential campaign, which attempted to link farmers, environmentalists, the poor, and minorities. Interestingly, many of the activists involved in environmental and farm protest movements are women—those who bear primary responsibility for family reproductive activities. Consumption issues may be easier to mobilize Americans rather than pure labor market and class issues. The dominant ideology is still one of blaming the victim for falling into poverty and for other failures to achieve in the labor market. But consequences of the economy visible outside the labor market such as homelessness or environmental degradation are less acceptable to most Americans (Schiller, 1980). Finally, mobilizing people along consumption fronts may lead them to eventually question the extent to which farming and industry serve popular interests and, ultimately, the legitimacy of the economic system as a whole. Changing consumption levels and quality engendered by the restructuring of farming and industry thus have important but often little recognized implications for political activism in the post-fordist era.

POLICY DIRECTIONS AND POPULAR INITIATIVES

The evolution of agriculture and industry has come increasingly into conflict with many of the needs of Americans. In the industrial sector, the organization of work and use of finance has come to be more directed toward the short-term interests of business rather than toward working people and their households (Harrison and Bluestone, 1988; Kolko, 1988). The development of the farm sector has not only jeopardized the financial and social well-being of family producers but also led to an increasingly undemocratic agricultural system that is now embroiled in a serious environmental debate. Despite these general economic trends, new ways of organizing production in some segments of farming and industry are developing that may provide the foundation for a post-fordist economy. These new social experiments also appear to bring some benefits to producers and their communities.

For instance, since the late 1970s Japanese have been establishing 'just-in-time' supplier-assemble systems mainly throughout the Midwest auto corridor. The just-in-time system involves smoothing out production levels, eliminating large inventories (in contrast to American auto manufacturers heavy inventory stocking, 'just-in-case'), using flexible machinery adaptable to short production runs, and maintaining close relationsips between the major firms that assemble autos and their smaller suppliers. By the early 1990s, these transplants will be turning out about one-fifth of all cars produced in America (Florida et al., 1988:3). Some advantages for workers in this system are that it minimizes the separation of mental and manual labor (allowing workers more control over the labor process), promotes skill acquisition and on-the-job training, and results in relatively high wages. An interesting implication for the relationship between agriculture and industry are the types of communities that these firms choose: rural localities close to established suppliers with high quality, relatively well-educated labor having 'good work ethics' and little factory experience and tradition of unionism—a work force with a farm background. While the Japanese system is not without its drawbacks, including a reluctance to work with American unions and obvious, broader issues of reducing national industrial autonomy, it appears to have some benefits for communities. The Japanese have reinvested in an area of the Midwest generally abandoned by large American firms and have tended to revitalize business for small local American suppliers and the general industrial base of small communities. High capital investments and tight supplier networks also make these Japanese firms less movable once established.

The deleterious environmental impacts of agriculture are also resulting in alternative production techniques that tend to be labor- rather than capital-intensive and thus may also reduce debt and increase the need for family labor (which, with the right commodities and alternative marketing strategies, may profitably keep a family in farming). For example, sustainable agriculture involves practices that retain natural resources such as soil health, water quality, and energy (Geisler, 1984). Integrated pest management reduces pesticide use and saves energy. Organic farming avoids chemical fertilizers and pesticides and synthetic growth regulators and feed additives.

While the previous productive experiments suggest that some positive aspects of agricultural and industrial change loom on the horizon, they are confined presently only to a very small segment of both sectors (or in the case of agricultural production techniques, are not fully implemented on most farm units). Dependence on such private sector initiatives will not quickly or fundamentally alter the course and costs of current economic trends.

Much of our social history can be viewed as an attempt to make the organization of economic production responsive to the needs of those actively involved in day-to-day productive activities, a process that has been pursued with varying degrees of enthusiasm by the state. Any serious program of economic development that reaches profoundly into the structure of society undermines the wealthy and powerful who benefit from the social order. It would be naive to suggest dismantling and rebuilding our present economic, social, and political institutions to fit the needs of most Americans, although that may establish more quickly and thoroughly the social justice needed by working people and advocated by activists and scholars of the working class. Rather, I will suggest some broad routes evident from this study and related research that can increase the social and economic security of producers, their households, and localities and that can provide the material basis and democratic planning necessary to achieve this security. My suggestions are premised on the idea that the organization of industry and farming will continue to change as we move away from the fordist epoch and that new policies under this transition period ought to be addressed.

I focus on the economic development of rural areas, although many of the initiatives are applicable to urban areas as well. As noted previously, more than three-quarters of the counties in the study are rural. These areas have historically lagged behind urban areas in jobs and income and recently the gap has widened. It should also be noted that the following discussion simply outlines general policy thrusts and other public initiatives. I have not attempted to give an account of farm policy alternatives, such as commodity or price support programs that have been adequately addressed elsewhere (Tweeten, 1970; Luttrell, 1989; Cochrane, 1979, 1986; Strange, 1988); to provide a comprehensive inventory of the rural development policies already in place (see Tweeten and Brinkman, 1976; Smith, 1988); or to discuss specific methods for policy implementation. While these are important issues, they are complex and have been treated comprehensively by other analysts. Moreover, I have attempted to develop policy suggestions that flow from the findings of this particular study and related research. A final issue is that although I focus on initiatives with local impacts, any development strategy must be undergirded by an expansionary national and international macro-economic policy; that is, the acceleration of growth by "boosting consumption, investment, government spending, or net export—the constituent components of the GNP" (Harrison and Bluestone, 1988:176).

A first step is that efforts should be broadened to make the internal organization of farm and industrial firms more responsive to the needs of those actively involved in production. This challenge can be met through the grassroots initiatives of producers themselves, through their organizations, and through appropriate government policy. At least two areas of increased business accountability appear critical. First, the occupational health and safety of workers need to be ensured through more aggressive elimination of health and environmental hazards and active enforcement of existing legislation. Family farmers would also benefit from shifting agricultural practices toward more sustainable systems. Second, the extension of workplace democracy is essential. Greater decision-making by workers should be promoted on the shop floor and up through the firm hierarchy. This can be achieved by supporting labor organizing efforts among the farm and non-farm workforce and related legislation; but even employers now recognize the need for greater worker decision-making in order to enhance profits. More fundamentally, employee ownership of firms should be supported by worker organizations and by government credit policies. Employee ownership profoundly alters the balance of power between capital and labor and addresses workers' long-term interests in job stability (as opposed to management interest in shorter-term profit). Undergirding the previous points is that unions must exert sustained pressure on capital and that they can be a progressive force in doing so. However, in order for unions to be successful, they must recognize the fundamental issues and strategies that will best allow them to advance workers' interests in post-fordist work environments. For example, unions should focus on organizing and articulating the needs of previously neglected segments of labor, such as women and minorities, service sector employees, and farm workers.

A second policy direction is to support the types of farming and industry that are amenable to local control and that have the most benefits to local people. This involves establishing industries and farms that will be economically viable in the future, correspond to local needs and resources, and remain wedded to the community. Localities can gain greater control over the type of farming system they desire through appropriate economic development policies. For instance, fostering the growth of trades and services can help sustain both smaller and larger family farming; high paying jobs will inevitably benefit smaller family farmers; and land use policies can regulate the activities of industrialized farms. More fundamentally, community land trusts can democratize access to land and increase family farmers' power in this exchange sphere. While smaller family farming is not particularly beneficial to communities, it may be the only alternative some producers have or represent a life-style choice they are willing to sacrifice for. This farming does have some potential benefits in that it creates a more heterogenous rural society and provides a last opportunity for people to remain in farming. Both larger and smaller family farmers, however, should be encouraged to find commodity niches, to engage in value-added production, and to use direct marketing strategies that will enable them to gain greater incomes for their efforts. In addition to pursuing activities that will enhance farm income, farmers should take a more active role in understanding and attempting to satisfy local food needs.

In the nonfarm sector, localities should try to retain what core sector employment remains, to diversify their industrial base, and promote local entrepreneurship. As noted by a number of analysts, localities should not attempt to attract large firms, as they did in the 1960s. At best, this is often an unnecessary strategy, at worst, it can create conflict and uneven economic development among communities (Falk and Lyson, 1988). Large firms are also more footloose than those that are community based. Smaller firms building on local resources and talents and using innovative practices should be encouraged. Manufacturing can be encouraged to adapt to flexible production techniques in order to capture new consumer markets and fluctuating demand. Rural services and other businesses can establish market niches, which may be based upon particular local resources such as handicrafts, traditional furniture or foods (Malecki, 1988; de Janvry et al.,

1987). Businesses should also recognize local needs in deciding on goods or services to produce. Local government programs can help foster an innovative as well as socially responsive business environment. Credit assistance can be provided for product innovation and transition and for promising start-up firms. Infrastructure, particularly transportation and communications, and managerial assistance should likewise center upon supporting local firms. It should also be recognized that while small, diverse local enterprises will generally not provide high the wage employment of core firms, they will serve to insulate communities more in the long run from macroeconomic instability.

A third policy issue is the need to redistribute the uneven benefit of state economic programs to rural localities and family farms. It has often been noted that the benefits of agriculture programs and research are captured disproportionately by larger farms (Strange, 1988; de Janvry et al., 1987; Geisler, 1984). Recently, analysts have argued that the only rural development funding directed to the farm sector ought to be to viable family farms (Swanson and Skees, 1987; de Janvry et al., 1987). Moderate-size family farms have been the most seriously affected by the farm crisis; they have sufficient assets and management potential as to be very productive (de Janvry et al., 1987); and as this study has shown, they have the greatest benefits to communities. Smaller family farms also might be assisted to allow them to cover a higher proportion of their subsistence needs or to help them become larger, more viable, self-sustaining units.

Direct or indirect spatial inequities in other government programs ought to be eliminated. For instance, the elimination of general revenue sharing in 1987 and restrictions in the use of tax-exempt municipal bonds in financing private development have dried up important sources of capital for rural areas (*The Wall Street Journal*, August 4, 1989:6). As a consequence of changes in medicare prospective pricing in 1983, rural hospitals have been reimbursed at lower payments per case than their urban counterpart based on misleading assumptions that the costs of treatment are lower for rural facilities. The general cuts in social programs during the Reagan administration also reinforced historical gaps between urban and rural areas in regard to socioeconomic conditions. The poorer health care, lower health status and education, and greater poverty of rural areas are symptomatic, in part, of the urban bias in federal programs.

A fourth issue is that the need for a comprehensive, rural economic development program has now reached a critical point. De Janvry et al. (1987) note that after World War II, the United States pursued a policy of national economic growth with little regard for its distribution. Rural areas subsidized the development of urban areas as cheap food benefitted industry as a wage subsidy and fostered the growth of input industries mainly in urban areas. Government support of large, industrialized farms through univeristy research, commodity programs, tax breaks, and extension services coupled with the general policy of national economic growth "were actually de-development policies for rural areas" (de Janvry et al., 1987:56). Significant efforts to deal with the rural poor were evident under the 1930s New

Deal legislation and in the Johnson administration's War on Poverty. While these efforts were in large part aimed at curbing social unrest (Piven and Cloward, 1971), they did improve the living standards of many rural people. The problem with these and nearly all other federal rural economic programs, however, is that have not been given sustained support. Attempts to foster privatized development is still the basic but ineffective strategy, "a trickle-down approach to the poor" (de Janvry et al., 1987:65).

For some time, analysts have argued that agriculturally based programs and extension efforts are insufficient for dealing with current rural economic development issues. Many have called for a comprehensive and sustained rural economic development initiative and the decoupling of farm programs from this initiative (Swanson, 1989; de Janvry et al., 1987; Swanson and Skees, 1987). Most analysts advocate prolonged federal policy initiatives to deal with issues such as employment, education and health, which would be differentially directed to communities, households, and other segments of rural society. As this study has shown, such a program would also promote the viability of family farming and thus would be an important supplement to any agricultural programs still in place. According to de Janvry et al. (1987), there are a number of reasons indicating why a comprehensive program is ripe for political action: the fiscal crisis of the state has made support of costly farm programs difficult; the gap between the rhetoric of protecting family farming and evidence about the growth of industrialized farming has grown so large that farm policy can longer be justified ideologically; consumer aversion to use of pesticides and environmental concerns about farming suggest that current farming practices will need to be drastically altered; the farm crisis created the political agitation and support for new policy initiatives; and finally, the increase in poverty in rural areas will be so great by the next recession that extensive government intervention will be necessary.

A fifth point is that any rural development initiative should focus on empowering people and their localities. This study and others have shown that market security, education, and the elimination of joblessness and discrimination are essential to local well-being. Expansion of social welfare programs, particularly in light of recent cuts, is needed to provide a safety net for those who can work and for those who have no alternative means of subsistence. Extending social welfare is also related to important gender issues and feminist objectives, such as the need for a national child care system, maternal and paternal leaves, equal pay, and health care coverage. Moreover, improvements in social welfare not only redistribute resources but "inject spendable income into the economy where it is most likely to be spent and have the largest 'multiplier' effect" (Harrison and Bluestone, 1988:190). The need for expanded worker organizing and new union strategies was also previously noted.

The role of education in empowering people and their localities merits special consideration. While counties with higher educational levels tend to have higher income levels at any one cross-sectional point, they do not always do so over time. A higher level of schooling thus does not, in and of itself, lead to higher income and lower poverty. Rather, at any historical point, employers may find it advantageous to develop those areas with higher education and at other points, to discount them. This does not mean that the role of education is unimportant; it does, however, indicate that the limitations of education in influencing economic well-being should be acknowledged. Efforts to improve educational attainments will have little bearing on local economic well-being unless accompanied by sufficient, good quality jobs. On the other hand, education broadens minds and increases the skills necessary for full social and political participation. Increasing educational attainments among poorly educated populations can allow them to compete for better quality jobs, reducing income inequality across areas (see Chapter 6). Significant upgrades in educational achievements, particularly of the young, however, cannot be accomplished without extensive investment in local schools, which makes such attempts more difficult for poorer communities. Thus, efforts to improve schools in poor, rural areas should receive greater subsidization from the federal government.

Finally, efforts beyond the policy arena, particularly the need for coalition building and political organizing, are essential in creating social and economic justice. While federal, state, and local governments can do much to counter the destabilizing effects of economic change and to redistribute power and wealth within and between urban and rural areas, they are inherently limited by the social order and by those who benefit from current inequities. Broad based coalitions of people historically and more recently excluded from the benefits of the fordist system have a window of opportunity in this transition stage. Such groups include minorities, women, the poor, family farmers, hired farm workers, and workers newly marginalized by economic change. They may be the real key to a socially responsive and environmentally sound agricultural and industrial system.

Appendix

Development of the Farm Structural Patterns

This appendix describes the development of the farm structural measures based upon Wimberley's (1986, 1987) work. Twenty indicators that are comparable for both the 1969 and 1978 Censuses of Agriculture are initially employed in constructing the indexes. The indicators reflect major aspects of county farm differentiation. They are briefly described below following Table A.1. Means and standard deviations for these variables are also reported in Table A.1. It should be noted that sales figures refer to annual, gross dollar amounts.

TABLE A.1

Means and Standard Deviations for Variables Used in the
Factor Analysis of U.S. Farm Structure

County Level Indicators	1969		1978	
	Mean	Standard Deviation	Mean	Standard Deviation
Scale				
1. No. of farms	896.53	644.96	741.34	537.40
2. % land in farms	60.29	31.31	56.35	30.43
3. Mean farm size	801.61	3,212.10	803.71	2,506.92
4. Small farms (v $2,500 gross)	327.24	299.62	151.97	139.16
5. Gross sales ($1,000)	14,963.24	21,201.74	35,162.31	52,868.12
6. Farm real estate value ($1,000)	67,875.27	75,060.74	207,339.39	218,300.07
Ownership				
7. Individual/family	486.17	404.37	504.10	389.96
8. Partnership	72.75	66.95	67.45	60.36
9. Legal incorporation	7.06	11.73	16.04	22.52
Operator Tenure				
10. Full owner	560.07	457.14	426.14	358.37
11. Part owner	220.54	163.17	223.66	160.58
12. Tenant	115.91	128.34	91.54	93.36

TABLE A.1 *continued*

	1969		1978	
County Level Indicators	Mean	Standard Deviation	Mean	Standard Deviation
Operator Characteristics				
13. Farm resident	651.06	490.93	520.65	400.18
14. Off-farm work	285.92	242.94	252.82	209.46
15. Age	51.54	2.23	50.71	2.18
Labor Requirements				
16. Farms with hired workers	457.92	364.41	312.57	263.56
17. No. of hired workers	1,898.31	4,288.11	1,709.55	4,458.16
18. Contract-labor expenses ($1,000)	151.93	910.30	295.11	1,749.26
19. Custom-work expenses ($1,000)	287.40	527.47	558.47	1,260.52
20. Machine/equipment value ($1,000)	8,332.30	7,216.93	25,484.88	24,025.48

Scale. The differentiation of farm structure should be observable through measures of scale. At the county level, land, sales, and number of farms are the basis for measuring scale. Indicators are: (1) the total number of farms in the county; (2) the proportion of county land in farming; (3) the mean acreage of county farms; (4) the number of small farms or those with annual sales of less than $2,500; (5) the total dollar value of agricultural product sales; and (6) the total dollar value of farm real estate or land and buildings in a county.

Organization: Ownership and Operator Tenure. The form of organizational holding or ownership and the tenure of the farm operator are further bases of differentiation. Ownership is measured by the number of operators in a county who are (7) independent or individual and family owners of unincorporated farms; (8) partnerships; and (9) corporations, including those held by families. Operator tenure is measured by the number of operators in a county who are (10) full owners; (11) part owners or operators of land they own and also land they rent from others; and (12) tenant farm operators who operate only land they do not own but rent from others.

Operator Characteristics. Operator/household characteristics are another aspect of differentiation that reflect off-farm work or demographic adjustments made as the market economy penetrates farming. While household characteristics would be a useful level to observe differentiation, the Census of Agriculture reports characteristics of the operator only. These measures are (13) the number of county operators residing on the farm; (14) the number of operators working 200 or more days off the farm; and (15) the median age of county farm operators.

Labor Requirements. These important organizational aspects of farm structure can be considered both in terms of wage labor, as measured by (16) the number of county farms with any hired workers; (17) the number of hired workers in the county; (18) annual expenses for contract labor incurred by county farms; and in terms of capital intensity as measured by (19) annual expenses for custom work, machine hire, and rental of machinery and equipment incurred by county farms; and (20) the estimated market value of farm machinery and equipment for all county farms.

While the previous indicators cover most of the major areas in which farm structural change or differentiation has occurred, there are limitations due to the nature of agricultural census data. The census provides no information regarding the demographic and off-farm labor contributions of farm household members other than the operator. In regard to farm operation, there is no information on the number of hired managers; neither do the 1969 and 1978 censuses provide information on farm debt. A second limitation is that while most of the indicators are based on information for all farms, the 1969 census reported information for six of the indicators based only on farms with sales of $2,500 or more. In order to ensure comparability, 1978 data for these indicators used the same base. Three of the indicators applied almost entirely to higher sales farms for which they were reported anyway: the total number of hired farm workers in a county and expenses for contract labor and custom work. The three other indicators involved the ownership categories: individual/family, partnership, and corporation. Whether the farm structural indexes are computed using the six indicators with all farms or only those with sales of $2,500 as the base seems to make little difference: employing the six indicators calculated on the basis of all farms for the 1982 Census of Agriculture revealed no appreciable differences between these measures and those developed for earlier years (which were based on $2,500 sales).

In order to develop the measures of farm structure, the problem of missing data had to be considered. This occurs when Census of Agriculture data are withheld to avoid disclosure of information in counties with few farms and when data are not applicable or unavailable for various reasons. There were few missing data on the variables for 1969, with the largest number of missing cases on any variable totalling about 1 percent. For the 1978 data, however, the problem of missing data was somewhat greater. Variables with the largest number of missing data were contract labor expenses (12 percent), number of hired workers (6 percent) and expenses for custom work (4 percent). All other 1978 variables had less than 1 percent missing cases. Missing values were generally replaced with state means. In some cases, however, where data were inapplicable or county values appeared low (e.g., where data were based on a very few farms), missing values were recoded to zero as this seemed to better approximate real values. Another discussion of this issue is presented in Wimberley (1987).

Factor analysis was employed to determine the dimensions of farm structure. This is a data reduction technique that allows the researcher to discern the underlying patterns of linear relationships among a set of variables. (See Kim and Mueller (1978) for a succinct description of factor analysis.) Following Wimberley (1987), the dimensions of farm structure are extracted by a principal axis factor analysis. The objective of this step is to determine the smallest number of common factors that would satisfactorily produce the observed correlations among the variables (Kim and Mueller, 1978). In order to extract these factors, the initial communalities or estimates of the variance of a variable accounted for by the common factors must be calculated. As in Wimberley's (1987) analysis, initial commonalities are estimated by the maximum $|r|$ of a variable's correlation with any other of the 19 variables. The principal axis factoring was performed for the variables for 1969 and 1978. For both years, conventional criteria used to determine the number of factors, such as the scree test, proportion of estimated variance explained, and the sizes of the eigenvalues for the unrotated factors, revealed a three factor solution.

Oblique, promax rotations, which allow for the determination of factor structure without imposing orthogonality among factors, were then performed. This produced a three factor pattern for 1969 and for 1978 with similar magnitudes of rotated loadings on variables on the same factors for both years. This indicated that the factor pattern for 1969 was similar to that found in 1978—therefore, farm structure could be delineated by the same indicators. Wimberley (1987) has further found essentially the same factor pattern among the variables for 1974 and 1982 as well.

Factor analysis thus indicated that three patterns or dimensions of county farm structure characterize U.S. counties from 1969 through 1982. Indexes were then created from the specific variables defining each dimension. First, variables with the highest loadings (analogous to standardized regression coefficients) or those over .7, were selected to represent each dimension. Further, the variables selected had to have similar high loadings for all time points so that comparable indexes could be developed and to ensure that the indexes remained stable measures of farm structure over time. The variables meeting these criteria and the loadings on the dimension they define are shown in Table A.2.

As noted in the text, to create the farm pattern indexes, each variable was then standardized to a mean of 50 and standard deviation of 10. Because the variables were all in different metrics, this allowed them to be equally weighed. The variables for each index were then summed. Finally, because each index was based upon a different number of variables, each index was standardized to a mean of 50, standard deviation of 10. This permits comparison across all three dimensions. While it would have been desirable to generate factor score indexes that would reflect the weights of a variable's loading on each factor, this was not possible due to the highly intercorrelated nature of the variables that attenuated the scoring coefficients. However, the indexes constructed from the previous variables had intercorrelations close to the intercorrelations among the factors themselves which suggests that the indexes are good approximations of the factor scores. More detailed dicsussion about the creation of the indexes can be found in Wimberley (1987).

TABLE A.2

Three Dimensions of 1969 and 1978 U.S. Farm Structure[a]

County Level Indicators	I Industrialized Farming		II Larger Family Farming		III Smaller Family Farming	
	1969	1978	1969	1978	1969	1978
Scale						
1. No. of farms	b				.753	.763
2. % land in farms			.794	.818		
3. Mean farm size						
4. Small farms (v $2,500 gross)					1.102	1.078
5. Gross sales	.766	.763				
6. Farm real estate value						
Ownership						
7. Individual/family						
8. Partnership						
9. Legal incorporation	.898	.789				
Operator Tenure						
10. Full owner					.959	.948
11. Part owner			.784	.744		
12. Tenant			.822	.821		
Operator Characteristics						
13. Farm resident					.705	.746
14. Off-farm work					.981	1.018
15. Age						
Labor Requirements						
16. Farm with hired workers						
17. No. of hired workers	.795	.843				
18. Contract-labor expenses	1.002	1.026				
19. Custom-work expenses	.841	.939				
20. Machine/equipment value			.757	.773		

[a] Items indicate obliquely rotated loadings for variables used in the structural index for each dimension. Factor loadings that are strongly obliquely rotated may have values greater than one. Orthogonal varimax rotations that create uncorrelated dimensions, despite the intrinsic nature of the relationships, indicate that such loadings are about 0.9 (see Wimberley, 1987).

[b] Variables not included in index due to low loadings over 1969-1978 time points.

Notes

Chapter One

1. "Factories in the field" is a term used by McWilliams (1969) to describe early large scale, farming enterprises dependent on hired labor.

2. The rate at which surplus value is extracted is defined as surplus value divided by variable capital. Historically, this rate has been increased in two major ways. The first is to increase the length of the work day without increasing wages or changing the nature of the labor process, a coercive strategy used under early stages of competitive capitalism, which increases surplus value absolutely. The second is to increase the productivity of labor per time unit by intensifying the labor process, thereby increasing relative surplus value. The second strategy "has been the major historical response to the limits set by the class struggle and state legislation on the length of the working day and on harsher forms of physical exploitation in the earlier period" (Wood, 1986:10). It is the basis for fordism, the modern accumulation regime of high-wage, capital-intensive production, mass consumption, and liberal welfare state.

3. The concept of 'community' is similar to that of 'locality.' Community has three general meanings in the sociological literature: a geographic entity, a local social system, and an expression of social bond (Bradley and Lowe, 1984:4). Bradley and Lowe (1984:5) note that the first meaning "is spatial descriptive but not social and hence, from a sociological perspective, of only passing interest as a descriptive category" while the third meaning "has no necessary spatial significance." The second meaning most closely captures the concept of locality used in this book. I chose the term *locality* rather than *community* because the conceptual perspective taken here is closer to that of the recent locality studies found in British and American geography and in British rural sociology: in contrast to much of American rural sociology, which treats the community from a functionalist standpoint, this latter literature tends to be grounded in political economic principles. For a review that contrasts the history of community studies with the development of perspectives on the locality, see Newby (1986b). The term *community* is also conventionally used to refer to a city or town and hence is not entirely appropriate for the unit of analysis, the county, employed in this book.

4. This description is grounded in the framework of locality studies. Newby (1986b:211) notes that in locality studies, "Localities are not studied for their own sake but as a method of obtaining data on. . . processes of social change." Locality researchers outline three ways in which the locality can be used to study social process. First, the locality can be viewed as mediating the effects of larger social structures and processes. Because localities have developed unevenly, current social structural processes, such as national agricultural policies and industrial organizational changes, cannot be expected

to have uniform effects. This approach is useful for outlining "contingent" local characteristics that modify nonlocal or national trends. A second way to employ the locality is to examine structures and processes specifically based at this level. For example, a particular locality may generate specific types of farming patterns, consumption levels, or political alignments. A third way locality can be used is through studying 'locality effect', different processes combining at the local level to create a distinctly local culture, such as the paternalistic cultures in traditional mill villages of the Southern textile industry and the frontier mentality of early pioneer settlements. This study considers the locality mainly for the first two purposes.

5. The compatibility between non-Marxist views on economic segmentation, such as those of Doeringer and Piore (1971) and Marxist orientations, such as those of Edwards (1979) and Gordon et al. (1982), has been discussed by Fine (1987) and Gordon (1972). According to Gordon (1972:87), a basic difference is that the non-Marxist view "does not provide an explicit analysis of conflict and. . . [seems] to place too great an emphasis on the mutual delight of all parties. . .as if a harmony of interest was driving the evolution of a dual structure."

6. Wayne (1986:63) notes that families face two problems in attempting to subsist solely on the basis of wages:

> On the one hand the price of the labour power sold on the market may not cover consumption costs for the family, because the price may be below the value of the commodities consumed in that household, because the family may be forced to pay prices for commodities above their values, or because some combination of the two circumstances prevails. On the other hand, the value of labour power itself is always subject to change, predicted on the long-run movement of the supply and demand for labour power, in the context of "the continuous struggle between capital and labour."

7. Family farmers occupy a web of positions that are not easily categorized into distinct classes and associated consumption conditions. Based upon their class position, smaller farmers who are situated closer to the proletariat should have worse socioeconomic conditions; however, this may vary empirically. For example, farming may be a part-time activity or a hobby or retirement strategy in which the majority of household income comes from nonfarm sources. The quality of off-farm employment may be the more salient predictor of family socioeconomic conditions than farming itself. Likewise, farmers who rent rather than own land may be pursuing a profit-oriented strategy depending upon their combination of family and mechanical resources. Specific historical conditions thus preclude a necessary one-to-one correspondence between class location and socioeconomic conditions.

Chapter Two

1. There have been a number of other critiques and revisions of segmented economy perspectives. Most broadly, Fine (1987:29) argues that economic segmentation theory

is a middle range theory that cannot explain the long-term development of the economy. Researchers have also argued that the causal mechanisms by which industrial structure affects individual outcomes require clearer delineation (Fine, 1987; Baron and Bielby, 1980). Others have questioned the correspondence between industrial sectors and labor market conditions. It is now generally recognized that primary and secondary labor markets and the presence of good or bad jobs do not neatly correlate with industrial structure (Kalleberg and Berg, 1987:110). The division of the industrial economy into two and three sectors also cannot capture the full extent of segmentation (Hall, 1986:144; Hodson, 1983; Hodson and Kaufman, 1982). On an empirical level, the extent to which a firm resembles a core or peripheral enterprise or the extent to which a particular industry is composed of such firms has been disputed (Hodson and Kaufman, 1982; Hodson, 1983). Despite these issues, segmented economy theory provides a number of useful insights. First, it recognizes the uneven development of capitalist enterprises as a consequence of conflict between capital and labor and among different fractions of capital over the distribution of surplus. Second, it situates the creation of inequality in the sphere of production rather than in the characteristics of individuals, thereby challenging seriously human capital and functionalist assumptions about inequality. Finally, there is substantial empirical evidence that industrial segmentation has a bearing on wages, benefits, and other aspects of employment quality (Averitt, 1968; Baron and Bielby, 1980; Hodson, 1978, 1983; Hodson and Kaufman, 1982; Edwards, 1979; Jacobs, 1985; Gordon et al., 1982).

2. Much of this section is drawn from Kenney et al. (1989), copyright permission from *Sociologia Ruralis*.

3. Many of the data in this chapter are from the agricultural censuses. From 1954 to 1974, an agricultural census was conducted in years ending in 4 and 9. Agricultural censuses were then conducted in 1978, 1982, and 1987, and from this point will be taken every five years. Albrecht and Murdock (1988:43) note that between 1850 and 1982 the census definition of a farm changed nine times. As a result, data from the various censuses are not strictly comparable, although this is less of a problem with recent data. In 1969, a place was counted as a farm if it had at least ten acres of land and sales of products of $50 or more; or if it had less than ten acres but estimated sales of $250 or more. In 1974, the criterion for acreage was deleted and places were counted as farms only if they had product sales of $1,000 or more. This last definition has been employed to the present.

4. Definitions of what consititutes a small, medium, large, or family farm vary. Sales criteria are most commonly used to define farm size. Acreage is another indicator but tends to be less useful because it varies by commodity. The United States Department of Agriculture conventionally defined small farms as units with less than $20,000 in annual sales. Tweeten (1984:2) notes that this definition was changed in 1979 to reflect low income, family operated and managed farms, which depended on farming for a substantial amount of income. According to Tweeten (1984:2), the following terms are sometimes associated with annual sales: rural residences, farms with sales less than $5,000; small farms, sales from $5,000 to $39,000; medium farms, sales from $40,000 to $199,999; and large farms, $200,000 and over. Tweeten's (1981:4) definition of a family farm includes characteristics commonly found in the literature: "a crop and/or livestock producing unit in which the

operator and his/her family...control most of the decisions...supply most of the labor [and] derive most of their income from farming."

5. The four major tenure categories used by the Census of Agriculture have been: full-owner operated farms, in which all land is owned by the operator; part-owner farms, in which the operator both rents and owns land; tenant farms, in which all land is rented; and hired manager farms in which the operator owns no land and receives a salary. Tenants are not homogenous but vary in the degree to which they own and supply means of production and their control over the production process (Albrecht and Murdock, 1988:43). Cash tenants pay money rent, provide all inputs but land, and have extensive control over the production process; crop and livestock share-tenants return a proportion of the product produced and share operation and input provisions with the landlord; sharecroppers are much like hired laborers in that they provide only labor, the landlord supplying the means of production and controlling the production process. After 1959, the number of share-croppers and farm managers ceased to be reported by the agricultural census. Post-Civil War Southern economic development and the growth and demise of sharecropping have been discussed by a number of writers (see Mandle, 1978; Wood, 1986; and James, 1986).

6. Tweeten (1984) provides empirical evidence of the dualism in American agriculture. According to Tweeten (1984:8), "The nation has lost over 4 million farms (net) since 1935, and most were family farms." While definitions of family farming vary, numerous analysts have pointed to a declining middle sector of such farms over time (Stockdale, 1982; Goss et al., 1980; Rodefeld, 1974). Large farms have also captured larger shares of the net income produced in the farm sector. 'Superfarms' increased their share of total net farm income from 25 percent in 1970 to 48 percent in 1982 (Gladwin and Zabawa, 1986:40).

7. The present crisis has been attributed to a deterioration in the social structure of accumulation (Gordon et al., 1982:240-241). Although I focus on the United States, the current accumulation crisis is a global one. As Kolko (1988:3) notes, for over a decade, the crisis "has been evident to observers, whether perceived as a series of crises—in energy, the monetary system, debt, trade, food, and the like—or as a general cyclical, structural, or systemic crisis." For various perspectives on the causes and consequences of the crisis, see Kolko (1988), Piore and Sabel (1984), Lash and Urry (1987), Gordon et al. (1982), Bluestone and Harrison (1982), Lipietz (1986), and Noel (1987).

8. De Janvry et al. (1987:71) note that the gains farm workers secured during the 1960s and 1970s have been undermined in the 1980s by illegal immigration, greater use of farm labor contractors, declining wages and union influence, and poor working conditions. They note that it remains to be seen whether or not the recent immigration law will be enforced effectively to stabilize the farm labor force.

9. There are a variety of theories on the spatial organization of production. To political economists, spatial divisions of labor in a society result from social relations and the process of accumulation at the national and international levels (see for example, Massey, 1984; Storper and Scott, 1986; Lipietz, 1986; Lash and Urry, 1987). Neoclassical economists stress industrial and firm level processes and decisions such as innovation, technological change, product life cycles, cost minimization, and local amenities as reasons for differential

location of firms and industries. Lever (1985) presents a comprehensive review of this literature. Horan and Tolbert (1984) review sociological and economic theories—central place theory, economic base and functional specialization approaches, and perspectives on rural industrialization—which consider the spatial agglomerations attendant to firms and industries.

Chapter Three

1. A later work by Goldschmidt (1978a) includes his study of Wasco, another California community, as well as Arvin and Dinuba. Wasco occupied a midpoint between Arvin and Dinuba in regard to farm size. The effects of Wasco's farm structure were evident in its class structure, as compared to the other two communities: 52 percent of employed persons were professionals, entrepreneurs, farmers, or white collar workers in Dinuba, as compared to 28 percent in Wasco, and 17 percent in Arvin. Goldschmidt does not examine Wasco's quality of life in as much detail as he studied Arvin and Dinuba. However, he argues that in both Arvin and Wasco, corporate agriculture has weakened community autonomy.

2. For reviews of the Goldschmidt and other studies on the relationship between farm structure and community outcomes see Moxley (1986), Nuckton et al. (1982), and Salant and Munoz (1981). An annotated bibliography of studies on farm structure and the community has been published by Leistritz and Ekstrom (1986). The bibliography lists hundreds of studies that have dealt with the Goldschmidt issue in either a central or peripheral way.

3. Of the previous studies, only a few are linked directly to wider social science perspectives. Heffernan (1972) used Marx's insights on stratification to test class-related differences among producers. Flora et al. (1977) generated and tested a series of hypotheses derived from internal colonialism development theory. Heffernan and Lasley (1978) used the theoretical perspective of C. Wright Mills to test the resemblance of nonfamily farmers to the "new middle class". Swanson (1982) employed a neo-Marxist perspective to examine the transition from independent commodity production to capitalist production in farming for Pennsylvania trade centers.

Chapter Four

1. Sources of worker power can at times fragment the working class (Fine, 1987). For example, to the extent that unions are concerned with protecting their members' interests alone, unionized workers may gain at the expense of nonunionized workers. Community organizations may pit workers in one locale against those from another.

2. A distinction is often made between craft and industrial unions. Through the early twentieth century, craft unions tended to be exclusionary organizations, protecting skilled and generally white, male labor at the expense of unskilled, ethnic labor. The merger

of the AFL and CIO in 1955 united craft and industrial unions so this distinction is less important today.

3. There is a large literature on the role of the state in advanced capitalist societies (see for example, Wright, 1978; Poulantzas, 1974; O'Connor, 1973; Offe, 1972). Political economists have often attributed the expansion of state welfare spending during periods of civil disorder to the co-optation of dissent (Piven and Cloward, 1971). Yet it is increasingly realized that the gains made during such periods represent real breakthroughs for working and poor people. This is particularly true in light of the current conservative ideological and fiscal attack against the welfare state programs, many of which grew out of the dissent of the 1960s (see Block et al., 1987).

4. Means-tested transfers are aimed at raising money or consumption levels of poor people and may be received in cash or in-kind. Of these, the main cash income transfer programs are AFDC, general assistance, supplemental social security income for the blind, disabled, and elderly poor, and assistance to poor veterans and their families. In-kind transfers are provided in three main forms: food, housing, and medical care. Burtless (1986) shows that in the early 1960s, about nine out of ten dollars in means-tested programs were paid out in cash; by 1986, only about three out of ten dollars were cash payments. This reflects the increasing climate of political conservatism, where income poverty is viewed as a deserved punishment for labor market failure but where starvation and homelessness are less tolerable and their amelioration (through noncash programs) can be more closely monitored (Burtless, 1986).

5. For example, because individuals with lower education are more likely to live in poverty, it has been popularly assumed that raising education of everyone in a particular labor market eliminates aggregate poverty.

Chapter Five

1. Some researchers have attempted to address the problem of imperfect correlation between structural processes and geographic boundaries by discussing labor markets built upon workers' commuting patterns. However, the use of these empirically derived labor markets would also have several limitations for this study. Most importantly, the boundaries of such labor markets necessarily change over time, making longitudinal analyses problematic. Also, because labor markets may overlap governmental administrative units such as states, the effects of policy may be difficult to disentangle and policy prescriptions cannot be directed to any one particular administrative level. A final limitation is that labor markets (as any ecological unit) do not incorporate all important social processes and relationships. For example, while empirically constructed labor markets are based upon a fundamental social relationship (the exchange of paid labor), they neglect the spatial structure of nonwage and informal sector work (which includes types of farming activities) as well as the structure of relationships outside the arena of production entirely, such as in the sphere of consumption.

2. It should be noted that data from the 1969 and 1978 Censuses of Agriculture are not exactly comparable due to the different definitions of farming employed in each year. In 1969, a place was counted as a farm by the Census if it had at least ten acres of land and sales of products of $50 or more; or if it had less than ten acres but estimated sales of $250 or more. In 1974, the criterion for acreage was deleted and places were counted as farms on the basis of sales alone. In 1974 and following censuses, places were counted as farms only if they had product sales of $1,000 or more. As a result of this definitional change, small farms with sales under $1000 which previously would have been included in the census have been omitted after 1969. Keeping in mind that any sales indicator is subject to inflation, had the $50/ten acre or $250 sales definition of 1969 been applied to determine a farm's inclusion in the 1974 census, at least 152,000 farms would have been added (Wimberley, 1983b). Researchers, however, routinely perform comparative analyses using data from the 1969 census and later censuses, arguing that minimal if any bias occurs (Buttel et al., 1986; Flora and Flora, 1986; Green, 1985; Heaton, 1980; MacCannell and Dolber-Smith, 1986; Skees and Swanson, 1986; van Es et al., 1986). Because this study centers on tracing causal relationships rather than on detailing changes in the aggregate number of farms, the definitional change is likely to have particularly minimal effect.

3. While studies in the Goldschmidt tradition are fundamentally concerned with the same issue—the effects of large-scale, hired labor dependent farming on well-being, researchers tend to emphasize different aspects of this causal relationship. Some approaches are more in line with political economy perspectives in that they emphasize social relations of production as the basis of farm impacts (e.g., Rodefeld, 1974; Swanson, 1982; Flora and Flora, 1986). Others, particularly by agricultural economists, follow the traditional Goldschmidt approach by focusing on scale, measured in acreage or sales (e.g., Heady and Sonka, 1974; Marousek, 1979). A populist approach focusing on control of agricultural production by large, nonfarm corporations also underlies some perspectives (e.g., Goldschmidt, 1978a; Rodefeld, 1974). Despite their conceptual orientation, researchers have tended to be eclectic in their choice of measures. For example, while the social relations of production, such as the presence or absence of wage labor, may be the suggested basis of farm impacts, measures of scale are often used in conjunction with other indicators to represent farm structure.

4. Using various samples and data sources, analysts have developed a number of classification schemes to tap the concept of industrial segmentation. For a comparison of Hodson's and other schemes see Hall (1986). It should also be noted that extractive employment in agriculture, forestry, and fisheries was placed in peripheral employment rather than analyzed as a separate sector. This corresponds to Hodson's (1978) and Bloomquist and Summers' (1982) classifications. Previous research (Reif, 1987) shows that extractive employment has a detrimental effect on county economic conditions, providing empirical justification for treating it as peripheral employment. Other reasons for not analyzing extractive employment separately are: that this concept is already tapped somewhat through including the percentage of farm population; and that it makes for a simpler, clearer analysis.

5. The metropolitan proximity index is coded as follows: 17, core metropolitan counties with more than one million population; 16, fringe counties with more than one million
population; 15, core counties with populations of 750,000 to 999,999; 14, fringe counties
with populations of 750,000 to 999,999; 13, core counties with populations of 500,000
to 749,999; 12, fringe counties with populations of 500,000 to 749,999; 11, core counties
with populations of 250,000 to 499,999; 10, fringe counties with populations of 250,000
to 499,999; 9, core counties with populations of 100,000 to 249,999; 8, fringe counties
with populations of 100,000 to 249,999; 7, metro counties of 99,999 or less in population; 6, nonmet, adjacent counties with a largest place of 10,000 or more; 5, nonmet,
adjacent counties with a largest place of 2,500 to 9,999; 4, nonmet, adjacent counties
with a largest place less than 2,500; 3, nonmet, nonadjacent counties with a largest place
of 10,000 or more; 2, nonmet, nonadjacent counties with a largest place from 2,500 to
9,999; 1, nonmet, nonadjacent counties with a largest place less than 2,500.

6. A critique of these approaches to inequality and well-being is presented by Smith
(1977).

7. The Gini coefficient is defined in terms of the Lorenz curve, which is a plot of
the cumulative proportion of the measured characteristic, in this case, income, against
the cumulative proportion of units (families) associated with each income level. If both
sets of proportions ascended with the same magnitude, the result would be a diagonal
line indicating that income was evenly distributed across family income categories and
consequently, that perfect equality existed. The Gini index is defined as the area between
this line of perfect equality and the plot of the observed distribution (Smith, 1982:28).

8. It should be noted that there are relatively few problems with missing data for
the nonfarm variables. All indicators excluding establishment size have 0 or under 1 percent
missing cases. The business censuses, which report the data used in constructing the variable
for establishment size omit data that would disclose the operation of a specific establishment. Where counties have only a few establishments, data will be undisclosed. For 1967
and 1977, the percentage of counties having data unavailable for this variable were 22
and 24 percent, respectively. While this appears high, publicly available data sources on
firms and establishments typically have such problems (Hodson, 1983:90–92). Missing
values on all variables were replaced with the mean county value by state.

9. Sources on multiple regression and related techniques include Asher (1983),
Kessler and Greenberg (1981), and Neter and Wasserman (1974).

Chapter Six

1. Much of the material from this chapter is drawn from Reif (1987), copyright permission from *Rural Sociology*, and from Lobao and Thomas (1988), copyright permission
from *Journal of the Community Development Society*.

2. The lagged value of the dependent variable is included in the panel models because
the initial value of a variable affects its level at subsequent time points and because statis-

tically it reduces specification bias by picking up any unmeasured variables that affect the dependent variable (Kessler and Greenberg, 1981). The panel models introduce the problem of autocorrelated error terms. An examination of the residuals indicated no extensive autocorrelation. However, in order to examine whether potential autocorrelation would bias the results, an alternative measure of the dependent variable was created that incorporated the effects of the lagged variable (and thus eliminated the possibility for autocorrelation over time). The dependent variable at 1980 was regressed on its 1970 value and the error term output. The error term was then used as the dependent variable (following Wachtel and Betsey, 1971). The results of these models closely followed those of models employing the lagged dependent variables. Thus the results reported in this study are unlikely to be an artifact of autocorrelation. Perry (1980) also confronts this problem. He notes that while panel designs may be questionable because of potential autocorrelation, relative values of estimates closely parallel those of the true parameters. Since estimates can be employed to determine which relationships are of negligible magnitude, a panel analysis is useful for determining causal links between variables, even though some autocorrelation may exist.

3. An issue not addressed in the models concerns potential interaction effects between farming and industry structure. Interaction terms for these variables were included but had inconsistent and trivial effects. The maximum amount of variance explained by any interaction was about one-half of one percent. Because of their small impact and because they do not alter the general pattern of relationships, the interactions are omitted from the final analysis. Interrelationships between farm and industry structures, such as locational coincidence, represent another important issue which is discussed in Chapter 8.

4. Whether one sets the significance level at .05 or lower is arbitrary and makes little difference in light of the large number of observations. For example, in Tables 6.2-6.4, nearly all variables significant at the .05 level are also significant at the .01 level and most are significant at the .0001 level.

5. Other methodological issues considered are colinearity and heteroscedasticity. There was no evidence of unacceptable levels of colinearity among the independent variables. Further, correlation coefficients of variables included in the same model did not exceed moderate levels with one set of exceptions: the correlations, slightly under .8 between education and median income and poverty, found only in the lagged models. However, an alternative set of models run without the lagged dependent variable (described in Note 2) produced similar results and colinearity diagnostics likewise revealed acceptable levels. Because national as well as regional analyses based on the inclusion of many of their subunits (e.g., counties, communities) are susceptible to heteroscedasticity, the residuals were analyzed. In addition, the models were reanalyzed using a split, random sample of counties. Both of these analyses indicate that there was no unacceptable heteroscedasticity. According to Bohrnstedt and Carter (1971:142), departures from homoscedasticity in regression "do not generally cause serious distortions."

6. The principal axis factoring produced an eigenvalue of 2.412 which explained 97 percent of the variance in the dimension for the concept of economic well-being. Factor scores give the index a mean of 0, standard deviation of 1.0. The factor analysis shows

that the three major indicators of inequality are highly intercorrelated. Counties where median family incomes are higher have less income inequality and poverty. As Lenski's (1966) well-known perspective on inequality in industrialized societies maintains, increases in income are likely to be shared in order to ensure social stability and increase production.

7. Zero-order correlations show that industrialized farming is related to higher peripheral and lower core employment; larger family farming is related to lower state employment. Chapter 8 details the specific industries associated with each type of farming.

8. Infant deaths are recorded on the basis of place of residence not the place of death. The infant mortality rate has two principal components, neonatal mortality and post-neonatal mortality. Neonatal mortality concerns deaths to infants during the first four weeks of life, while post-neonatal mortality concerns infant deaths after this period to one year. Congenital factors, life style of mothers, and prenatal care—related to characteristics and behavior of the mother and present before or occuring during birth—particularly influence neonatal mortality. These rates tend to be more sensitive to the socioeconomic status of the population (Farmer et al., 1984). Post-neonatal mortality is influenced more by environmental factors such as infectious diseases, accidents, and home care (Gortmaker, 1979; Pampel and Pillai, 1986). Neonatal mortality rates typically are larger than the post-neonatal rates, which means that infant mortality tends to be dominated by neonatal rates (Grossman and Jacobwitz, 1981:698).

9. The elimination of counties with under fifteen infant deaths over three years is a conventional procedure (Farmer et al., 1984) and still leaves a greater proportion of rural counties in the analysis. About 840 (58 percent) of the 1,440 counties were nonmetropolitan in 1980 as compared to 2,349 (77 percent) out of the original 3,037. The mean infant mortality rate was 14.2. The means for per capita physicians and teenage fertility rate were .001 and 2.93, respectively.

10. Using conventional statistical guidelines, paths (relationships) that were not statistically significant ($p > .05$) were deleted from the model. The model was then re-estimated, including only those paths that were significant. The result of this standard procedure is to eliminate trivial relationships, thereby reducing a complex set of relationships into a more parsimonoius model. For the results of this final model see Table 6.8.

11. Indirect and total effects are calculated from the path coefficients in Table 6.9. See Kenny (1979:70–73) for a description of the computational procedures involved. The total effect of a variable equals its direct effect on the dependent variable plus the sum of its indirect effects (those which occur through intervening variables).

12. For example, farm and industry structure also could affect infant mortality through nutritional levels, housing and sanitation quality, and health insurance coverage. The analysis incorporates these and other stratification related factors to some extent by controlling for income and educational levels. In earlier analyses, I also examined county health and hospital expenditures and fertilizer and agricultural chemical expenditures per cropped acre (possible farm-related environmental hazards) as potential intervening variables but found little relationship between these variables and infant mortality.

13. While falling population in farming and rural areas is often used to explain the decline and subsequent consolidation of services, evidence is mounting that such processes occur even when the population is growing (Lewis, 1983). This appears to reflect national (rather than specifically rural) tendencies toward the increased service specialization of cities and upward shift in the hierarchy of services. Rural consumers appear to deal with these changes by making multipurpose trips to more centralized service locations.

14. This was verified through a set of analyses regressing 1980 levels of state employment on 1970 levels of income related well-being and the other independent variables. Income well-being (poverty, median income, income inequality) in 1970 had no significant impact on the level of state employment in 1980.

Chapter Seven

1. Behavioral location theories are a related set of perspectives that modify the neoclassical assumptions and focus on the decisions made at the level of the firm. These perspectives show that entrepreneurs sometimes make conscious choices of location "away from the optimal one, in the full knowledge that profits were not being maximized" (Lever, 1985:21). For example, depending upon an individual entrepreneur's place of birth or leisure pursuits, a location decision might involve social or environmental attributes over profit.

2. For a systematic treatment of the economic forces contributing to regional differentiation, see Markusen (1987). She attributes regional differences to three factors: (1) differential rates of economic growth, (2) the structure of class and ownership relations, and (3) the uneven distribution of market power in relationships of exchange among regions.

3. Focusing on a specific commodity is also a methodological convenience: it holds production characteristics constant so that social relations internal to a particular production system can be more clearly observed.

4. Controlling for regional location per se will not allow one to sort out how agroclimatic effects, social relations or other regional characteristics influence farm impacts. If the purpose is truly in examining the whether for example, agroclimatic factors affect relationships, these ought to be defined, measured, and incorporated into the analysis. While selecting a region on the basis of agroclimatic factors may allow one to narrow down potential causes of regional differences, the question of other factors would still remain.

5. The Office of Technology of Assessment studies were originally published as a series of background papers in 1986 and later compiled into a edited volume by Swanson (1988).

6. There are several reasons for this focus. First, the social bases of regional variations in the effects of farm structure have not been explicitly examined in any empirical study. Second, the multiple ways in which 'region' can mediate farm impacts cannot be captured in any single analysis so that these influences had to be limited. Finally, the availability of data for all parts of the country for the 1970–1980 period was a consideration.

7. To explore this issue, I examined agriculturally dependent counties (as defined by Bender et al., 1985) in Texas, California, Arizona, and Florida, the same states used by MacCannell and Dolber-Smith. These counties were slightly above the national average in larger family farming, under the national average for smaller family farming, and almost one standard deviation unit above the national average for industrialized farming. Economic well-being in these counties was considerably lower than the rest of the nation. However, median education and employment in core industries were also lower, there was a higher nonwhite population, and distance from metropolitan centers was greater. Multiple regression analyses in the same form as those presented in Tables 7.3–7.5 were run for these counties. Given the small sample size (N=84), few of the coefficients were significant. The only significant relationship found for any of the three farm structure variables was a negative relationship for smaller family farming and well-being in the 1970 model. Education and industrial structure were the strongest and only consistent predictors of well-being. The way in which the models of any test of the Goldschmidt hypothesis are specified will obviously affect the results. In the MacCannell and Dolber-Smith (1986) study, few controls could be incorporated, which may account for the varying findings. The descriptive data, however, do support MacCannell and Dolber-Smith's (1986) contentions in regard to the impoverishment of these counties, though one might attribute its causality not only to industrialized farming but to other factors as well.

Chapter Eight

1. Although industrial structure and locational characteristics tend to be regarded as the major local determinants of farm structure, it is recognized that other factors unanalyzed by this study also affect farming. Beaulieu et al. (1988) posit that in addition to socioeconomic influences (economic and sociodemographic structure) other local influences include community values and governance (taxing, zoning, spending, and regulatory activities). Like Beaulieu et al. (1988) I leave the latter two influences largely unanalyzed in part because they would require extensive primary data collection efforts for each county. Also, to some extent worker power and other local attributes incorporate these latter influences. For example, the level at which welfare payments are set reflects social norms and government support for family subsistence levels. Unionization rates are an indicator of whether or not public values side with the interests of capital or labor. The size of the state sector also is related to levels of government spending (Gurr and King, 1987).

2. There are a couple of reasons for eliminating counties that do not have consistent farming patterns for both years. First, in order to compare if different discriminators characterize farming patterns in the 1970 and 1980 periods, the same group of counties must be examined in each pattern. That way, observed changes will not be a function of the shifting of counties from one group to another. Second, counties that did not have stable patterns can be viewed as marginal examples of a particular type of farming. Eliminating these from the analyses substantially improved the ability to discriminant among the farming patterns.

3. The stepwise procedure begins with no variables in the model. It progressively adds variables that significantly ($p \leq .05$) contribute to separating the functions and then eliminates those selected earlier that no longer satisfy the significance criterion given the other variables now in the equation.

References

Agnew, John.
1987 *Place and Politics: The Geographical Mediation of State and Society.* Boston: Allen & Unwin.

Ahern, Mary.
1986 "An income comparison of farm and nonfarm people." Pp. 79–88 in Ronald C. Wimberley, Dale Jahr, and Jerry W. Johnson (eds.), *New Dimensions in Rural Policy: Building Upon Our Heritage.* Studies prepared for the use of the Subcommittee on Agriculture and Transportation of the Joint Economic Committee, Congress of the United States. Washington, D.C.: U.S. Government Printing Office.

Albrecht, Don E. and Steve H. Murdock.
1988 "The structural characteristics of U.S. Agriculture: historical patterns and precursors of producers' adaptations to the crisis." Pp. 29–44 in Steve H. Murdock and F. Larry Leistritz (eds.), *The Farm Financial Crisis: Socioeconomic Dimensions and Implications for Producers and Rural Areas.* Boulder, Colorado: Westview Press.

Allison, Paul D.
1978 "Measures of inequality." *American Sociological Review* 43 (December):865–880.

Althauser, Robert P. and Arne L. Kalleberg.
1981 "Firms, occupations and the structure of labor markets: a conceptual analysis." Pp. 120–149 in Ivar Berg (ed.), *Sociological Perspectives on Labor Markets.* New York: Academic Press.

Andrews, Frank, and Steve B. Withey.
1976 *Social Indicators of Well-being: Americans' Perceptions of the Quality of Life.* New York: Plenum Press.

Aronowitz, Stanley.
1973 *False Promises: The Shaping of American Working-Class Consciousness.* New York: McGraw-Hill.

Asher, Herbert B.
1983 Causal Modelling. 2nd ed. Beverly Hills: Sage Publications.

Ashton, David N.
1986 *Unemployment under Capitalism: The Sociology of British and American Labour Markets.* Brighton, Sussex: Harvester Press.

Averitt, Richard T.
1968 *The Dual Economy: The Dynamics of American Industry Structure.* New York: W.W. Norton.

Babb, E.M.
1979 "Some causes of structural change in U.S. agriculture." Pp. 51–60 in *Structure Issues of American Agriculture*. Washington, D.C.: U.S. Department of Agriculture, Economics, Statistics, and Cooperatives Service, Agricultural Economic Report 438.

Banaji, Jarius.
1980 "Summary of selected parts of Kautsky's *The Agrarian Question*." Pp. 39–82 in Frederick Buttel and Howard Newby (eds.), *The Rural Sociology of the Advanced Societies*. Montclair, N.J.: Allanheld, Osmun.

Barkin, David.
1982 "The impact of agribusiness on rural development." Pp. 1–25 in Scott McNall (ed.), *Current Perspectives in Social Theory*. Greenwich, Conn.: JAI Press Inc.

Barlett, Peggy F.
1986 "Part-time farming: saving the farm or saving the life-style." *Rural Sociology* 51 (Fall):289–313.

Baron, James N. and William T. Bielby.
1980 "Bringing the firms back in: stratification, segmentation, and the organization of work." *American Sociological Review* 45 (October):737–765.

1984 "The organization of work in a segmented economy." *American Sociological Review* 49 (August):454–473.

Beauford, E. Yvonne and Mack C. Nelson.
1988 "Social and economic conditions of black farm households: status and prospects." Pp. 99–119 in Lionel J. Beaulieu (ed.), *The Rural South in Crisis: Challenges for the Future*. Boulder, Colorado: Westview Press.

Beaulieu, Lionel J. and Joseph J. Molnar.
1984 "Community change and the farm sector: impacts of rural development in agriculture." Paper presented at the annual meetings of the Rural Sociological Society, College Station, Texas.

Beaulieu, Lionel J., Michael K. Miller, and David Mulkey.
1988 "Community forces and their influence on farm structure." Pp. 211–232 in Lionel J. Beaulieu (ed.), *The Rural South in Crisis: Challenges for the Future*. Boulder, Colorado: Westview Press.

Beck, E.M., Patrick M. Horan and Charles M. Tolbert II.
1978 "Stratification in a dual economy: a sectoral model of earnings determination." *American Sociological Review* 43 (October):704–720.

Becker, G.S.
1964 *Human Capital*. New York: Columbia University Press.

Beeghley, Leonard.
1988 *Living Poorly in America*. New York: Praeger.

Belyea, Michael J. and Linda M. Lobao.
1990 "The psychosocial consequences of agricultural transformation: the farm crisis and depression." *Rural Sociology* 55 (Spring):58–75.

Bender, Lloyd D., Bernal L. Green, Thomas F. Hady, John A. Kuehn, Marlys K. Nelson, Leon B. Perkinson, and Peggy J. Ross.
1985 *The Diverse Social and Economic Structure of Nonmetropolitan America.* Washington, D.C.: United States Department of Agriculture, Economic Research Service.

Berg, Ivar, Robert Bibb, T. Aldrich Finegan, and Michael Swafford.
1981 "Toward model specification in the structural unemployment thesis: issues and prospects." Pp. 347–367 in Ivar Berg (ed.), *Sociological Perspectives on Labor Markets.* New York: Academic Press.

Betz, D.M.
1974 "A comparative study of income inequality in cities." *Pacific Sociological Review* 17 (October):435–454.

Bibb, Robert and William H. Form.
1977 "The effects of industrial, occupational, and sex stratification on wages in blue-collar markets." *Social Forces* 55 (June):974–996.

Blank, Rebecca M. and Alan S. Blinder.
1986 "Macroeconomics, income distribution, and poverty." Pp. 180–208 in Sheldon H. Danziger and Daniel H. Weinberg (eds.), *Fighting Poverty: What Works and What Doesn't.* Cambridge, Mass.: Harvard University Press.

Blau, Judith R. and Peter M. Blau.
1982 "The cost of inequality: metropolitan structure and violent crime." *American Sociological Review* 47 (February):114–129.

Blau, Peter and Otis D. Duncan.
1967 *The American Occupational Structure.* New York: Wiley.

Blaug, Mark.
1976 "The empirical status of human capital theory: a slightly jaundiced survey." *Journal of Economic Literature* 14 (3):827–855.

Block, Fred.
1987 "Rethinking the political economy of the welfare state." Pp. 109–160 in Fred Block, Richard A. Cloward, Barbara Ehrenreich, and Frances Fox Piven (eds.), *The Mean Season: The Attack on the Welfare State.* New York: Pantheon Books.

Block, Fred, Richard A. Cloward, Barbara Ehrenreich, and Frances Fox Piven.
1987 "Introduction." Pp. ix–xvi in Fred Block, Richard A. Cloward, Barbara Ehrenreich, and Frances Fox Piven (eds.), *The Mean Season: The Attack on the Welfare State.* New York: Pantheon Books.

Bloomquist, Leonard E. and Gene F. Summers.
1982 "Organization of production and community income distributions." *American Sociological Review* 47 (June):325–338.

Bluestone, Barry.
1982 "Deindustrialization and the abandonment of community." Pp. 38–61 in John C. Raines, Lenora E. Berson, and David M. Gracie (eds.), *Community and Capital in Conflict: Plant Closings and Job Loss*. Philadelphia: Temple University Press.

Bluestone, Barry and Bennet Harrison.
1982 *The Deindustrialization of America: Plant Closings, Community Abandonment, and the Dismantling of Basic Industry*. New York: Basic Books.

Blumberg, Paul.
1980 *Inequality in an Age of Decline*. New York: Oxford University Press.

Boehm, William.
1979 "Farm structure and a changing food policy environment." Pp. 263–268 in *Structure Issues of American Agriculture*. Washington, D.C.: U.S. Department of Agriculture, Economics, Statistics, and Cooperatives Service, Agricultural Economic Report 438.

Bohrnstedt, G.W. and T.M. Carter.
1971 "Robustness in regression analysis." Pp. 118–146 in H.L. Costner (ed.), *Sociological Methodology*. San Francisco: Jossey-Bass.

Bonanno, Alessandro.
1987 *Small Farms: Persistence with Legitimation*. Boulder, Colorado: Westview Press.

Bowles, Samuel and H. Gintis.
1976 *Schooling in Capitalist America: Educational Reform and the Contradictions of Economic Life*. New York: Basic Books.

Boxley, Robert F. and Larry Walker.
1979 "Impact of rising land values on agricultural structure." Pp. 88–96 in *Structure Issues of American Agriculture*. Washington, D.C.: U.S. Department of Agriculture, Economics, Statistics, and Cooperatives Service, Agricultural Economic Report 438.

Bradley, Tony and Philip Lowe.
1984 "Introduction: locality, rurality and social theory." Pp. 1–23 in Tony Bradley and Philip Lowe (eds.), *Locality and Rurality*. Norwich, England: Geo Books.

Bradsaw, Ted K. and Edward J. Blakely.
1979 *Rural Communities in Advanced Industrial Society: Development and Developers*. New York: Praeger.

Braverman, Harry.
1974 *Labor and Monopoly Capital*. New York: Monthly Review Press.

Breault, K.D. and Augustine J. Kposowa.
1987 "Explaining divorce in the United States: a study of 3,111 counties, 1980." *Journal of Marriage and the Family* 49 (August):549–558.

Brenner, R.
1977 "The origins of capitalist development: a critique of neo-Smithian Marxism." *New Left Review* 104:25–92.

Briggs, Vernon M.
1981 "Unemployment and underemployment." Pp. 359–381 in Amos H. Hawley and Sara Mills Madie (eds.), *Nonmetropolitan America in Transition*. Chapel Hill: The Univeristy of North Carolina Press.

Brooks, Nora L., Thomas A. Stucker, and Jennifer Bailey.
1986 "Income and well-being of farmers and the farm financial crisis." *Rural Sociology* 51 (Winter):391–405.

Brown, David L. and Calvin L. Beale.
1981 "Diversity in post-1970 population trends." Pp. 27–71 in Amos H. Hawley and Sara Mills Mazie (eds.), *Nonmetropolitan American in Transition*. Chapel Hill: The University of North Carolina Press.

Bultena, Gordon, Paul Lasley, and Jack Geller.
1986 "The farm crisis: patterns and impacts of financial distress among Iowa farm families." *Rural Sociology* 51 (Winter):436–448.

Burawoy, Michael.
1983 "Factory regimes under advanced capitalism." *American Sociological Review* 48 (October):587–605.

Burtless, Gary.
1986 "Public spending for the poor: trends, prospects, and economic limits." Pp. 18–49 in Sheldon H. Danziger and Daniel H. Weinberg (eds.), *Fighting Poverty: What Works and What Doesn't*. Cambridge, Mass.: Harvard University Press.

Buttel, Frederick H.
1980a "Agricultural structure and rural development." *Sociologia Ruralis* 20 (1–2):44–61.

———.
1980 b "W(h)ither the family farm? Toward a sociological perspective on independent commodity production in U.S. agriculture." *Cornell Journal of Social Relations* 15:10–37.

———.
1982 "The political economy of agriculture in advanced industrial societies: some observations on theory and method." Pp. 27–55 in Scott G. McNall (ed.), *Current Perspectives in Social Theory*. Greenwich, Conn.: JAI Press.

———. 1983a "Beyond the family farm." Pp. 87–107 in Gene Summers (ed.), *Technology and Social Change in Rural Areas*. Boulder, Colorado: Westview Press.

———. 1983b "Farm structure and rural development." Pp. 103–124 in David E. Brewster, Wayne D. Rasmussen, and Garth Youngbert (eds.), *Farms in Transition*. Ames, Iowa: The Iowa State University Press.

Buttel, Frederick H. and Oscar W. Larson, III.
1979 "Farm size, structure, and energy intensity: an ecological analysis of U.S. agriculture." *Rural Sociology* 44 (Fall):471–488.

Buttel, Frederick H., Mark Lancelle, and David R. Lee.
1986 "Emerging agricultural technologies, farm structural change, public policy, and rural communities in the Northeast." Pp. 213–372 in *Technology, Public Policy and the Changing Structure of American Agriculture*. Vol. 2, *Background Papers*, Part D: *Rural Communities*. Washington, D.C.: Office of Technology Assessment.

Campbell, Angus, Phillip E. Converse, and Willard L. Rodgers.
1976 *The Quality of American Life: Perceptions, Evaluations, and Satisfaction*. New York: Russell Sage Foundation.

Carlin, Thomas A. and John Crecink.
1979 "Small farm definition and public policy." *American Journal of Agricultural Economics* 61 (December):933–939.

Carlin, Thomas A. and Bernal L. Green.
1988 *Local Farm Structure and Community Ties*. United States Department of Agriculture, Economic Research Service, Rural Development Research Report Number 68.

Chandler, Alfred D.
1977 *The Invisible Hand*. Cambridge, Mass.: The Belknap of Harvard University Press.

Christenson, James A.
1976 "Quality of community service: a macro-unidimensional approach with experiential data." *Rural Sociology* 41 (Winter):509–525.

Clark, Gordon L.
1986 "The crisis of the midwest auto industry." Pp. 127–148 in Allen J. Scott and Michael Storper (eds.), *Production, Work and Territory: The Geographical Anatomy of Industrial Capitalism*. Boston: Allen & Unwin.

Clifford, William B. and Yevonne S. Brannon.
1985 "Rural-urban differentials in mortality." *Rural Sociology* 50 (Summer):210–224.

Cochrane, Willard.
1979 *The Development of American Agriculture*. Minneapolis: University of Minnesota Press.

————.
1986 "The need to rethink agricultural policy in general and to perform some radical surgery on commodity programs in particular." Pp. 391–411 in Joseph J. Molnar (ed.), *Agricultural Change: Consequences for Southern Farms and Rural Communities.* Boulder, Colorado: Westview Press.

Collins, Randall.
1974 *Conflict Sociology: Toward an Explanatory Science.* New York: Academic Press.

Connor, John M.
1979 "Manufacturing and food retailing." Pp. 226–234 in *Structural Issues of American Agriculture.* Agricultural Economics Report 438. Washington, D.C.: Economics, Statistics, and Cooperatives Service, U.S. Department of Agriculture.

Coughenour, C. Milton.
1984 "Social ecology and agriculture." *Rural Sociology* 49 (1):1–22.

Coye, Molly Joel.
1986 "The health effects of agricultural production." Pp. 165–197 in Kenneth A. Dahlberg (ed.), *New Directions for Agriculture and Agricultural Research: Neglected Dimensions and Emerging Alternatives.* Totowa, N.J.: Rowman and Allanheld.

Cummings, Scott.
1987 "Vulnerability to the effects of recession: minority and female workers." *Social Forces* 65 (3):834–857.

Cutright, Phillip.
1987 "Cross-sectional and longitudinal models of 1977 national social insurance expenditures." *Sociological Focus* 20 (4):295–307.

Danziger, Sheldon H. and Daniel H. Weinberg.
1986 "Introduction." Pp. 1–17 in Sheldon H. Danziger and Daniel H. Weinberg (eds.), *Fighting Poverty: What Works and What Doesn't.* Cambridge, Mass.: Harvard University Press.

Danziger, Sheldon H., Robert H. Haveman, and Robert D. Plotnick.
1986 "Antipoverty policy: effects on the poor and the nonpoor." Pp. 50–77 in Sheldon H. Danziger and Daniel H. Weinerg (eds.), *Fighting Poverty: What Works and What Doesn't.* Cambridge, Mass.: Harvard University Press.

Davis, John Emmeus.
1980 "Capitalist agricultural development and the exploitation of the propertied laborer." Pp. 133–154 in Frederick Buttel and Howard Newby (eds.), *The Rural Sociology of the Advanced Societies: Critical Perspectives.* Montclair, N.J.: Allanheld, Osmun.

Davis, Kingsley and Wilbert E. Moore.
1945 "Some principles of stratification." *American Sociological Review* 10 (April): 242–249.

Davis, Mike.
1978 " 'Fordism' in crisis: a review of Michel Aglietta's *Régulation et crises: L'expérience des Etats-Unis." Review* 2 (2):207–269.

Deavers, Kenneth L.
1987 "Rural economic conditions and rural development policy for the 1980s and 1990s." Pp. 113–123 in Gene F. Summers, John Bryden, Kenneth Deavers, Howard Newby, and Susan Sechler (eds.), *Agriculture and Beyond: Rural Economic Development.* Madison: University of Wisconsin, College of Agricultural and Life Sciences.

de Janvry, Alain.
1980 "Social differentiation in agriculture and the ideology of neopopulism." Pp. 155–168 in Frederick Buttel and Howard Newby (eds.), *The Rural Sociology of the Advanced Societies: Critical Perspectives.* Montclair, N.J.: Allanheld, Osmun.

de Janvry, Alain and Phillip LeVeen.
1986 "Historical forces that have shaped world agriculture: a structural perspective." Pp. 83–104 in Kenneth A. Dahlberg (ed.), *New Directions for Agriculture and Agricultural Research: Neglected Dimensions and Emerging Alternatives.* Totowa, N.J.: Rowman and Allanheld.

de Janvry, Alain, David Runsten, and Elisabeth Sadoulet.
1987 "Toward a rural development program for the United States: a proposal." Pp. 55–93 in Gene F. Summers, John Bryden, Kenneth Deavers, Howard Newby, and Susan Sechler (eds.), *Agriculture and Beyond: Rural Economic Development.* Madison: University of Wisconsin, College of Agricultural and Life Sciences.

Denis, Wilfrid B.
1982 "Capital and agriculture: a review of Marxist problematics." *Studies in Political Economy* 7 (Winter):127–154.

Deseran, Forrest A. and Ann Z. Dellenbarger.
1988 "Local labor markets in agricultural policy dependent areas of the South." Pp. 170–180 in Lionel J. Beaulieu (ed.), *The Rural South in Crisis: Challenges for the Future.* Boulder, Colorado: Westview Press.

Devine, Joel A.
1985 "State and state expenditure: determinants of social investment and social consumption spending in the postwar United States." *American Soiological Review* 50 (2):150–165.

Doeringer, Peter and Michael Piore.
1971 *Internal Labor Markets and Manpower Analysis.* Lexington, Mass.: D.C. Heath Books.

Dunlap, Riley E. and Kenneth E. Martin.
1983 "Bringing environment into the study of agriculture: observations and suggestions regarding the sociology of agriculture." *Rural Sociology* 48 (Summer):201–218.

Dyson, Lowell K.
1986 *Farmers' Organizations.* New York: Greenwood Press.

Eberstein, Isaac W. and Jan Reese Parker.
1984 "Racial differences in infant mortality by cause of death: the impact of birth weight and maternal age." *Demography* 21 (August):309–321.

Eberts, Paul R.
1979a "Growth and the quality of life: some logical and methodological issues." Pp. 159–184 in Gene F. Summers and Arne Selvik (eds.), *Nonmetropolitan Industrial Growth and Community Change.* Lexington, Mass.: D.C. Heath.

_____.
1979b "The changing structure of agriculture and its effects on community life in northeastern U.S. counties." Paper presented at the annual meetings of the Rural Sociological Society, Burlington, Vermont.

_____.
1982 "Social indicators of well-being." Pp. 284–295 in Don A. Dillman and Daryl J. Hobbs (eds.), *Rural Society in the U.S.: Issues for the 1980s.* Boulder, Colorado: Westview Press.

Edwards, Richard.
1979 *Contested Terrain: The Transformation of the Workplace in the Twentieth Century.* New York: Basic Books.

Emerson, Robert D.
1984 "Migration in farm labor markets." Pp. 104–135 in Robert D. Emerson (ed.), *Seasonal Agricultural Labor Markets in the United States.* Ames: The Iowa State University Press.

Erven, Bernard L.
1984 "Impact of labor laws and regulations on agricultural labor markets." Pp. 375–405 in Robert D. Emerson (ed.), *Seasonal Agricultural Labor Markets in the United States.* Ames, Iowa: The Iowa State University Press.

Falk, William W. and Thomas A. Lyson.
1988 *High Tech, Low Tech, No Tech: Recent Industrial and Occupational Change in the South.* Albany, N.Y.: State University of New York Press.

Farmer, Frank L., Michael K. Miller, and Donald E. Voth.
1984 "Evaluation of rural health care programs employing unobserved variable models: impact on infant mortality." *Rural Sociology* 49 (Summer):127–142.

Fine, Ben.
1987 "Segmented labour market theory: a critical assessment." Discussion paper, Department of Economics, Birkbeck College, London, England, July.

FitzSimmons, Margaret.
1986 "The new industrial agriculture: the regional integration of specialty crop production." *Economic Geography* 62 (4):334–353.

Fligstein, Neil, Alexander Hicks, and S. Philip Morgan.
1983 "Toward a theory of income determination." *Work and Occupations* 10 (3):289–306.

Flora, Jan L. and Cornelia Butler Flora.
1986 "Emerging agricultural technologies, farm size, public policy, and rural communities: the Great Plains and the West." Pp. 168–212 in *Technology, Public Policy and the Changing Structure of American Agriculture.* Vol. 2, *Background Papers,* Part D: *Rural Communities.* Washington, D.C.: Office of Technology Assessment.

Flora, Jan L., Ivan Brown, and Judith Lee Conby.
1977 "Impact of type of agriculture on class structure, social well-being, and inequalities." Paper presented at the annual meetings of the Rural Sociological Society, Burlington, Vermont.

Florida, Richard, Martin Kenney, and Andrew Mair.
1988 "The transplant phenomenon." *Economic Development Commentary* (Winter):3–9.

Foley, J.M.
1977 "Trends, determinants and policy implications of income inequality in U.S. counties." *Sociology and Social Research* 61 (July):441–461.

Freeman, Richard B. and James L. Medoff.
1984 *What Do Unions Do?* New York: Basic Books.

Frey, William H.
1987 "Migration and depopulation of the metropolis: regional restructuring or rural renaissance?" *American Sociological Review* 52 (2):240–257.

Friedland, William H.
1982 "The end of rural society and the future of rural sociology." *Rural Sociology* 47 (Winter):589–608.

Friedland, William H., Amy E. Barton, and Robert J. Thomas.
1981 *Manufacturing Green Gold.* Cambridge: Cambridge University Press.

Friedmann, Harriet.
1978 "World market, state, and family farm: social bases of household production in an era of wage labor." *Comparative Studies in Society and History* 20:545–586.

————.
1981 "The family farm in advanced capitalism: outline of a theory of simple commodity production in agriculture." Paper presented at the annual meetings of the American Sociological Association, Toronto.

——.
1987 "Agro-food industries and export agriculture: the changing international division of labor, 1945-73." Paper presented at the annual meetings of the Rural Sociological Society, Madison, Wisconsin, August.

Fritsch, Conrad F.
1984 "Seasonality of farm labor use patterns in the United States." Pp. 64–95 in Robert D. Emerson (ed.), *Seasonal Agricultural labor markets in the United States.* Ames, Iowa: The Iowa State University Press.

Fuchs, V.R.
1984 *Who Shall Live? Health, Economics, and Social Choice.* New York: Basic Books.

Fuguitt, Glenn and Calvin Beale.
1978 "Population trends of nonmetropolitan cities and villages in subregions of the United States." *Demography* 15 (4):605–620.

Fujimoto, Isao.
1977 "The communities of the San Joaquin Valley: the relation between scale of farming, water use, and quality of life." Pp. 480–500 in U.S. Congress, House of Representatives, Obstacles to Strengthening the Family Farm System. Hearings Before the Subcommittee on Family Farms, Rural Development, and Special Studies of the Committee on Agriculture, 95th Congress, first session. Washington, D.C.: U.S. Government Printing Office.

Fuller, Anthony M.
1984 "Part-time farming: the enigmas and the realities." Pp. 187-219 in Harry K. Schwarzweller (ed.), *Research in Rural Sociology and Development*, Volume I. Greenwich, Conn.: JAI Press.

Gans, Herbert.
1972 "The positive functions of poverty." *American Journal of Sociology* 78 (2):275–289.

Gasson, Ruth.
1988 *The Economics of Part-Time Farming.* New York: John Wiley and Sons.

Geisler, Charles C., J. Tadlock Cowan, Michael R. Hattery, and Harvey M. Jacobs.
1984 "Sustained land productivity: equity consequences of alternative agricultural technologies." Pp. 213–236 in Gigi M. Beradi and Charles C. Geisler (eds.), *The Social Consequences of New Agricultural Technologies.* Boulder, Colorado: Westview Press.

Giddens, Anthony.
1981 *A Contemporary Critique of Historical Materialism.* London: MacMillan.

Gilbert, Jess and Raymond Akor.
1988 "Increasing structural divergence in U.S. dairying: California and Wisconsin since 1950." *Rural Sociology* 53 (1):56–73.

Gilles, Jere.
1980 "Farm size, farm structure, energy and climate: an alternative ecological analysis of United States agriculture." *Rural Sociology* 45 (Summer):332–339.

Gilles, Jere Lee and Dalecki, Michael.
1988 "Rural well-being and agricultural change in two farming regions." *Rural Sociology* 53 (Spring):40–55.

Gladwin, Christina H.
1985 "Values and goals of Florida farm women: do they help the family farm survive?" *Agriculture and Human Values* 2 (Winter):40–47.

Gladwin, Christina H. and Robert Zabawa.
1986 "After structural change: are part-time or full-time operators better off?" Pp. 39–60 in Joseph J. Molnar (ed.), *Agricultural Change: Consequences for Southern Farms and Rural Communities.* Boulder, Colorado: Westview Press.

Glover, Robert W.
1984 "Unstructured labor markets and alternative labor market forms." Pp. 254-285 in Robert D. Emerson (ed.), *Seasonal Agricultural Labor markets in the United States.* Ames, Iowa: The Iowa State University Press.

Goldfield, Michael.
1987 *The Decline of Organized Labor in the United States.* Chicago: The University of Chicago Press.

Goldschmidt, Walter.
1968 "Small business and the community: a study in the central valley of California on effects of scale of farm operations." Pp. 303–433 in U.S. Congress, Senate, Corporation Farming, Hearings Before the Subcommittee on Monopoly of the Select Committee on Small Business, U.S. Senate, 90th Congress, 2nd session, May and July 1968. Washington, D.C.: U.S. Government Printing Office.

———.
1978a *As You Sow: Three Studies in the Social Consequences of Agribusiness.* Montclair, N.J.: Allanheld, Osmun and Company.

———.
1978b "Large-scale farming and the rural social structure." *Rural Sociology* 43 (Fall):362–366.

Goodman, David and Michael Redclift.
1985 "Capitalism, petty commodity production and the farm enterprise." *Sociologia Ruralis* 25 (3–4):231–247.

Gordon, David.
1972 *Theories of Poverty and Unemployment.* Lexington, Mass.: D.C. Heath.

Gordon, David, Richard Edwards, and Michael Reich.
1982 *Segmented Work, Divided Workers: The Historical Transformation of Labor in the United States.* Cambridge: Cambridge University Press.

Gortmaker, Steven L.
1979 "Poverty and infant mortality in the United States." *American Sociological Review* 84 (April):280–297.

Goss, Kevin F. and Richard D. Rodefeld.
1979 "Review of Goldschmidt, *As You Sow.*" *Rural Sociology* 44 (Winter):802–806.

Goss, Kevin, Richard Rodefeld, and Frederick Buttel.
1980 "The political economy of class structure in U.S. agriculture." Pp. 83–132 in Frederick Buttel and Howard Newby (eds.), *The Rural Sociology of Advanced Societies.* Montclair, N.J.: Allanheld Osmun.

Green, Gary P.
1985 "Large-scale farming and the quality of life in rural communities: further specification of the Goldschmidt hypothesis." *Rural Sociology* 50 (Summer):262–273.

Grossman, Michael and Steven Jacobwitz.
1981 "Variations in infant mortality among counties of the United States: The roles of public policies and programs." *Demography* 18 (November):695–713.

Gurr, Ted Robert and Desmond S. King.
1987 *The State and the City.* Chicago: The University of Chicago Press.

Hall, Richard H.
1986 *Dimensions of Work.* Beverly Hills: Sage.

Hamm, L.G.
1979 "Farm input industries and farm structure." Pp. 218–225 in *Structural Issues of American Agriculture.* Agricultural Economics Report 438. Washington, D.C.: Economics, Statistics, and Cooperatives Service, U.S. Department of Agriculture.

Hanushek, Eric A.
1973 "Regional differences in the structure of earning." *Review of Economics and Statistics* 55 (2):204–232.

Harris, Craig and Jess Gilbert.
1982 "Large-scale farming, rural income, and Goldschmidt's agrarian thesis." *Rural Sociology* 47 (Fall):449–458.

Harrison, Bennett.
1984 "Regional restructuring and 'good business climates': the economic transformation of New England since World War II." Pp. 48–96 in Larry Sawers and William K. Tabb (eds.), *Sunbelt/Snowbelt: Urban Development and Regional Restructuring.* New York: Oxford University Press.

Harrison, Bennett and Barry Bluestone.
1988 *The Great U-Turn: Corporate Restructuring and the Polarizing of America*. New York: Basic Books.

Harvey, David.
1973 *Social Justice and the City*. Baltimore: The Johns Hopkins University Press.

———.
1975 "The geography of capitalist accumulation: a reconstruction of the Marxian theory." *Antipode* 7 (2):9–21.

———.
1988 "The geographical and geopolitical consequences of the transition from fordist to flexible accumulation." Pp. 101–134 in George Steenlieb and James W. Hughes (eds.), *America's New Market Geography*. New Brunswick, N.J.: Rutgers University Press.

Hauser, Robert M. and David L. Featherman.
1977 *The Process of Stratification: Trends and Analysis*. New York: Academic Press.

Havens, A. Eugene.
1986 "Capitalist development in the United States: state, accumulation, and agricultural production systems." Pp. 26–59 in A. Eugene Havens (ed.) with Gregory Hooks, Patrick H. Mooney, and Max J. Pfeffer, *Studies in the Transformation of U.S. Agriculture*. Boulder, Colorado: Westview Press.

Hayes, Michael N., and Alan L. Olmstead.
1984 "Farm size and community quality: Arvin and Dinuba revisited." *American Journal of Agricultural Economics* 66 (November):430–436.

Heady, Earl O. and Steven T. Sonka.
1974 "Farm side, rural community income, and consumer welfare." *American Journal of Agricultural Economics* 56 (August):534–542.

Heaton, Tim B.
1980 "Metropolitan influence on United States farmland use and capital intensivity." *Rural Sociology* 45 (Fall):501–508.

Heaton, Tim B. and David L. Brown.
1982 "Farm structure and energy intensity: another look." *Rural Sociology* 47 (Spring):17–31.

Heffernan, William D.
1972 "Sociological dimensions of agricultural structures in the United States." *Sociologia Ruralis* 12 (October):481–499.

———.
1982a "Reducing uncertainty: changes in the U.S. poultry industry." Paper presented at the Sociology of Agriculture Conference, Davis, University of California.

———.
1982b "Structure of agriculture and quality of life in rural communities." Pp. 337–346 in Don A. Dillman and Daryl J. Hobbs (eds.), *Rural Society in the U.S.: Issues for the 1980s.* Boulder, Colorado: Westview Press.

Heffernan, William D. and Judith B. Heffernan.
1986 "The farm crisis and the rural community." Pp. 273–280 in Dale Jahr, Jerry W. Johnson, and Ronald C. Wimberley (eds.), *New Dimensions in Rural Policy: Building Upon Our Heritage*, Studies prepared for the use of the Subcommittee on Agriculture and Transportation of the Joint Economic Committee of the United States. Washington, D.C.: U.S. Government Printing Office.

Heffernan, William D. and Paul Lasley.
1978 "Agricultural structure and interaction in the local community: a case study." *Rural Sociology* 43 (Fall):348–361.

Heffernan, William D., Gary Green, R. Paul Lasley, and Michael F. Nolan.
1981 "Part-time farming and the rural community." *Rural Sociology* 46 (Summer):245–262.

Heise, David R.
1970 "Causal inference from panel data." Pp. 3–27 in Edgar F. Borgatta and George W. Bohrnstedt (eds.), *Sociological Methodology 1970.* San Francisco: Jossey-Bass.

Helfgott, Roy B.
1980 *Labor Economics* (2nd ed.). New York: Random House.

Henry, Mark, Mark Drabenstott, and Lynn Gibson.
1988 "A changing rural economy." Pp. 15–37 in Mark Drabenstott and Lynn Gibson (eds.), *Rural America in Transition.* The Federal Reserve Bank of Kansas City Research Division.

Hightower, Jim.
1973 *Hard Tomatoes, Hard Times: A Report of the Agribusiness Accountability Project on the Failure of the Land Grant College Complex.* Cambridge, Mass.: Schenkman.

Hodge, Robert W. and Barbara A. Laslett.
1980 "Poverty and status attainment." Pp. 126–163 in Vincent T. Covello (ed.), *Poverty and Public Policy: An Evaluation of Social Science Research.* Cambridge, Mass.: G.K. Hall.

Hodson, Randy.
1978 "Labor in the monopoly, competitive, and state sectors of production." *Politics and Society* 8:429–480.

———.
1983 *Worker's Earnings and Corporate Economic Structure.* New York: Academic Press.

———.
1984 "Companies, industries and the measurement of economic segmentation." *American Sociological Review* 49 (June):335–348.

Hodson, Randy D. and Robert L. Kaufman.
1982 "Economic dualism: a critical review." *American Sociological Review* 47 (December): 727–739.

Holland, David and Joe Carvalho.
1985 "The changing mode of production in American agriculture: emerging conflicts in agriculture's role in the reproduction of advanced capitalism." *Review of Radical Political Economics* 17 (4):1–27.

Hollingsworth, J. Rogers.
1986 *A Political Economy of Medicine: Great Britain and the United States*. Baltimore: The Johns Hopkins University Press.

Holt, James S.
1984 "Introduction to the seasonal farm labor problem." Pp. 3–32 in Robert D. Emerson (ed.), *Seasonal Agricultural Labor Markets in the United States*. Ames, Iowa: The Iowa State University Press.

Hoppe, Robert A.
1987 "Shifting income patterns: implications for nonmetro America." *Rural Development Perspectives* 4 (February):2–5.

Horan, Patrick M. and Charles M. Tolbert II.
1984 *The Organization of Work in Rural and Urban Labor Markets*. Boulder, Colorado: Westview Press.

Hosokawa, Michael C.
1986 "Issues in rural health care." Pp. 470–476 in Dale Jahr, Jerry W. Johnson, and Ronald C. Wimberley (eds.), *New Dimensions in Rural Policy: Building Upon Our Heritage*, studies prepared for the use of the Subcommittee on Agriculture and Transportation of the Joint Economic Committee Congress of the United States. Washington, D.C.: U.S. Government Printing Office.

Howes, Candace and Ann R. Markusen.
1981 "Poverty: a regional political economy perspective." Pp. 437–463 in Amos H. Hawley and Sara Mills Mazie (eds.), *Nonmetropolitan American in Transition*. Chapel Hill: The University of North Carolina Press.

Huffman, Wallace E.
1984 "Some analytical approaches for human resource issues of seasonal farm labor." Pp. 33–63 in Robert D. Emerson (ed.), *Seasonal Agricultural Labor Markets in the United States*. Ames, Iowa: The Iowa State University Press.

Jacobs, David.
1982 "Competition, scale and political explanations: an integrated study of sectoral explanatons at the aggregate level." *American Sociological Review* 47 (5):600–614.

———.
1985 "Unequal organizations or unequal attainments? An empirical comparison of sectoral and individualistic explanations for aggregate inequality." *American Sociological Review* 50 (April):166–180.

James, David R.
1986 "Local state structure and the transformation of Southern agriculture." Pp. 150–178 in A. Eugene Havens (ed.) with Gregory Hooks, Patrick H. Mooney, and Max J. Pfeffer, *Studies in the Transformation of U.S. Agriculture*. Boulder, Colorado: Westview Press.

Johnston, R.J.
1986 "The state, the region, and the spatial division of labor." Pp. 265–280 in Allen J. Scott and Michael Storper (eds.), *Production, Work, Territory: The Geographical Anatomy of Industrial Capitalism*. Boston: Allen & Unwin.

Jonas, Andrew.
1988 "A new regional geography of localities." *Area* 20 (1):1–10.

Kalleberg, Arne L. and Ivar Berg.
1987 *Work and Industry: Structures, Markets, and Processes*. New York: Plenum Press.

Kalleberg, Arne L. and Aage B. Sørensen.
1979 "The sociology of labor markets." *Annual Review of Sociology* 5:351–379.

Kalleberg, Arne L., Michael Wallace, and Robert P. Althauser.
1981 "Economic segmentation, worker power, and income inequality." *American Journal of Sociology* 87 (June):651–683.

Kaufman, Robert L., Randy Hodson, and Neil D. Fligstein.
1981 "Defrocking dualism: a new approach to defining industrial sectors." *Social Science Research* 10 (March):1–31.

Kautsky, Karl.
1988 *The Agrarian Question*, Volumes 1 and 2 (translated by Pete Burgess, originally published in 1899). London: Zwan Publications.

Keating, Norah C.
1987 "Reducing stress of farm men and women." *Family Relations* 36 (4):358–363.

Kendal, M.G. and A. Stuart.
1961 *The Advanced Theory of Statistics*. London: Griffin

Kenney, Martin, Linda M. Lobao, James Curry, and W. Richard Goe.
1989 "Midwestern agriculture in U.S. fordism: from the New Deal to economic restructuring." *Sociologia Ruralis* 29 (2):130–148.

Kenny, David A.
1979 *Correlation and Causality*. New York: John Wiley and Sons.

Kessler, Ronald C. and David F. Greenberg.
1981 *Linear Panel Analysis: Models of Quantitative Change.* New York: Academic Press.

Kim, Jae-On and Charles W. Mueller.
1978 *Factor Analysis: Statistical Methods and Practical Issues.* Beverly Hills: Sage.

Klecka, William R.
1984 *Discriminant Analysis* (fifth printing). Beverly Hills: Sage.

Kodras, Janet E.
1982 "The geographic perspective in social policy evaluation: a conceptual approach with application to the U.S. food stamp program." Ph.D. dissertation, Department of Geography, The Ohio State University.

————.
1986 "Labor market and policy constraints on the work disincentive effect of welfare." *Annals of the Association of American Geographers* 76 (2):228–246.

Kolko, Joyce.
1988 *Restructuring the World Economy.* New York: Pantheon Books.

Korsching, Peter F. and Curtis W. Stofferahn.
1984 "Impact of the changing farm structure on rural communities." Paper presented at the 1984 annual meetings of the Rural Sociological Society, College Station, Texas.

————.
1985a "Farm and non-farm interdependencies in agricultural communities." Paper presented at the annual meetings of the Rural Sociological Society, Blacksburg, Virginia.

————.
1985b "Interrelationships between the farm and non-farm sectors in agricultural communities." Paper presented at the annual meetings of the Rural Sociology Section, Southern Association of Agricultural Scientists, Biloxi, Mississippi.

————.
1986 "Agricultural and rural community interdependencies." Pp. 245–266 in Joseph Molnar (ed.), *Agricultural Change: Consequences for Southern Farms and Rural Communities.* Boulder, Colorado: Westview Press.

Krause, Kenneth.
1987 *Corporate Farming, 1969-1982.* Washington, USDA, Economic Research Service. Agricultural Economic Report Number 578 (December).

Langwell, Kathryn, Shelly Nelson, Daniel Calvin, and John Drabek.
1985 "Characteristics of rural communities and the changing geographic distribution of physicians." *The Journal of Rural Health* 1 (July):42–55.

Larson, Olaf F.
1981 "Agriculture and the community." Pp. 147–193 in Amos H. Hawley and Sara Mills Mazie (eds.), *Nonmetropolitan America in Transition*. Chapel Hill: The University of North Carolina Press.

Larson, Oscar W., III and Frederick H. Buttel.
1980 "Farm size, structure, climate, and energy: a reconsideration." *Rural Sociology* 45 (Summer):340–348.

Larson, Oscar W., Gilbert W. Gillespie, and Frederick H. Buttel.
1983 "Social class identification among farmers." *Rural Sociology* 48 (Spring):82–103.

Lash, Scott and John Urry.
1987 *The End of Organized Capitalism*. Cambridge: Polity Press.

Lawrence, Kathleen.
1987 "Changing rural landscapes." *Choices* (Fourth Quarter):4–7.

Leistritz, F. Larry and Brenda L. Ekstrom.
1986 *Interdependencies of Agriculture and Rural Communities: An annotated Bibliography*. New York: Garland Publishing, Inc.

———.
1988 "The financial characteristics of production units and producers experiencing financial stress." Pp. 73–95 in Steve H. Murdock and F. Larry Leistritz (eds.), *The Farm Financial Crisis: Socioeconomic Dimensions and Implications for Producers and Rural Areas*. Boulder, Colorado: Westview Press.

Leistritz, F. Larry and Steve H. Murdock.
1988 "Financial characteristics of farms and of farm financial markets and policies in the United States." Pp. 13–28 in Steve H. Murdock and F. Larry Leistritz (eds.), *The Farm Financial Crisis: Socioeconomic Dimensions and Implications for Producers and Rural Areas*. Boulder, Colorado: Westview Press.

Lenin, V.I.
1934 *Capitalism and Agriculture in the United States*. New York: International Publishers.

———.
1974 *The Development of Capitalism in Russia*. Moscow: Progress Publishers.

Lenski, Gerhard.
1966 *Power and Privilege: A Theory of Social Stratification*. New York: McGraw-Hill.

Lever, W.F.
1985 "Theory and methodology in industrial geography." Pp. 10–39 in Michael Pacione (ed.), *Progress in Industrial Geography*. London: Croom Helm.

Levy, Frank.
1988 "Incomes, families and living standards." Pp. 108–153 in Robert E. Litan, Robert Z. Lawrence, and Charles L. Schultze (eds.), *American Living Standards*. Washington, D.C.: The Brookings Institution.

Lewis, G.J.
1983 "Rural communities." Pp. 149–172 in Michael Pacione (ed.), *Progress in Rural Geography*. London: Croom Helm.

Lewis, Oscar.
1968 *La Vida*. New York: Vintage.

Lipietz, Alain.
1986 "New tendencies in the international division of labor: regimes of accumulation and modes of regulation." Pp. 16–40 in Allen J. Scott and Michael Storper (eds.), *Production, Work, Territory: The Geographical Anatomy of Industrial Capitalism*. Boston: Allen & Unwin.

Litan, Robert.
1988 "The risks of recession." Pp. 66–107 in Robert E. Litan, Robert Z. Lawrence and Charles L. Schultze (eds.), *American Living Standards*. Washington, D.C.: The Brookings Institution.

Liu, Ben-Chieh.
1976 *Quality of Life Indicators in U.S. Metropolitan Areas: A Statistical Analysis*. New York: Praeger Progressive.

Lobao, Linda M. and Donald W. Thomas.
1988 "Farm structure and infant mortality: an analysis of nonmetropolitan counties." *Journal of Community Development Society* 19 (2):1–29.

Luttrell, Clifton B.
1989 *The High Cost of Farm Welfare*. Washington, D.C.: Cato Institute.

MacCannell, Dean.
1988 "Industrial agriculture and rural commodity degradation." Pp. 15–75 in Louis E. Swanson (ed.), *Agriculture and Community Change in the U.S.: The Congressorial Research Reports*. Boulder, Colorado: Westview Press.

MacCannell, Dean, and Edward Dolber-Smith.
1986 "Report on the structure of agriculture and impacts of new technologies on rural communities in Arizona, California, Florida, and Texas." Pp. 19–167 in *Technology, Public Policy and the Changing Structure of American Agriculture*. Vol. 2, *Background Papers*, Part D: *Rural Communities*, Washington D.C.: Office of Technology Assessment.

Majka, Linda C. and Theo J. Majka.
1982 *Farm Workers, Agribusiness, and the State*. Philadelphia: Temple University Press.

Malecki, Edward J.
1988 "New firm startups: key to rural growth." *Rural Development Perspectives* 5 (February):18–23.

Mamer, John W.
1984 "Occupational structure and the industrialization of agriculture." Pp. 286–327 in Robert D. Emerson (ed.) *Seasonal Agricultural Labor Markets in the United States.* Ames, Iowa: The Iowa State University Press.

Mandel, Ernest.
1980 *Long Waves of Capitalist Development: The Marxist Interpretation.* Cambridge: Cambridge University Press.

Mandle, Jay R.
1978 *The Roots of Black Poverty: The Southern Plantation Economy after the Civil War.* Durham, N.C.: Duke University Press.

Mann, Susan A., and James M. Dickinson.
1978 "Obstacles to the development of a capitalist agriculture." *Journal of Peasant Studies* 5 (July):466–481.

Markides, Kyriakos S. and Connie McFarland.
1982 "A note on recent trends in the infant mortality-socioeconomic status relationship." *Social Forces* 61 (1):268–276.

Markus, Gregory B.
1979 *Analyzing Panel Data.* Beverly Hills: Sage.

Markusen, Ann.
1987 *Regions: The Economics and Politics of Territory.* Totowa, N.J.: Rowman and Littlefield.

Marousek, Gerald.
1979 "Farm size and rural communities: some economic relationships." *Southern Journal of Agricultural Economics* 11 (December):57–61.

Martin, Philip L. and David S. North.
1984 "Nonimmigrant aliens in American agriculture." Pp. 168–198 in Robert D. Emerson (ed.), *Seasonal Agricultural Labor Markets in the United States.* Ames: The Iowa State University Press.

Martinson, Oscar B., Eugene A. Wilkening, and Richard D. Rodefeld.
1976 "Feelings of powerlessness and social isolation among 'large-scale' farm personnel." *Rural Sociology* 41 (Winter):452–472.

Marx, Karl
1967 *Capital: A Critique of Political Economy* (edited by Frederick Engels). Volume 3. New York: International Publishers.

Maslow, Abraham H.
1954 *Motivation and Personality*. New York: Harper and Row.

Massey, Doreen.
1978 Regionalism: Some Current Issues. *Capital and Class* 6:106–125.

———.
1984 *Spatial Divisions of Labour: Social Structures and the Geography of Production*. London: Macmillan.

Matta, Benjamin N.
1984 "The off-farm work of hired farm workers." Pp. 140–164 in Robert D. Emerson (ed.), *Seasonal Agricultural Labor Markets in the United States*. Ames, Iowa: The Iowa State University Press.

McGranhan, David A.
1980 "The spatial structure of income distribution in rural regions." *American Sociological Review* 45 (April):313–324.

McWilliams, Carey.
1969 *Factories in the Field: The Story of Migratory Farm Labor in California*. Hamden, Conn.: Archon Books (originally published in 1939).

Meir, Kenneth J. and William P. Browne.
1983 "Interest groups and farm structure." Pp. 47–56 in David E. Brewster, Wayne D. Rasmusser, and Garth Youngberg (eds.), *Farms in Transition*. Ames, Iowa: Iowa State University Press.

Menchik, Mark David.
1981 "The service sector." Pp. 231–254 in Amos H. Hawley and Sara Mills Mazie (eds.), *Nonmetropolitan America in Transition*. Chapel Hill: The University of North Carolina Press.

Miller, C.A.
1985 "Infant mortality in the United States." *Scientific American* 253 (1):31–37.

Miller, Michael K., Donald E. Voth, and Diana Danforth Chapman.
1984 "Estimating the effects of community resource development efforts on county quality of life." *Rural Sociology* 49 (Spring):37–66.

Mincer, J.
1970 "The distribution of labor's income." *Journal of Economic Literature* 8:1–26.

Molnar, Joseph J. and Lionel J. Beaulieu.
1984 "Societal implications of changes in the organization of agricultural production." Paper presented at the annual meetings of the Rural Sociological Society, College Station, Texas.

Mooney, Patrick.
1982 "Labor time, production time, and capitalist development in agriculture: a reconsideration of the Mann-Dickinson Thesis." *Sociologia Ruralis* 12 (3–4):279–292.

———.
1983 "Toward a class analysis of Midwestern agriculture." *Rural Sociology* 48 (4):563–584.

———.
1987 "Desperately seeking: one-dimensional Mann and Dickinson." *Rural Sociology*
52 (2):286–295.

Morrill, Richard L. and Ernest H. Wohlenberg.
1971 *The Geography of Poverty in the United States.* New York: McGraw-Hill.

Morris, Michael and John B. Williamson.
1986 *Poverty and Public Policy: An Analysis of Federal Intervention Efforts.* New York:
Greenwood Press.

Mottura, Giovanni and Enrico Pugliese.
1980 "Capitalism in agriculture and capitalist agriculture: the Italian case." Pp. 171–199
in Frederick Buttel and Howard Newby (eds.), *The Rural Sociology of the Advanced
Societies: Critical Perspectives.* Montclair, N.J.: Allanheld, Osmun.

Moxley, Robert L.
1986 "Agriculture, communities, and urban areas." Pp. 322–332 in Ronald C. Wimberley,
Dale Jahr, and Jerry W. Johnson (eds.), *New Dimensions in Rural Policy: Building Upon
Our Heritage.* Studies prepared for the use of the Subcommittee on Agriculture and
Transportation of the Joint Economic Committee, Congress of the United States.
Washington, D.C.: U.S. Government Printing Office.

Murdock, Steve H. and F. Larry Leistritz.
1988 "Introduction." Pp. 1–9 in Steve H. Murdock and F. Larry Leistritz (eds.), *The
Farm Financial Crisis: Socioeconomic Dimensions and Implications for Producers and
Rural Areas.* Boulder, Colorado: Westview Press.

Murdock, Steve H., Don E. Albrecht, Rita Hamm, F. Larry Leistritz, and Arlen G. Leholm.
1986 "The farm crisis in the Great Plains: implications for theory and policy development." *Rural Sociology* 51 (Winter):406–435.

Murdock, Steve H., Lloyd B. Potter, Rita R. Hamm, Kenneth Backman, Don E. Albrecht
and F. Larry Leistritz.
1988 "The implications of the current farm crisis for rural America." Pp. 141–168 in
Steve H. Murdock and F. Larry Leistritz (eds.), *The Farm Financial Crisis: Socioeconomic
Dimensions and Implications for Producers and Rural Areas.* Boulder, Colorado:
Westview Press.

Murray, Charles.
1984 *Losing Ground: American Social Policy, 1950–1980.* New York: Basic Books.

The National Commission on Agricultural Trade and Export Policy.
1986 *New Realities: Toward a Program of Effective Competition.* Washington, D.C.: U.S. Department of Agriculture.

Neter, John and William Wasserman.
1974 *Applied Linear Statistical Models.* Homewood, Illinois: Richard D. Irwin.

Newby, Howard.
1978 "The rural sociology of advanced capitalist societies." Pp. 3–30 in Howard Newby (ed.), *International Perspectives in Rural Sociology.* Chichester, England: John Wiley and Sons.

————.
1980 "Rural sociology: a trend report." *Current Sociology* 28 (Spring):3–41.

————.
1983 "The sociology of agriculture: toward a new rural sociology." Pp. 67–81 in Ralph H. Turner and James F. Short, Jr. (eds.), *Annual Review of Sociology.* Volume 9. Palo Alto, California: Annual Reviews Inc.

————.
1986a "Emergent issues in theories of agrarian development." Pp. 7–22 in Daniel Thorniley (ed.), *The Economics of Rural Communities: East-West Perspectives.* Aldershot, England: Avebury.

————.
1986b "Locality and rurality: the restructuring of social relations." *Regional Studies* 20 (3):209–215.

————.
1987 "Economic restructuring and rural labor markets in Europe: current policy options." Pp. 41–54 in Gene F. Summers, John Brydon, Kenneth Deavers, Howard Newby and Susan Sechler (eds.), *Agriculture and Beyond Rural Economic Development.* Madison: University of Wisconsin, College of Agriculture and Life Sciences.

Newby, Howard and Frederick H. Buttel.
1980 "Toward a critical rural sociology." Pp. 1–35 in Frederick H. Buttel and Howard Newby (eds.), *The Rural Sociology of the Advanced Societies.* Montclair: Allanheld Osmun.

Nielson, Elizabeth G. and Linda K. Lee.
1987 *The Magnitude and Costs of Groundwater Contamination from Agricultural Chemicals: A National Perspective.* U.S. Department of Agriculture, Natural Resources Economics Division, Economic Research Service, June.

Noel, Alain.
1987 "Accumulation, regulation, and social change: an essay on French political economy." *International Organization* 41 (2):303–333.

North, David S. and Philip L. Martin.
1984 "Nonimmigrant aliens in American agriculture." Pp. 168–193 in Robert D. Emerson (ed.), *Seasonal Agricultural Labor Markets in the United States*. Ames, Iowa: Iowa State University Press.

Nuckton, Carole Frank, Refugio I. Rochin, and Douglas Gwynn.
1982 "Farm size and rural community welfare: an interdisciplinary approach." *Rural Sociology* 47 (Spring):32–46.

O'Connor, James.
1973 *The Fiscal Crisis of the State*. New York: St. Martin's Press.

Offe, Claus.
1972 "Advanced capitalism and the welfare state." *Politics and Society* 1:479–488.

O'Hare, William P.
1988 The Rise of Poverty in Rural America. Occasional paper Number 15, July. Washington, D.C.: The Population Reference Bureau, Inc.

Pampel, Fred C. Vijayan K. Pillai.
1986 "Patterns and determinants of infant mortality in developed nations, 1950–1975." *Demography* 23 (November):525–541.

Parcel, Toby L.
1979 "Race, regional labor markets and earnings." *American Sociological Review* 44 (2):262–279.

Parcel, Toby L. and C.W. Mueller.
1983 *Ascription and Labor Markets: Race and Sex Differences in Earnings*. New York: Academic Press.

Penn, J.B.
1979 "The structure of agriculture: an overview of the issue." Pp. 1–23 in *Structure Issues of American Agriculture*. Washington, D.C.: U.S. Department of Agriculture, Economics, Statistics, and Cooperatives Service, Agricultural Economic Report 438.

————.
1981 "Economic developments in U.S. Agriculture during the 1970s." Pp. 3–47 in D. Gale Johnson (ed.), *Food and Agricultural Policy for the 1980s*. Washington: American Enterprise Institute for Public Policy Research.

Perry, Charles S.
1980 "Industrialization, income, and inequality: further considerations." *Rural Sociology* 45 (Spring):139–146.

————.
1982 "The rationalization of U.S. farm labor: trends between 1956 and 1979." *Rural Sociology* 47 (Winter):670–691.

Pfeffer, Max.
1983 "Social origins of three systems of farm production in the United States." *Rural Sociology* 48 (Winter):540–562.

Piore, Michael.
1985 "American labor and the industrial crisis." Pp. 142–149 in Richard L. Rowan (ed.), *Readings in Labor Economics.* Homewood, Ill.: Richard D. Irwin, Inc.

Piore, Michael and Charles Sable.
1984 *The Second Industrial Divide.* New York: Basic Books.

Piven, Frances Fox and Richard Cloward.
1971 *Regulating the Poor.* New York: Vintage.

———.
1987 "The historical sources of the contemporary relief debate." Pp. 3–43 in Fred Block, Richard A. Cloward, Barbara Ehrenreich, and Frances Fox Piven (eds.), *The Mean Season: The Attack on the Welfare State.* New York: Pantheon Books.

Poole, Dennis L.
1981 "Farm scale, family life, and community participation." *Rural Sociology* 46 (Spring):112–127.

Poulantzos, Nico.
1974 *Classes in Contemporary Capitalism.* London: Verso Editions.

Rasmussen, Wayne D.
1980 "The structure of farming and American history." Pp. 3–17 in *Farm Structure: A Historical Perspective on Changes in the Number and Sizes of Farms.* The Committee on Agriculture, Nutrition, and Forestry, United States Senate, Washington: U.S. Government Printing Office.

Raup, Phillip M.
1973 "Needed research into the effects of large scale farm and business firms on rural America." In U.S. Congress, Senate, Committee on Small Business, *Hearings before the Subcommittee on Monopoly,* 92nd Congress, 1st and 2nd Sessions, Role of Giant Corporations. Washington, D.C.: U.S. Government Printing Office.

Rees, Gareth.
1984 "Rural regions in national and international economies." Pp. 27–44 in Tony Bradley and Philip Lowe (eds.), *Locality and Rurality.* Norwich, England: Geo Books.

Reif, Linda Lobao.
1986 "Farm structure, industry structure and socioeconomic conditions: a longitudinal study in economy and society." Ph.D. diss., North Carolina State University, Raleigh.

———.
1987 "Farm structure, industry structure, and socioeconomic conditions in the United States." *Rural Sociology* 52 (Winter):462–482.

Rodefeld, Richard D.
1974 The changing organization and occupational structure of farming and the implications for farm work force individuals, families and communities. Ph.D. diss., The University of Wisconsin, Madison.

Rosenblatt, Roger and Ira S. Moscovice.
1982 *Rural Health Care.* New York: John Wiley and Sons.

Rosenfeld, Rachael A.
1985 *Farm Women: Work, Farm, and Family in the United States.* Chapel Hill, N.C.: The University of North Carolina Press.

Ross, Peggy J., Herman Bluestone, and Fred K. Hines.
1979 *Indicators of Social Well-Being for U.S. counties.* U.S. Department of Agriculture, Economics, Statistics, and Cooperatives Service: Rural Development Research Report No. 10.

Salant, Priscilla and Robert Munoz.
1981 *Rural Industrialization and Its Impact on the Agricultural Community: A Review of the Literature.* Washington, D.C.: U.S. Department of Agriculture, Economics and Statistics Service Staff Report.

Sanders, Jimy M.
1988 "A test of the new structural critique of the welfare state." Pp. 130–162 in Donald Tomaskovic-Devey (ed.), *Poverty and Social Welfare in the United States.* Boulder: Westview.

Savage, Mike, James Barlow, Simon Duncan, and Peter Saunders.
1987 "'Locality research': the Sussex programme on economic restructuring, social change and the locality." *Quarterly Journal of Social Affairs* 31:27–51

Sayer, Andrew.
1986 "Industrial location on a world scale: the case of the semiconductor industry." Pp. 107–122 in Allen J. Scott and Michael Storper (eds.), *Production, Work and Territory: The Geographical Anatomy of Industrial Capitalism.* Boston: Allen & Unwin.

Schervish, Paul G.
1983 *The Structural Determinants of Unemployment.* New York: Academic Press.

Schiller, Bradley R.
1980 *The Economics of Poverty and Discrimination* (3rd ed.). Englewood CLiffs, N.J.: Prentice-Hall, Inc.

Schulman, Michael D. and Linda M. Lobao.
1989 "Agrarian origins, industrial experience, and militancy: an analysis of Southern textile workers." *Sociological Spectrum* 9:379–401.

Scott, A.J. and M. Storper.
1986 "Industrial Change and territorial organization: a summing up." Pp. 301–311 in Allen J. Scott and Michael Storper (eds.), *Production, Work, Territory: The Geographical Anatomy of Industrial Capitalism.* Boston: Allen & Unwin.

Seninger, Stephen F. and Timothy M. Smeeding.
1981 "Poverty: a human resource-income maintenance perspective." Pp. 382–436 in Amos H. Hawley and Sara Mills Mazie (eds.), *Nonmetropolitan America in Transition.* Chapel Hill: The University of North Carolina Press.

Sewell, William H., and Robert M. Hauser.
1975 *Education, Occupation, and Earnings: Achievement in the Early Career.* New York: Academic Press.

Shaffer, Ron E.
1979 "The general economic impact of industrial growth on the private sector of nonmetropolitan communities." Pp. 103–118 in Richard E. Lonsdale and H.L. Seyler (eds.), *Nonmetropolitan Industrialization.* Washington, D.C.: V.H. Winston and Sons.

Sheets, Robert E., Steven Nord, and John J. Phelps.
1987 *The Impact of Service Industries on Underemployment in Metropolitan Economies.* Lexington, Mass.: D.C. Heath & Company.

Singer, Edward G., Gary P. Green, and Jere L. Gilles.
1983 "The Mann-Dickinson thesis: reject or revise?" *Sociologia Ruralis* 23(3–4):276–287.

Skees, Jerry R. and Louis E. Swanson.
1986 "Examining policy and emerging technologies affecting farm structure in the South and the interaction between farm structure and well-being of rural areas." Pp. 373–495 in *Technology, Public Policy and the Changing Structure of American Agriculture.* Vol. 2, *Background Papers,* Part D: *Rural Communities.* Washington, D.C.: Office of Technology Assessment.

———.
1988 "Farm structure and rural well-being in the South." Pp. 238–321 in Louis E. Swanson (ed.), *Agriculture and Community Change in the U.S.: The Congressional Research Reports.* Boulder: Westview.

Small Farm Viability Project.
1977 *The Family Farm in California: Report of the Small Farm Viability Project.* Sacramento, California: Employment Development, the Governor's Office of Planning and Research, the Department of Food and Agriculture and the Department of Housing and Community Development.

Smith, David M.
1982 *Where The Grass Is Greener: Living in an Unequal World.* Baltimore: The Johns Hopkins University Press.

———.
1977 *Human Geography: A Welfare Approach.* London: Edward Arnold.

Smith, Matthew G., Clark Edwards, and R. Neal Peterson.
1987 "How many farms? Projecting U.S. farm numbers and sizes." *Rural Development Perspectives* 4 (June):16–20.

Smith, Neil.
1984 *Uneven Development: Nature, Capital, and the Production of Space.* Oxford: Basil Blackwell.

Smith, Stewart N.
1988 "Six ways states can spur their rural economics." *Rural Development Perspectives* 5 (February):8–14.

Smith, T. Lynn
1969 "A study of social stratification in the agricultural sections of the U.S.: nature, data, procedures, and preliminary results." *Rural Sociology* 34 (Winter):497–510.

Sørenson, Aage B.
1983 "Sociological research on the labor market: conceptual and methodological issues." *Work and Occupations* 10 (August):261–287.

Stockdale, Jerry D.
1982 "Who will speak for agriculture?" Pp. 317–327 in Don A. Dillman and Daryl J. Hobbs (eds.), *Rural Society in the U.S.: Issues for the 1980s.* Boulder, Colorado: Westview.

Stolzenberg, Ross M.
1978 "Bringing the boss back in: employer size, employee schooling, and socioeconomic achievement." *American Sociological Review* 43 (6):831–828.

Storper, M. and A.J. Scott.
1986 "Production, work, territory: contemporary realities and theoretical tasks." Pp. 3–15 in Allen J. Scott and Michael Storper (eds.), *Production, Work, Territory: The Geographical Anatomy of Industrial Capitalism.* Boston: Allen & Unwin.

Storper, Michael and Richard Walker.
1984 "The spatial division of labor: labor and the location of industries." Pp. 19–47 in Larry Sawers and William K. Tabb (eds.), *Sunbelt/Snowbelt: Urban Development and Regional Restructuring.* New York: Oxford University Press.

Strange, Marty.
1988 *Family Farming: The New Economic Vision.* Lincoln: University of Nebraska Press and San Francisco Institute for Food and Development Policy.

Summers, Gene F., Sharon D. Evans, Frank Clemente, E.M. Beck, and John Minkoff.
1976 *Industrialization of Nonmetropolitan America.* New York: Praeger.

Swanson, Larry.
1980 "A study in socioeconomic development: changing farm structure and rural community decline in the context of the technological transformation of American agriculture." Ph.D. diss., University of Nebraska, Lincoln.

Swanson, Louis E.
1982 "Farm and trade center transition in an industrial society: Pennsylvania, 1930–1960." Ph.D. diss., The Pennsylvania State University, University Park, Pennsylvania.

———.
1988 *Agriculture and Community Change in the U.S.: The Congressional Research Reports.* Boulder, Colorado: Westview Press.

———.
1989 "The sociology of agriculture: the research agenda." *The Rural Sociologist* (Spring): 27–31.

———.
1990 "Rethinking assumptions about farm and community change." Pp. 19–33 in A.E. Luloff and Louis E. Swanson (eds.), *American Rural Communities.* Boulder, Colorado: Westview Press.

Swanson, Louis E. and Jerry R. Skees.
1987 "Finding new ideas for old objectives: the current case for rural development programs." *Choices* 4 (Fourth Quarter): 8–32.

Tetreau, E.D.
1938 "The people of Arizona's irrigated areas." *Rural Sociology* 3 (June):177–187.

———.
1940 "Social organization in Arizona's irrigated areas." *Rural Sociology* 5 (June):192–205.

Thomas, Robert J.
1982 "The social organization of industrial agriculture." *The Insurgent Sociologist* 3:5–20.

Thurow, Lester C.
1975 *Generating Inequality.* New York: Basic Books.

Tigges, Leann M.
1988 "Age, earnings, and change within the dual economy." *Social Forces* 66 (3):676–698.

Till, Thomas E.
1981 "Manufacturing industry: trends and impacts." Pp. 194–230 in Amos H. Hawley and Sara Mills Mazie (eds.), *Nonmetropolitan America in Transition.* Chapel Hill: The University of North Carolina Press.

Tolbert, Charles M., II.
1983 "Industrial segmentation and men's intergenerational mobility." *Social Forces* 61 (June):1119–1137.

Tomaskovic-Devey, Donald.
1987 "Labor markets, industrial structure, and poverty: a theoretical discussion and empirical example." *Rural Sociology* 52 (1):56-74.

———.
1988a "Industrial structure, relative labor power, and poverty rates." Pp. 104–129 in Donald Tomaskovic-Devey (ed.), *Poverty and Social Welfare in the United States*. Boulder, Colorado: Westview Press.

———.
1988b "Poverty and social welfare in the United States." Pp. 1–26 in Donald Tomaskovic-Devey (ed.), *Poverty and Social Welfare in the United States*. Boulder, Colorado: Westview Press.

———.
1988c "The impact of industrial structure, labor market organization, and income transfers on changes in U.S. poverty, 1959-1979." Paper presented at the annual meetings of the American Sociological Society, Atlanta, August.

Townsend, Peter.
1979 *Poverty in the United Kingdom: A Survey of Household Resources and Standards of Living*. Berkeley: University of California Press.

Tweeten, Luther.
1970 *Foundations of Farm Policy*. Lincoln: The University of Nebraska Press.

———.
1981 "Prospective changes in U.S. agricultural structure." Pp. 113–146 in D. Gale Johnson (ed.), *Food and Agricultural Policy for the 1980s*. Washington: American Enterprise Institute for Public Policy Research.

———.
1984 *Causes and Consequences of Structural Change in the Farming Industry. Food and Agriculture Committee, Des Moines, Iowa, Report #2* and National Planning Association, Washington D.C., Report #207.

Tweeten, Luther and George L. Brinkman.
1976 *Micropolitan Development: Theory and Practice of Greater Rural Economic Development*. Ames, Iowa: Iowa State University Press.

Urry, John.
1984 "Capitalist restructuring, recomposition and the regions." Pp. 45–64 in Tony Bradley and Philip Lowe (eds.), *Locality and Rurality*. Norwich, England: Geo Books.

———.
1985 "Deindustrialization, households, and politics." Pp. 13–29 in Linda Murgatroyd, Mike Savage, Dan Shapiro, John Urry, Sylvia Walby, Alan Ward with Jane Mark-Lawson (eds.), *Localities, Class and Gender*. London: Pion Limited.

Urry, John and Alan Ward.
1985 "Introduction." Pp. 1–12 in Linda Murgatroyd, Mike Savage, Dan Shapiro, John Urry, Sylvia Walby, Alan Ward with Jane Mark-Lawson (eds.), *Localities, Class, and Gender.* London: Pion Limited.

U.S. Bureau of the Census.
1978 *County and City Data Book, 1977.* Washington, D.C.: United States Government Printing Office.

————.
1983a *County and City Data Book, 1983.* Washington, D.C.: United States Government Printing Office.

————.
1983b *Statistical Abstract of the United States: 1984* (104th edition). Washington, D.C.: United States Government Printing Office.

————.
1984 *1982 Census of Agriculture.* Vol. 1, Part 51. Washington, D.C.: U.S. Department of Commerce.

————.
1986 *Statistical Abstract of the United States: 1987* (107th edition). Washington, D.C.: United States Government Printing Office.

USDA (United States Department of Agriculture).
1987 *Economic Indicators of the Farm Sector: National Financial Summary, 1986.* Washington, D.C.: Economic Research Service, December.

————.
1988 *Farm Sector Review, 1986.* Washington, D.C.: Economic Research Service, January.

van Es, J.C., David L. Chicoine, and Mark A. Flotow.
1986 "Agricultural technologies, farm structure, and rural communities in the Cornbelt: policy changes and implications for 2000." Pp. 496–570 in *Technology, Public Policy and the Changing Structure of American Agriculture.* Vol. 2, *Background Papers*, Part D: *Rural Communities.* Washington, D.C.: Office of Technology Assessment.

Wachtel, Howard M. and Charles Betsey.
1971 "Employment at low wages." *The Review of Economics and Statistics* 54 (May): 121–129.

Wallace, Michael and Arne Kalleberg.
1981 "Economic organization of firms and labor market consequences: toward a specification of dual economy theory." Pp. 119–149 in Ivar Berg (ed.), *Sociological Perspectives on Labor Markets,* New York: Academic Press.

Ward, Alan.
1985 "Comparable localities: some problems of method." Pp. 54–76 in Linda Mugatroyd, Mike Savage, Dan Shapiro, John Urry, Sylvia Walby, Alan Ward with Jane Mark-Lawson (eds.), *Localities, Class, and Gender.* London: Pion Limited.

Wayne, Jack.
1986 "The function of social welfare in a capitalist economy." Pp. 56–84 in James Dickinson and Bob Russell (eds.), *Family, Economy, and State: The Social Reproduction Process Under Capitalism.* London: Croom Helm.

Wells, Miriam J.
1984 "The resurgence of sharecropping: historical anomaly or political strategy." *American Journal of Sociology* 90 (1):1–29.

Wheelock, Gerald C.
1979 "Farm size, community structure and growth: specification of a structural equation model." Paper presented at the annual meetings of the Rural Sociological Society, Burlington, Vermont.

Wicks, Jerry W. and Edward G. Stockwell.
1984 "A comment on the neonatal mortality-socioeconomic status relationship." *Social Forces* 62 (4):1035–1039.

Wilson, William Julius and Kathryn M. Neckerman.
1986 "Poverty and family structure: the widening gap between evidence and public policy issues." Pp. 232–259 in Sheldon H. Danziger and Daniel H. Weinberg (eds.), *Fighting Poverty: What Works and What Doesn't.* Cambridge, Mass: Harvard University Press.

Wimberley, Ronald C.
1983a "Structural profiles of American agriculture." Paper presented at the annual meetings of the Rural Sociological Society, Lexington, Kentucky.

———.
1983b "The emergence of part-time farming as a social form of agriculture." Pp. 325–356 in Ida H. Simpson and Richard L. Simpson (eds.), *Research in the Sociology of Work: Peripheral Workers.* Volume 2. Greenwich, Connecticut: JAI Press Inc.

———.
1984 "Recent trends in stability and change among dimensions of U.S. agricultural structure." Paper presented at the annual meetings of the Rural Sociological Society, College Station, Texas.

———.
1985 "Testimony before the Joint Economic Committee of the Congress of the United States." Pp. 49–74 in the Joint Economic Committee, Congress of the United States, 98th Congress 2nd session (ed.), *The Economic Evolution of Agriculture.* Washington, D.C.: U.S. The Joint Economic Committee.

———.
1987 "Dimensions of U.S. agristructure: 1969–1982." *Rural Sociology* 52 (4):445–61.

Wimberley, Ronald C. and Linda Lobao Reif.
1988 "The measurement of farm structure and the Goldschmidt hypothesis." Paper presented at the annual meetings of the Rural Sociological Society, Athens, Georgia, August.

Winter, Michael.
1984 "Agrarian class structure and family farming." Pp. 91–128 in Tony Bradley and Philip Lowe (eds.), *Locality and Rurality: Economy and Society in Rural Regions.* Norwich, England: Geo Books.

Wood, Phillip J.
1986 *Southern Capitalism: The Political Economy of North Carolina, 1880–1980.* Durham, N.C.: Duke University Press.

Wright, Erik Olin.
1978 *Class, Crisis, and the State.* London: New Left Books.

———.
1979 *Class Structure and Income Determination.* New York: Academic Press.

Wright, J. Stephen and Dale W. Lick.
1986 "Health in rural America: problems and recommendations." Pp. 461–469 in Dale Jahr, Jerry W. Johnson, and Ronald C. Wimberley (eds.), *New Dimensions in Rural Policy: Building Upon Our Heritage*, studies prepared for the use of the Subcommittee on Agriculture and Transportation of the Joint Economic Committee Congress of the United States. Washington, D.C.: U.S. Government Printing Office.

Index